W9-AES-295

THE JOURNAL OF
A LONDON PLAYGOER

THE VICTORIAN LIBRARY

THE JOURNAL OF
A LONDON PLAYGOER

HENRY MORLEY

WITH AN INTRODUCTION BY
MICHAEL R. BOOTH

LEICESTER UNIVERSITY PRESS
1974

First published in 1866
Second edition published in 1891
Victorian Library edition (reprinting 1891 text)
published in 1974 by
Leicester University Press

Distributed in North America by
Humanities Press Inc., New York

Introduction copyright © Michael R. Booth 1974

Printed in Great Britain by
Unwin Brothers Limited, The Gresham Press
Old Woking, Surrey

ISBN 0 7185 5031 5

THE VICTORIAN LIBRARY

There is a growing demand for the classics of Victorian literature in many fields, in political and social history, architecture, topography, religion, education, and science. Hitherto this demand has been met, in the main, from the second-hand market. But the prices of second-hand books are rising sharply, and the supply of them is very uncertain. It is the object of this series, THE VICTORIAN LIBRARY, to make some of these classics available again at a reasonable cost. Since most of the volumes in it are reprinted photographically from the first edition, or another chosen because it has some special value, an accurate text is ensured. Each work carries a substantial introduction, written specially for this series by a well-known authority on the author or his subject, and a bibliographical note on the text.

The volumes necessarily vary in size. In planning the newly-set pages the designer, Arthur Lockwood, has maintained a consistent style for the principal features. The uniform design of binding and jackets provides for ready recognition of the various books in the series when shelved under different subject classifications.

Recommendation of titles for THE VICTORIAN LIBRARY and of scholars to contribute the introductions is made by a joint committee of the Board of the University Press and the Victorian Studies Centre of the University of Leicester.

INTRODUCTION

In his later days, and after he died, Henry Morley's
primary reputation was not that of a drama critic or even
a journalist, but of a leading educationist and humanist
whose extensive lecturing, writing, and editing activities
were of great importance in making English literature
a field of respectable academic study inside schools and
universities and in stimulating interest in reading and
culture in the general populace. He achieved this
eminence toward the end of his life, however, and in the
period covered by *The Journal of a London Playgoer* was
a working drama critic, journalist at large, and newspaper editor.

Born in Hatton Garden, London, in 1822, the son of
an apothecary, Morley was sent to school in Germany
and intended for his father's calling. In 1838 he entered
King's College, London, to pursue medical studies, and
graduated in 1843. He became a physician's assistant in
Somerset; then went into partnership in Shropshire,
but was ruined when his partner proved dishonest.
Leaving medicine, Morley established a school in
Lancashire embodying certain principles of German
education, and at the same time wrote medical articles
for periodicals. This kind of writing attracted the attention of Dickens, and Morley was asked to London to

write for and help edit *Household Words* and its successor
All the Year Round. At the same time he was taken on
the staff of the *Examiner*, then edited by John Forster,
and almost at once he found himself writing dramatic
reviews. With the *Examiner* he became sub-editor and
finally, from 1861 to 1867, editor. In 1852 Morley married
Mary Anne Sayer from the Isle of Wight, and in 1857
began a long career in higher education by being
appointed lecturer in English language and literature to
evening classes at King's College. Over the years he
taught working men in adult education classes and
gave frequent public lectures. In 1865 he was made
professor of English at University College, London, and
in 1878 was given a similar position at Queen's College.
He received an honorary LL.D from the University of
Edinburgh in 1879 and was appointed principal of
University Hall in Gordon Square, London, in 1882.
In 1890 Morley resigned his university positions in order
to devote more time to writing and editing, and retired
to Carisbrooke in the Isle of Wight, where he died in
1894.

Morley's output as author and editor was prodigious,
and even more significant than his teaching, although
in the ultimate sense they cannot be separated. A great
deal of this output was embodied in six substantial series
of which he was general editor, and to which he contributed introductions and editorial work of his own:
Cassell's Library of English Literature in five volumes
(1875–81), *Morley's Universal Library* in 64 volumes,
published by Routledge (1883–8), *Cassell's National
Library* in no less than 209 volumes (1886–90), the
Carisbrooke Library in 14 volumes (1889–92), and *Com-*

panion Poets in nine volumes (1891–2), both published by Routledge. The tremendous mass of editing and writing that Morley accomplished can be divided into roughly three categories: drama, poetry, and prose (tales, romances, treatises, novels, and essays). In drama Morley wrote introductions to plays by Aeschylus, Marlowe, Shakespeare, Molière, Sheridan, Goldsmith, Goethe, and Schiller. In poetry, in addition to the poets in *Companion Poets*, Morley produced editions of ballads, Cowper, Crabbe, Schiller, Scott, and Macaulay. By far the largest category is prose, and here the list is too long to enumerate. More, Bacon, Swift, Defoe, Johnson, Boswell, Southey, Dickens, and Carlyle were among the English authors whom Morley separately edited; Aristotle, à Kempis, Cervantes, Rabelais, and Voltaire several of the classical and European writers. In addition, Morley wrote many original works of biography and criticism. His criticism dealt especially with English literature: *Tables of English Literature* (1870), *A First Sketch of English Literature* (1873), and notably a massive history, *English Writers* (1887–95), projected in 20 volumes of which Morley lived to complete only ten, carrying the study as far as Shakespeare. Evidence for his own life is obtainable in *Early Papers and Some Memories* (1891), and in 1898 there appeared *The Life of Henry Morley*, by Henry S. Solly, the only biography.

The Journal of a London Playgoer was first published in 1866 and reprinted with an index in 1891. Because of the usefulness of the index the latter edition is reprinted here. The book is a selection of Morley's dramatic criticism for the Sunday weekly, the *Examiner*, founded in 1808

by Leigh Hunt and his brother John. The former
became its first and, together with William Hazlitt,
who reviewed for the *Examiner* from 1814 to 1817,
its most eminent dramatic critic. A later drama re-
viewer for the paper was Macready's friend John
Forster, but he was not of the same quality. Under the
editorship of Forster and Morley the *Examiner* declined
from the high reputation it possessed as a radical paper
under Leigh Hunt and Albany Fonblanque, its owner and
editor in the 'thirties and 'forties. But that matter is not
really germane to Morley's achievement as a theatre
critic.

When Morley began to write dramatic reviews for the
Examiner in 1851, the theatre was, according to several
uninformed modern historians of the drama, going
through a period analogically akin to the Dark Ages.
In actuality, the merest glance at the diversity and
richness of the material he reviewed is sufficient to
contradict such as assumption; but it is still all too
common for critics and historians today, especially
those with a literary bias, to regard the nineteenth
century as a whole as the doldrums of the English drama,
and the 1850s and 1860s in particular – between the
retirement of William Charles Macready in 1851 and the
coming of Tom Robertson and the Bancrofts in the
mid-'sixties – as the uttermost point of calm and stag-
nation in that period. In actuality again, the 15 years
covered by Morley's reviews include many significant
developments and a continuous process of evolutionary
change, extending back to the beginning of the century
and forward to its end, which by no means came to a
dead halt in the 1850s and 1860s.

At the date of Macready's retirement, three notable managements were operating in London, two of them especially – Charles Kean's at the Princess's and Samuel Phelps's at Sadler's Wells[1] – doing significant and valuable work, both in terms of the classical repertory, particularly Shakespeare, and the presentation of new plays by the best available playwrights. The third management, that of Madame Vestris and her husband Charles Mathews at the Lyceum,[2] was marked by the elegant and refined production of comedy and the fairy extravaganzas of James Robinson Planché, a dramatist whose writing in this area strongly influenced W. S. Gilbert and the whole style and tone of the Savoy operas.

During his tenancy of the Princess's, Kean offered theatregoers a series of elaborately mounted and archaeologically motivated productions of Shakespeare.[3] Kean estimated that in one season he had spent £50,000 in a theatre where £200 a night was considered a good house.[4] In this way of treating Shakespeare he had his enemies,[5] and his own performances did not meet with universal approbation, but no one could deny Kean's constant endeavour to achieve the highest ensemble and production standards, an endeavour that continued the excellent work of Macready and Phelps in the same areas,[6] and of Vestris and Mathews in the lighter part of the repertory.[7] By his deliberately educational and simultaneously spectacular approach to Shakespeare, Kean, who was himself an eminently respectable personage with an impeccable private life, succeeded in drawing back into his audiences some elements of the fashionable classes who years before largely deserted the theatre for opera and ballet, as well as increasing numbers of the respectable and educated middle class – Morley's theatrical touchstone. The fact that Kean had since 1848 been patronized by Queen Victoria, who frequently visited the Princess's and for whom he for several years arranged the private theatricals at Windsor Castle, did not exactly do him any harm.

Phelps's achievement at Sadler's Wells was even greater than Kean's. Morley was devoted to him and usually noticed him at greater length than he did Kean. In eighteen years of management in unfashionable and distant Islington, Phelps produced no fewer than 31 of Shakespeare's plays, as well as a large number of what contemporary audiences and critics, including Morley, believed to be significant new plays of serious intent and revivals from the drama of Shakespeare's contemporaries at a time when nobody else was reviving these plays. Indeed, when one realizes that together with his substantial accomplishments in the repertory Phelps was unflagging in his attempts to maintain and improve all aspects of artistic direction, without being able to spend nearly the sums of money on production that Kean had at his disposal, it is obvious that Sadler's Wells at this period was the closest thing England possessed to a National Theatre.[8] Morley has left us full and valuable accounts of several of Phelps's Shakespearean productions.

In addition to these three managements, whose offerings appear regularly in the pages of the *Journal of a London Playgoer*, there were others whose quality Morley commended, their existence demonstrating that even below the heights attained by such well-known managements as those of Kean, Phelps, and Vestris and

Mathews, work of a high standard was going on in well-organized and well-directed companies working towards definite artistic goals. One such company Morley frequently praised was that of Alfred Wigan at the Olympic from 1853 to 1857. Wigan, with a repertory of domestic middle-class drawing-room drama and comedy mainly adapted from the French, was careful to establish a realistic mise-en-scène and develop a company acting style firmly rooted in Victorian bourgeois life. With experience behind him in the Covent Garden management of Vestris and Mathews and Kean's Princess's company, Wigan was, as an actor, a reformer and modernist. He was highly polished, gentlemanly, and realistic, specializing in roles of dramatic power contained within the well-bred restraints of ordinary domestic intercourse, his chief characteristics being, according to Westland Marston, "extreme refinement, delicate perception, and truth to nature, combined with deep, though quiet feeling."[9] Other managements of lesser stature but undoubted competence also attracted Morley's attention. He was frequently at the Haymarket, which in the 'fifties and 'sixties was the premier comedy company in London, unmatched in the performance of classical English comedy such as the plays of Sheridan and of new comedies written for its especial talents.[10] Morley also admired the "excellent company" gathered together by Madame Celeste in her brief tenure of the Lyceum,[11] and reviewed the opening production of Charles Fechter's innovative Lyceum management in 1863.[12] Fechter mechanized the Lyceum stage and introduced various reforms in scenery, lighting, and costuming that won him the praise of many besides Morley.

A Frenchmen who was quite at home acting in English, Fechter was also a dashing stage romantic, a performer of cloak-and-sword melodrama without peer, and a tragedian of stature. He serves as only one example of the wide range of acting ability that Morley could and did witness during the period of his reviewing for the *Examiner*. He saw Fechter, for instance, at the Princess's in Hugo's *Ruy Blas* (adapted by Edmund Falconer), Dion Boucicault's *The Corsican Brothers*, *Othello* (as Othello and Iago), and *Hamlet* – a remarkable interpretation of Hamlet that swept away much stage tradition attached to the part, an interpretation that stressed modernity, familiarity, and realism. A review of Fechter's Hamlet was not included in the *Journal*, but a notice of Emil Devrient's Hamlet was; the German tragedian also played Goethe and Schiller at the St James's in 1852. The Italian tragedienne Adelaide Ristori was also in London in the 1850s and 1860s, and Morley saw her, among other parts, play Phèdre, Schiller's Mary Stuart, Bianca in Henry Hart Milman's *Fazio*, Lady Macbeth, and Scribe's Adrienne Lecouvreur.[13] In all these characters Morley records the tragic power that made her one of the greatest European actresses of any age.

The list of fine English-speaking performers active in Morley's time is of course much longer. In addition to Kean, Phelps, Wigan, Vestris, and Mathews, Morley reviewed numerous actors with considerable contemporary reputations. One of his favourites was Frederick Robson, equally eminent in farce, burlesque parts with tragic overtones (such as Shylock and Medea), and serious parts with an admixture of the grotesque that allowed for sudden outbursts of intense passion. Two favourite players of comedy and pathos were Robert Keeley and his wife Mary Ann: the former was one of the outstanding comedians of his time; the latter was accomplished in melodrama as well as low comedy. The Haymarket comedians Buckstone and Henry Compton, E. A. Sothern in his famous rendering of Lord Dundreary in Tom Taylor's *Our American Cousin*, the farceur J. L. Toole at the beginning of his long and popular career, the American actor Joseph Jefferson in his star part of Rip Van Winkle – these were a few of the great comic performers on the English stage in the nineteenth century, most of them with a performance range that could be extended far beyond the bounds of comedy and farce.[14] At the same time the English theatre was very strong in actors of melodrama and 'drama', and Morley saw the greatest of these: Phelps as Cardinal Richelieu in Bulwer-Lytton's *Richelieu*, Fechter and Kean in non-Shakespearean roles such as the former's dashing and heroic Chevalier Lagardère in *The Duke's Motto*, by Paul Féval *via* the English adaptation of John Brougham, and the latter's demonic and malignant Louis XI in Boucicault's adaptation from the French of that title. Boucicault himself appears in the pages of the *Journal* as an actor in various melodramatic roles, as does the American Charlotte Cushman in her sensational interpretation of the mad, haunted Meg Merrilies in a version of *Guy Mannering*, one of the great character performances of the century. In 1857 Morley was delighted with the sailor hero of the veteran T. P. Cooke in such classical roles of nautical melodrama as Long Tom Coffin in Edward Fitzball's *The Pilot* and Harry Halyard in J. T. Haines's *My Poll and My Partner Joe*. In Shakespeare, as well as the productions noted, Morley saw Kate Terry, Ellen's sister and a much admired actress before her early retirement from the stage in 1867, play Viola and Sebastian; he also heard Fanny Kemble reading *A Midsummer Night's Dream* accompanied by Mendelssohn's music, and witnessed the return to the stage in 1864 of Helen Faucit, Macready's leading actress, reviewing at some length her Imogen, Rosalind, and Lady Macbeth (the play still with Locke's music and the singing, dancing witches, much to Morley's annoyance).

Italian singers as well as English actors occupied space in Morley's columns; he reviewed opera regularly. At Covent Garden and at Her Majesty's in the Haymarket he saw the best singers of the day, including Luigi Lablache, Giulia Grisi, Guiseppe Mario, Antonio Tamburini, Giorgio Ronconi, Marietta Piccolomini, Marietta Alboni, and Adelina Patti. Finally, Morley went to Christmas pantomimes (out of duty, perhaps, rather than pleasure), enjoyed entertainments as diverse as marionettes and equestrian spectacle, and was a keen observer of amateur theatricals, giving Dickens his due as an actor in Wilkie Collins's melodrama, *The Lighthouse*.

The purpose of summarizing the quality and range of theatrical performance available to Morley during the years he was reviewing for the *Examiner* has not been merely to compile a list of performers seen, but rather to show what the London stage had to offer at a period since condemned as a wasteland of trivia and badness. Morley himself was not slow to condemn the trivial and the bad, yet it is evident from the above record that he was able to experience a wide variety of the very best acting (and singing, if opera is included) that native and foreign performers could offer, often in companies of particular merit with high standards of ensemble and production, and exercised upon a considerable extent of dramatic material – tragedy, comedy, opera, farce, burlesque, melodrama, pantomine – contained in both the traditional repertory and the new theatre. One receives the impression while reading the *Journal* that despite the gloomy *pronunciamento* of the prologue and the animadversions and occasional denunciation in the reviews themselves, Morley was often satisfied and pleased with the interest and merit of the work he was seeing from day to day. That this could be so – and Morley was a discerning critic – is at least one testimonial to the worth of the London stage in the 1850s and 1860s.

The kind of drama that Morley was reviewing, as distinct from its theatrical performance (if one can be permitted such an artificial distinction for the sake of the very briefest of outlines), was of course thoroughly representative of mid-Victorian playwriting. It was, like the taste of its audiences, conservative and un-experimental. Many plays of the time, whether comedies, farces, or melodramas, were taken from the French. Authors like Boucicault and Taylor were constantly reworking French originals: the two most popular new plays of the 'fifties and 'sixties respectively, Boucicault's *The Corsican Brothers* and Taylor's *The Ticket-of-Leave Man*, were borrowed from France. The staple fare of the West End theatre, Morley's principal territory as a critic, was in his day revivals of Shakespeare and a few

other classics, survivals of the older repertory; the
melodramas, comedies, and farces of Taylor, Boucicault,
J. S. Coyne, Edmund Falconer, John Oxenford, Watts
Phillips, Charles Reade, J. P. Simpson, Edward Stirling,
and Charles Selby; the farces of John Maddison Morton,
William Brough, and Andrew Halliday; the extravaganzas of Planché and Robert Brough; the burlesques of
H. J. Byron and F. C. Burnand; and the Christmas
pantomimes of E. L. Blanchard.[15] The strong domestic
tendencies of Victorian artistic expression suffused all
these forms of drama, and an equal proclivity for
realism in all aspects of staging combined with them to
convey a surface impression of household and family
reality in a drama whose essential content was fantastic.
Such a paradox was as true of farce as of melodrama,
and in Victorian pantomime the extremes of fairyland
fantasy alternated with domestic low comedy and
reference to contemporary events to produce an extra-
ordinary and unique theatrical genre of great social and
psychological interest. Indeed, nineteenth-century drama
is fully comprehensible only if one understands the social
and psychological context in which theatre audiences
lived, worked, and thought; much may be deduced
from the *Journal*, but such an analysis is well beyond the
limited scope of this introduction.

In his 1866 prologue Morley states that there are
twenty-five theatres in London, including two opera
houses, and estimated the average nightly audience at
15,000. An appendix to a parliamentary committee's
report of the same year on theatrical licences and
regulations lists the number of metropolitan theatres
and opera houses as twenty-seven. Exclusive of the two

opera houses, Covent Garden and Her Majesty's, the appendix assigns a total capacity of over 48,000 to those remaining.[16] The *Journal* records visits to nine of these twenty-five, only two of them – Sadler's Wells and the Marylebone (one visit) – outside the West End. Reviews of performances at the others – the Princess's, the Haymarket, the Olympic, Drury Lane, the Lyceum, the St James's, and the Adelphi – constitute the bulk of the *Journal*.[17] These nine theatres had a capacity, according to the appendix, of 16,000 or about 33 per cent of the total. Although Morley's prologue mentions the Pavilion in Whitechapel, the *Journal* does not review a performance there, or at any other East End theatre of significance, such as the Britannia or the Grecian. Nor, it seems, did Morley attend – at least on a reviewing basis – the Surrey or the Victoria south of the Thames, both of them theatres typical, as were the East End theatres, of working and lower middle-class dramatic taste. It is therefore important to remember that when Morley writes of the London stage in the *Journal*, he is writing almost entirely of the middle-class West End,[18] a minority theatre in terms of audience numbers and of plays produced, by no means completely characteristic of London drama and theatre as a whole. That whole was in large part constituted by the thriving working and lower middle-class theatres of the East End and South Bank, whose loyal neighbourhood audiences subsisted principally upon a diet of melodrama, farce, and pantomime (comedy and burlesque, middle-class concerns, were almost unknown) different in content, style, and class orientation from the same forms as practised in the West End theatres. Except for the occasional visit out of curiosity, the middle-class critic ignored the existence of this theatre, which was not in the mainstream of development and has (wrongly so) passed largely unnoticed in subsequent critical and historical estimates of nineteenth-century drama and theatre.

Morley's middle-class bias, instinctive and unconscious with every drama critic of his period, is reflected not only in attendance at particular theatres, but also in his expressed preferences and opinions. He tended to admire middle-class managers, like Kean and Wigan, who were highly conscious of their own status and made every effort to protect and assert it.[19] He wrote his reviews for the educated middle class, appealed to them on more than one occasion to rescue the theatre from triviality and mindlessness, and expected the theatre manager to "take for standard of the people he would please an honest Englishman of the educated middle-class, akin to all that is human, trained not only in school or college, but in daily active stir of life, to interest in all true thinking and true feeling, to habitual notice of varieties of character, and to a habit of noting its depths in real life."[20] The support of this class for the theatre was essential to that theatre's health; the less educated and other classes might have gone to be entertained, but they did not matter, and the implication is that their presence harmed the cause of good theatre.[21]

Along with Morley's middle-class point of view went, quite naturally, a Victorian morality that was an integral part of it. One of the reasons Morley objected so strongly to burlesque – at least in principle, if not always in the course of reviewing – was that he thought it fundamentally immoral, especially in the broadest sense, since on the first page of his book he declared explicitly that "the better the stage the better the town". The purpose of the stage should be educational, for it is "one of the strongest of all secular aids towards the intellectual refinements of the people";[22] such a purpose understandably embraced moral principles. Examples of moral attitudes can often be found in the *Journal*. Morley disliked Verdi, for instance, notably *La Traviata*, on the grounds of the moral offensiveness of the libretto as well as the music (he also attacked *La Dame aux Camélias*). He found opera libretti in general immoral, the immorality being "rather the rule than the exception".[23] As Taylor's *The Fool's Revenge*, *Rigoletto* was acceptable, since Verdi's lax morality had been improved and because "the sense of right and justice in an English audience" had been satisfied.[24] An adaptation of Farquhar's *The Inconstant* was approved because the original had now been freed "not only from immorality of speech but also from immorality of spirit".[25] English plays of past ages could be mended in this way, but too many French plays were corrupt; "it would be easier as well as wholesomer to pare the sound old English apple than to scoop and cook and sugar those rotten French windfalls to the English taste".[26] Other examples could be given but they are all in the book; Morley's moral principles are clear, and they inform much of the criticism in the *Journal*.

What is most impressive about this criticism is Morley's boundless admiration for the art and power of good acting, a respect for the collective wisdom and, as it were, the representative nationalism of a good English audience sitting at a good English play, and an unshakeable faith in the essential worth and stature of the stage as a national institution of the highest standing. That is why Morley protested so strongly about anything in the theatre that would seem to tarnish that worth, and why he worried about the level and quality of public taste. The acted drama and the stage that performed it were as treasure-trove in the care of a principled and uncorruptible guardian, who discharged his trust carefully and honourably over the fifteen years of his stewardship. It would not be an exaggeration to describe Henry Morley's view of the theatre and his exercise of his critical duties in those terms.

Michael R. Booth
University of Warwick

NOTES

1 Kean's management lasted from 1850 to 1859, Phelps's from 1844 to 1862.

2 (1847–1855). During its last year the illness of Vestris compelled Mathews to continue virtually on his own, under great financial difficulties.

3 The Duke of Newcastle, in proposing the health of Kean at a banquet in his honour in 1859, declared that "his sceneries are not only lessons in art, but they are lessons in history. . . . I look upon Mr. Kean as one of the greatest archaeologists of the day. . . . You may see living representatives of Shakespeare's characters, with the exact costume, the exact scenery, the exact furniture of the rooms which, there is every reason to believe, from pictures and other sources, existed at the time Shakespeare represented." (John William Cole, *The Life and Theatrical Times of Charles Kean, F.S.A.*, (2nd edn, 1859), II, 366.)

4 *Ibid.*, II, 383.

5 A good example of Kean's method was his treatment of the siege of Harfleur in *Henry V* (1859); in his own words "it was no ideal battle, no imaginary fight; it was a correct representation of what had actually taken place; the engines of war, the guns, banners, fire balls, the attack and defence, the barricades at the breach, the conflagration within the town, the assault and capitulation, were all taken from the account left to us by a priest who accompanied the army, was an eye-witness, and whose Latin MS. is now in the British Museum. . . . whatever I have done had been sanctioned by history, to which I have adhered in every minute particular." (*ibid.*, II, 382).

6 Macready managed Covent Garden from 1837 to 1839, and Drury Lane from 1841 to 1843.

7 Particularly in Vestris's management of the Olympic (1831–9) and, with Mathews, of Covent Garden (1839–42).

8 The most recent study of Phelps is Shirley Allen's *Samuel Phelps and Sadler's Wells Theatre* (1971), which

shows what Phelps contributed to Shakespearean production and nineteenth-century theatre as a whole: he was by no means a conventional traditionalist, and some of his methods were essentially modern.

9 *Our Recent Actors* (1888), II, 252. Interesting especially for its conclusions is David Rinear's 'Alfred Wigan: Victorian Realist', *Theatre Survey*, XIII (November 1972), 44–59.

10 J. B. Buckstone managed the Haymarket from 1853 to 1879, although only nominally in the last few years.

11 From 1858 to 1861.

12 Fechter's management lasted until 1867.

13 Unlike Fechter, Ristori performed only in Italian, and these plays were Italian adaptations of the originals tailored especially for her.

14 No reviews of the Marie Wilton and Squire Bancroft management of the Prince of Wales's Theatre, which began in 1865, appear in the *Journal*. It is a pity that we do not have Morley's impressions of Tom Robertson's first success there, *Society*.

15 If I could refer the reader to my own work, the four volumes so far published (1969–1973) of *English Plays of the Nineteenth Century* might serve as a good introduction to the drama of the period.

16 *Report from the Select Committee on Theatrical Licences and Regulations* (1866), 295.

17 Morley was obviously conscious of this limitation, clearly a self-imposed one. He says in his prologue: "In our provinces and colonies the form of entertainment will be, as it is now, mainly determined by the example of the eight or nine theatres in or near the West-end of London, of which I hold the performance to be worth serious attention." (15).

18 He did go regularly to Sadler's Wells, mostly to see Phelps's Shakespeare. But this was hardly venturing outside middle-class 'establishment' territory.

19 Wigan once wrote to Joseph Chute, who managed at Bristol and Bath, that "he did not like to puff himself,

but that he and his wife's chief characteristics were variety and versatility and their social position." (Quoted in a marginal note in a copy, owned by one Wedmore, of Westland Marston's *Our Recent Actors*.)

20 *Journal*, 20.
21 See for instance pp. 6, 19, 25, 52, and 244 in the *Journal*.
22 *Journal*, 9.
23 *Ibid.*, 126.
24 *Ibid.*, 200.
25 *Ibid.*, 127.
26 *Ibid.*, 23.

BIBLIOGRAPHICAL NOTE

The Journal of a London Playgoer from 1851 to 1866, by
Henry Morley, was first published in London by Routledge in 1866. In 1891 a new edition of the work was
produced by the same publisher. For this edition the
type was re-set and some alterations were made in the
text. An index was included in the volume. The 1891
edition also differed from its predecessor in format,
pagination and running heads. A half-title announced
the edition as volume II in a series of *Books and Papers
of Henry Morley 1851–1866*.

Because of the value of the index the present volume
reprints photographically the text of the 1891 edition.
No subsequent editions of the work have been published.

J. L. Madden

BOOKS AND PAPERS

BY

HENRY MORLEY

1851—1866

II

THE JOURNAL

OF A

LONDON PLAYGOER

From 1851 to 1866

BY

HENRY MORLEY, LL.D.,

EMERITUS PROFESSOR OF ENGLISH LITERATURE IN UNIVERSITY COLLEGE,
LONDON

LONDON

GEORGE ROUTLEDGE AND SONS, Limited

Broadway, Ludgate Hill

GLASGOW, MANCHESTER, AND NEW YORK

1891

PROLOGUE.

THE writer who first taught Englishmen to look for principles worth study in the common use of speech, expecting censure for choice of a topic without dignity, excused himself with this tale out of Aristotle. When Heraclitus lived, a famous Greek, there were some persons, led by curiosity to see him, who found him warming himself in his kitchen, and paused at the threshold because of the meanness of the place. But the philosopher said to them, "Enter boldly, for here too there are Gods". "The Gods" in the playhouse are, indeed, those who receive outside its walls least honour among men, and they have a present right to be its Gods, I fear, not only because they are throned aloft, but also because theirs is the mind that regulates the action of the mimic world below. They rule, and why? Is not the educated man himself to blame when he turns with a shrug from the too often humiliating list of an evening's performances at all the theatres, to say lightly that the stage is ruined, and thereupon make merit of withdrawing all attention from the players? The better the stage the better the town. If the stage were what it ought to be, and what good actors heartily desire to make it, it would teach the public to appreciate what is most worthy also in the sister arts, while its own influence would be very strong for good. The great want of the stage in our day is an educated public that will care for its successes, honestly inquire into its failures, and make managers and actors feel that they are not dependent for appreciation of their efforts on the verdict that comes of the one mind divided into fragments between Mr. Dapperwit in the stalls, Lord Froth in the side-boxes, and Pompey Doodle in the gallery. The playgoer who would find in our London theatres a dramatic literature, in which England is rich beyond all other nations, fitly housed, may be indignant at much that he sees in them. But what if Doodle, Dapperwit, and Froth do clap their hands at pieces which are all leg and no brains; in which the male actor's highest ambition is to caper, slide, and stamp with the energy of a street-boy on a cellar-flap, the actress shows plenty of thigh, and the dialogue, running entirely on the sound of words, hardly admits that they have any use at all as signs of thought? Whose fault is it that the applauders of these dismal antics sit so frequently as umpires in the judgment of dramatic literature?

Take, for example, that notorious burlesque of *Ixion*, in which the brother of a Viscount not long ago made his *début* as an actor, and was thus advertised : "Great success of the Hon. Lewis Wingfield as Minerva. Other characters by the loveliest women in England." That burlesque of *Ixion* has no story to develop, or only as much plot as can be told in a sentence. Ixion, scouted by his wife and people, is invited to dinner by Jove, accepts the invitation, goes, flirts with Venus, leaves her for Juno, and is doomed by Jove to lead off the speaking of a tag to the audience from behind a wheel. The whole success of the piece was made by dressing up good-looking girls as immortals lavish in display of leg, and setting them to sing and dance, or rather kick wretched burlesque capers, for the recreation of fast blockheads. If Miss Pelham only knew how she looks in the eyes of the better half of any audience when she comes forward with sandy beard and moustaches disfiguring her face, and with long pink legs wriggling her body into the ungainly gestures of burlesque toeing and heeling, the woman in her would rise in rebellion against the miserable vulgarity of the display. As for the Hon. Lewis Wingfield, who dressed his thin figure in petticoats and spoke falsetto as Minerva—every man to his taste ! His great success was an idiotic dance in petticoats that might stand for something in competitive examination for admission into the Earlswood Asylum, but as a gentleman's first bid for the honours of the English stage was a distressing sight to see.

They who care for the past literature of their country, and look for the right maintaining of its honour by the writers to whose hands it is committed in our day, must blame themselves in part for the too frequent perversion of the stage into an agent for the ruin of the written drama. They turn back from the threshold of the playhouse, flinching from the present meanness of the place, and in vain the actor who desires fit company would bid them enter boldly, and help his desire to reverence the gods they seek.

Most of us who have been often to the play have seen the occasional flashing of undeveloped power even from actors who are esteemed third-rate, when they have something to do which plucks well at their energies. Good parts would breed in a·few years many good players ; and we, who have in our literature the finest drama in the world, stay at home and scold at the players whom we never see, or go abroad only to be entertained or depressed by them with prosy and ill-written melodramas, or with the bright scenery of bad burlesques.

It is not quite so true now as it was but a few years ago —for there has sprung up during the last three or four years in several of our journals a healthy little breeze of public criticism—but it is still too commonly the case, that the mistaken kindness of his friends by indiscriminate praise robs the player of his best encouragement to strive to a high mark, win definite appreciation for himself, and honour for his calling. The best actor exercising his delightful art upon material that will bring all the subtlest powers into use—although, indeed, it is his ill-fortune to work in the most transient material, that cannot survive, except in memory, the moment of its full expression—is not the less as true an artist as the poet or the painter or the sculptor, and even more worthy than these are of immediate repute, since that alone is his reward. The sculptor, painter, poet, misunderstood in his own time, leaves his work to do him right. The actor's labour is for ever lost if it miss instant recognition. The public owes, therefore, for its own sake, and in common justice, generous attention to the stage. There has been too much of the disdainful inattentive generosity that shames an honourable profession, and drives many a good actor almost to despair by confounding good and bad under the same cant form of empty, supercilious praise.

The London playgoer who in this book adds up the sum of his experience has found much to attack, and thinks it worth attacking seriously, because he has a firm faith in the future of the English stage.

Some ways of writing come in and go out with the fashions, but the Drama is too natural a part of us to be cast off. It may be an ailing limb of the great body of our Literature, but it is a limb, and a main limb. Sense of dramatic action appears in the year-old infant, and enlivens almost every form of child's play. The maturest acts and busiest scenes of life, in proportion as a community is vigorous and has high motives for its energy, quicken the sense that all the world's a stage. In the chief city of such a community—in London—where every man lives in active daily perception of the characters and humours and relations to each other of the persons about him, if there be any literary life at all, there is dramatic power.

We have a rich soil that grows weeds because we disdain tillage. In the field of our Drama we need never want good wheat; but we must not flinch when the ploughshare is tearing through the thistledown and poppies. There will be no want of good plays when they have room to come up, and are not choked by the bad burlesques and French translations that now occupy the ground. Nor will there be any want of good actors when good acting shall be honestly appreciated, instead of being thoughtlessly confounded with the bad by undue exaltation of pretenders, or by slight of indiscriminate applause. As it is, we have among our playwrights clever writers, and upon the stage good actors and actresses, to whom this book pays honour. The actor has not now fair play, and will not have it till the educated public honestly comes forward to take the patronage of the English drama out of the hands of Doodle, Dapperwit, and Froth.

The main purpose of this volume is to show the need and use of such an intervention. During the last fourteen or fifteen years, while studying our literature, I have been in professional attendance at the bedside of our modern Drama, seeing nearly every piece produced, with or without music, at the chief London theatres. At first now and then as a supernumerary clinical clerk, and afterwards more regularly, I have furnished the *Examiner* with notes from my case-book upon the succession of symptoms. A warm interest in the patient never affected the determination to set down precisely what I took for truth. Always, also, I have watched the case from the same point of view; desiring to see our Drama, with a clean tongue and a steady pulse, able to resume its place in society as a chief form of Literature, with a stage fitly interpreting its thoughts and in wide honour as one of the strongest of all secular aids towards the intellectual refinement of the people. From the occasional notes thus made, I have wished to collect into this volume only as much as will sketch faithfully an individual impression of our stage as it now is, the indications of health in it and the remedies for its disease. Small things will be chronicled sometimes, where they may aid in producing a right general idea. Sometimes, also, important incidents will be passed over, perhaps because the current notes of them were furnished by another hand. But although such notes as were of my own taking are but a tithe of all there might have been, to reprint the whole even of these would be, as the stage now is, to emulate the learned gentleman who wrote six volumes on a dot. Starting, then, far enough back to show that suggestions in the later pages of this little book, if wrong, were at any rate not made until after more than a seven years' apprenticeship to critical playgoing, I shall endeavour to connect together only such comments, and fragments of comment, as may stand for a fair speaking of one mind upon the present condition of the English stage. Of some of the best acting it has had to show during the last fourteen or fifteen years, little as it may be, I wish to give what definite account I can, both for its own sake, and as the best way of saying what qualities appear to me most worthy of appreciation in an actor. To secure material enough for criticism of this kind, I shall look also to some of the best foreign actors who have played in London.

As far as lies in me, I shall wish to enforce the argument of this book by a cordial appreciation of every sign of a regard for the true credit of the acted drama. The players who uphold most worthily the honour of their living art should suffer by no grudging estimate of their desert. They should be used as Shakespeare himself, through *Hamlet*, bade us use them. We, indeed, of the present generation see no perfect acting of a part demanding all the highest powers of an artist for its full realisation. But we do now and then find an actor by whom much of the poetical intention of a dramatist has been felt rightly, and not unworthily expressed. Wherever that is so, it is to the best interest of our drama that the actor's reward shall not be chilled with censure for his falling short of an ideal standard. The actors who are dead and gone are only names to us. They have carried their art with them, and can do nothing for us if memory of their worth do not inspire the present with an active emulation. Better for us at least that they had never been, than that their names should be used as part of a grim superstition for the quelling of all faith and hope in efforts yet to come. The actor's future reputation depends wholly upon the opinion of his day. When he is gone no after time is able to supply omissions in the record, or revise a careless judgment. And that judgment may be a careless one which shall seem strict and true, when it notes chiefly those defects of manner which may be, in some cases, more obvious than the delicacies of true art expressed through an imperfect instrument. Mr. Phelps, for example, plays his parts with various degrees of merit, and impairs the force of almost all by an undue slowness of delivery. This he acquired, probably, at Sadler's Wells, when he was training a rude audience to the enjoyment of dramatic poetry, and endeavoured to assure life in slow minds to every word by dwelling upon each with a slight excess of the weight in utterance which, within certain limits, is required of all who would give value to the reading of good poetry. In course of time the deliberately measured pace of speech has hardened into mannerism ; and, considering its origin, the blemish is like that of a scar won in honourable war. But it is still a blemish, the more conspicuous when it is seen also that something of the impulse of young blood has gone, here and there, out of the acting of familiar parts. But such obvious and accidental qualities as these in a true actor, or as the French accent of Mr. Fechter, when they have been once mentioned, I prefer to put aside. It is little to say that reference to them should not supersede, it ought hardly to intrude upon, apt estimation of the actor's mind employed upon the reading of his part. Let but the contemporary praise earned by good acting be definitely just, and lack of ifs and buts will mislead nobody; the critics will be free and competent hundreds of years hence to form, from the character of the praise earned, a right estimate of the relative worth of actors appraised by successive critics in successive generations. A vague exaggeration of applause discourages true effort, and tends to defraud good actors of their chance of lasting fame.

But this little book will not fulfil its purpose if it do not include also a few definite censures. There are mistakes of policy behind the foot-lights and misjudgments by the public that lead only to the degradation of the stage, which means the loss to English literature of an acted drama. I shall erase from this record many a sharp censure spoken when it was deserved, of which the repetition might give pain without serving a useful purpose. The reader accustomed to dramatic criticism in great lakes of milk and honey may think mine but a bitter streamlet, water of Mara flowing through a desert, with an oasis here and there, where the critical mirage had suggested universal Paradise. A little bitterness of flavour my small stream must needs take from the soil through which it flows; but I do know that too much of that quality would take away its wholesomeness.

I wish also to avoid laying undue stress on my own judgment, as that of one playgoer, upon any one player or playwright. There is an Italian proverb, "Tutto il cervello non è in una testa." All the brains are not in one head. Every man is bound to do whatever it may lie in him to do with all his might, and be a firm centre to his own small circle of experience and thought. But he is not called upon to think himself the axis of the Cosmos. He knows nothing, and is able to learn nothing, who has not learnt that upon many points he may be wrong. Yet one is not the less bound to uphold every cause that he thinks right, if it fall within the proper scheme of his life's work to do active battle for it. I trust, therefore, that the readers of this book will allow throughout for the underlying reservation of respect to differing opinions, even in those passages which may contain firmest expression of my own belief. The strongest individual conviction ought not to be inconsistent with a power of applying to oneself the law that is applicable to all other men. We see every day men whom we think none the less wrong because they are positive ; and we ought to admit, each for himself, the difference between a personal conviction and an abstract truth.

A critic to whom I look up holds Mr. Phelps to be no actor. A veteran man of letters, who has a clear judgment, has astonished me with glowing admiration of the Juliet of Miss Bateman. Intellectual men have accredited Mr. Charles Kean, in his most honourable career as a manager and actor, with poetic insight that I fail to recognise. It is well for the world, and for every section of work done in it, that opinions thus differ. Without such difference there would be no scouting of rash assertions, no constant shaking to and fro of the great sieve of argument, no exercising of the thews of a man's intellect, no divine energy at work in men, who labour well only when labouring in concert with their fellows, and only with their help can rise, by studying in the endless uses and graces of life the pattern of true wisdom in the will of the Creator.

The mind that does not shut itself out from the world, or hold itself the universal arbiter, will find in all that breathes a spark of the Divine. God, who gave to the moth his dainty wings, and to the violet a scent whose use is but the creation of pleasure, gave to man, with the delights of speech, faculties that weave them by the subtlest of his arts into a flower-world of intellect and feeling. At the playhouse-door, then, we may say to the doubting, Enter boldly, for here, too, there are gods.

There are in London twenty-five theatres. Her Majesty's

Theatre will hold 3,000 persons; the Pavilion, in White-chapel, holds even 3,500; the Marylebone, 2,000; the new Adelphi, 1,400; and others in proportion. Except during the autumn holidays, and after all allowance for thin houses, and houses occasionally closed, the London public must be going in daily detachments averaging at least 15,000 persons to the play for recreation; and the audiences are changed every night. What is accounted in London good entertainment is adopted by provincial and colonial theatres. Add all their audiences to such an estimate, and we shall hardly ask again, Why care for what it is that the stage offers to the daily renewed army of playgoers? Our theatre is able to maintain in health a noble branch of English literature, and the literature is able in return to make the stage partaker of its health. We may owe to the stage a leavening of the intelligence of thousands who, while thoroughly amused, are imbued with some fit sense of art; or it may be, as it seems, content with all its mischievous defects. Wherever the English language is spoken, here or at the other side of the world, theatres there will always be, with daily thousands looking to them for amusement. In our provinces and colonies the form of entertainment will be, as it now is, mainly determined by the example of the eight or nine theatres in or near the West-end of London, of which I hold the performances to be worth serious attention. If they who wish well to English literature disdain to stretch out a hand in friendship to the players, and will make no effort at all to recover the old wholesome alliance between good wit and good acting, they not only assent to the ruin of what has hitherto been, in this country at least, one of the chief strongholds of good wit, but their neglect snaps one of the surest bonds of union between true literature and the main body of the people. Plays that address the eye for sensual appreciation, and reduce their dialogue and action to the meanest level of an unformed taste, will even damage for those who are entertained by them the power of appreciating thought in books.

But let this prologue include a recognition of the fact that, in speaking of the theatres, we may be liable to over-estimate the real extent of our ground of complaint. In comment on shortcomings of the stage, let us remember that in its best and in its worst days it has been equally abused. In 1597, when Shakespeare himself was a player —it was the very year in which his success as a dramatist enabled him to buy one of the best houses in his native town—Joseph Hall, afterwards a bishop, published his satires ; and therein, while he condemned the dramatist's big sounding sentences and words of state, he was yet more grieved that on our stage russet and royal state had equal place, and ended one satire by crying—

> " Shame that the Muses should be bought and sold,
> For every peasant's brass, on each scaffold."

Joseph Hall, who had at least read Chaucer and Skelton, reckoned himself to be the first English satirist, upon no other ground than that he was the first who imitated Juvenal. Good literature, in his eyes, was for the educated courtier, and was discredited when it was brought home to "each base clown". The glory of the drama was for him its shame. That bowl of small-change taken at the play-house-door gave a more sure support to men of genius who earned their share from it, than Royal favour and the being in high fashion among courtiers.

It was dependence upon courtly favour that destroyed in the stage of the Restoration its old national character. But whether the stage were good or bad—though it were adorned by Shakespeare or by Garrick—the tide of com-plaint flowed on, and did not owe its whole strength to the protests of the Puritans. Ben Jonson, in revolt from tyranny of the bad taste before the curtain, vigorously con-

demned "the loathed stage". Pope in his day decried
excesses of the scene in which

> "Hell rises, Heaven descends, and dance on Earth
> Gods, imps, and monsters, music, rage, and mirth,
> A fire, a jig, a battle, and a ball,
> Till one wide conflagration swallow all,"—

and that was in the days of Cibber, Wilkes, and Booth.
Then Garrick came, of whom Quin said, that, "if the young
fellow was right, he and the rest of the players had been all
wrong." When Garrick was at his brightest, even Churchill
said, in scorn of authors who would wait on actors :

> "Bow down, ye slaves ! before these idols fall ;
> Let genius stoop to them who've none at all."

Yet Churchill was in truth the strong maintainer of the
actors' honour, as the keenest and best critic they have ever
had. The fame, in his own day, of Garrick, as of those
who came before and those who followed him, was blemished
by the unfailing custom of exalting actors who are gone.
Quin claimed supremacy, as of the school of Betterton and
Booth.

> "For how should moderns, mushrooms of the day,
> Who ne'er those masters knew, know how to play?"

Churchill opposed to the

> "Greybearded veterans, who, with partial tongue,
> Extol the times when they themselves were young ;
> Who, having lost all relish for the stage,
> See not their own defects, but lash the age,"

emphatic recognition of the genius of Garrick. One says
he is too short,

> "Another can't forgive the paltry arts
> By which he makes his way to shallow hearts ;
> Mere pieces of finesse, traps for applause.—
> 'Avaunt, unnatural start—affected pause !'"

But of the starts and pauses condemned by the veterans who thus had lost their relish for the stage, Churchill said for his own time,

> "When in the features all the soul's portrayed,
> And passions such as Garrick's are displayed,
> To me they seem from quickest feelings caught :
> Each start, is nature ; and each pause, is thought."

As it was said in Garrick's day that there were no more Booths and Bettertons, so in our day it may be said that there are no more Kembles, no more Listons and Farrens, no more of any of the actors who have become traditions of perfection since they were no more. This strain of lamentation I have no wish to take up. In John Kemble, the last of the great bygone actors, even the highest eulogy of his acting in such a part as Coriolanus would be blended, while he was yet on the stage, with the observation that he was inapt for comedy ; that his face, capable of depicting powerful emotion, could not represent by play of feature delicacies of expression, so that his acting might be as well appreciated from the gallery as from the front row of the pit ; that his tone of voice was too sepulchral ; that his study led to the substituting of an ostentatious style of acting for a natural one. A glance at bygone censure should suffice to warn us against taking a hopeless view of our own matters of complaint.

In one respect considerable advance has been made during the last few years. The growth of civilisation has brought even into the homes of the poor comforts unknown to the rich in the days of Elizabeth. The million, who then could only satisfy their mental appetite by taking good thought through their ears from stage or pulpit, may now sit at ease by their own fireside and read what they will. In perfect rest of body they may feast their fancies upon tales rich in dramatic incident and speech of men—dramas, in fact, wherein well-written description takes the place of

scenery, and the author's own way of analysis supplants the
actor's power of interpreting the humours and the passions
of the scene.   The best of these novels are more original in
their construction, paint character with more skill, and have
a better dialogue than may be found in any of the new
plays acted on the stage.   The play, if, after its kind, as
good as the novel and well acted, gives a greater pleasure.
But is it a pleasure so much greater as to tempt people
away from their home comforts after the labours of the day,
induce them to submit to the trouble of a journey to and
from the theatre, and sit there during four, or sometimes
five hours, bound to one allotted seat?   The changes to
which this question points have almost all been recognised
during the last fifteen years, and for even so much progress
we have reason to be thankful.   One theatre after another
has lost its old aspect of discomfort before the curtain ; and
petty exactions that interfere with perfect rest of mind are
gradually disappearing, though they are not yet altogether
gone.   The payment for a seat should be made to secure,
within the theatre, every service necessary to the right
enjoyment of it.   Not only the seats but the approaches to
them should be easy.   Seats in the pit should be cushioned,
backed, and not overcrowded ; in the boxes and stalls,
always comfortable chairs.   Desire to reap quickly the fruit
of every success still tempts nearly all managers to crowd
their seats together, and grudge lines of open space for
movement to and fro.   They crowd, if they can, with extra
chairs, or sell as " standing-room" even the few narrow path-
ways which they are compelled unwillingly to leave.   In
this they are not just to their public, and I believe also that
they are less kind to themselves than the state of their
treasury on any single night might lead them to suppose.
First catch your customer, then truss him, and stew him four
hours in a hot closet, is a recipe that involves some risk of
at least not catching your rational customer a second time.

Having received company pleasantly, and suppressed all levies of blackmail within the theatre ; having also placed every one at ease on seats which rest the body, and are so arranged that even a lady may without much trouble relieve the weariness of long fixture in one position by a little movement from her chair during some interval between the acts ; having recognised thoroughly all natural requirements of his audience, even down to the fact that footstools are a necessary compensation for the difference of height in male and female ; having done all that can be done to secure ventilation and to keep out draughts ; and having made it a fixed rule never, except on occasion of some incident that will not be repeated, to admit into the house more persons than it will comfortably hold ; what next is the model manager to do ?

He is next, I think, to have faith in his patrons, not to look down on them and treat them as if he fancied that a witless man about town could be taken for their standard of capacity. There is a large half-intelligent population now in London that by bold puffing can be got into a theatre. It numbers golden lads and lasses as well as chimney-sweeps. The population is, indeed, so large that it takes many nights to pass it through a theatre, each night's theatre-full being as a bucket-full dipped out of a big stagnant pond. Any manager may, if he will, set his face against intelligent opinion, and, falling back upon the half-intelligent, go the right way to that pond, bale patiently, and send nearly the whole of it through his house. But its credit will not be the cleaner for that process, though it may secure the specu-lator against loss by misplaced costliness of scenery, and may enable him to set against the condemnation of his piece by every educated man the advertisement that Duchesses and Viscounts have been to see it, and that it is being acted for its millionth night. That is not being a model manager.

But if this mythical being ought not to accept too low a standard of the public taste, and should remember that a good piece will answer as well as a bad one for drawing the untaught crowd, who will freely follow a good lead, it does not therefore follow that he should see a standard of the public taste in any section of those critical highflyers who affect the sort of fastidiousness over which Ben Jonson justly broke the seven vials of his wrath—

> " Let their fastidious, vain
> Commission of the brain
> Run on and rage, sweat, censure, and condemn ;
> They were not made for thee, less thou for them."

In the theatre let our escape be complete from every sort of pedantry. Our model manager should take for standard of the people he would please an honest Englishman of the educated middle-class, akin to all that is human, trained not only in school and college, but in daily active stir of life, to interest in all true thinking and true feeling, to habitual notice of varieties of character, and to a habit of noting its depths in real life. He may take its soundings more or less inaccurately, but at any rate he has so constantly endeavoured to map out the depths and shoals of character in definite cases that he is bred to a keen relish of those suggestions of yet subtler exploration which should be among the highest charms of a good drama. Let the model manager give to his public of every kind of true dramatic entertainment that which is most thorough. The practical jokes of the short farce, devised to satisfy a homely relish of that kind of fun, are in their place as legitimate as the soliloquies of Hamlet. Let us still have our melo-dramas blending jest with earnest, and let no manager permit the tragic Muse to be robbed of her dagger and bowl. Let our playwrights still be free to take any good story which they can put into a good dramatic form, and adapt modern French plays if they can do no better—only I am sure they might do better. But, whatever they do, let it be something real, not like burlesque, vacuity of thought giving itself all the airs of wit, and most dependent for success on a display of women's legs and servile copies of the humour of the music-halls. Let the playgoer, when he has settled himself down in his easy seat, have reason to respect his entertainers. He cannot do that if he has been brought into his place within the theatre by bills and advertisements that trumpeted as real what he finds to be either a forced success or no success at all. He cannot do so if he finds that the "original play" he has come out to see, the original play with an English writer's name placed in unmodified connection with it, is the French play that he saw when he was last in Paris. It does not lessen the general, though it will remove particular, occasion for complaint, if this form of untruth has been carried so far that, when a dramatist is honestly original, nine playgoers out of ten suppose that he, too, bought the chief part of his wit and invention for a shilling in the Burlington Arcade. Whenever a French piece has been adapted for use in an English theatre, there should be honest, definite acknowledgment—the name of the French piece and its author being given in the bills, with some indication of the greater or less degree of manipulation to which it has been subjected ; one, say, "translated", another "adapted", another "freely altered", from the *Pomme Pourrie* of MM. Péché and Bonbon.

The poor thought and unreal sentiment of these translations from French plays arise from the fact that they are based not even on a true study of French life, but only upon a shrewd perception of the French varieties of stage-effect and of stage-character. In the best days of our drama plays were founded on perception of essentials of character acquired from a direct study of life itself, and for this reason the elements of an unfading interest are to be found in very many of our pieces. With less pains than are spent by a clever English adapter on the flashy stage-effects of a French drama of the present day, such plays of ours could have the rust rubbed off, the points of discord with existing ways of thought removed, and they might thus restore to us the old enjoyment of sound wit or poetry spent on the painting of men's humours and passions. John Kemble, at the beginning of our century, revised many a good English play for modern acting : one of Beaumont and Fletcher's, one of Massinger's, one of Wycherley's, two of Congreve's, even a play of Mrs. Aphra Behn's, besides one of Rowe's, two of Nat. Lee's, Young's *Revenge*, and plays by Holcroft, Moore, and Murphy, were among his adaptations. They were not all worth adapting ; and John Kemble's literary skill was far beneath that of our best dramatic authors, who are also skilled adapters of inferior material. I might cite several, but for example dare venture to name Mr. Tom Taylor and Mr. Oxenford as writers of our time who join a true appreciation of good literature to a remarkable stage-tact and some real dramatic genius. It might be said that men with good reputations to lose would flinch justly from the charge of a rash meddling with the works of any standard English writer. But the works of our best dramatists will remain untouched in all their editions, and will certainly not be the less read for a free quarrying among their treasures by those who can make the good old names at home as they should be upon English playbills, and their best passages of jest or earnest familiar again in the mouths of our good actors. And, in fact, skilful adapters would have less trouble in remodelling for present use the best of our old English plays than they now frequently take with modern French ones. In those old plays of ours there is sometimes a conventional indelicacy which comes only of honest recognition of the whole nature of man, who has a body as well as a soul. In too many of the new French plays adapted for us there is a conventional delicacy to content the ear where the understanding can find only rottenness to bite into. It would be easier as well as wholesomer to pare the sound old English apple than to scoop and cook and sugar those rotten French windfalls to the English taste.

Our range of choice, too, in this matter is wider than the sheepwalk of the latest fashions. We dare go back even to Marlowe, whose *Edward the Second* needs but few touches to make it a good acting play. Now that *Faust* is in the ascendant, it might even be said that freedom of omission in the comic scenes, with elsewhere two or three skilful modifications, would give to our stage in Marlowe's *Faustus* a grand part for a good actor. In Marlowe's *Jew of Malta*, that dark mediæval painting of a man of a detested race, there may be too much of nightmare ; but an English audience still likes a play with plenty of good downright villainy, and would be strongly impressed, even in our day, by such figures as those of Barabas and Ithamore, set in a play without any fine shades of character-painting, yet full of a grand strength of invention and of sounding lines that are not sound alone. It is something, too, that the play is capable of rich picturesque decoration, and would give to the eye Spanish knights, magnificent Turks, slaves, monks, nuns, Jews. It would admit, too, of effective acting in some boldly-coloured parts ; while a few easy changes in the scenes with Bellamira, and omission from the other dialogue of some half-dozen jests, would be all the alteration absolutely necessary. In fact, I am speaking of plays that no one hopes ever to see acted again in England, to show how, even in cases apparently hopeless, when one comes to look narrowly at the construction of one of these old masses of dramatic energy, the work of adaptation to the modern stage appears much easier than vague recollection of their character might lead one to suppose. Of course, in the case of a play like the *Jew of Malta*, questions of obsolete stage-effect would here and there arise.   In this play, for example, Friar Barnardine might have to be strangled off the stage, and the setting up of his dead body to be struck down by Friar Jacomo could hardly be in the presence of the people.   But if we supposed it to be set up on the other side of a central open door at the back of the stage, not only might the whole incident remain, but every word of the text with it.   Friar Jacomo, standing in the doorway, might even be seen to strike at the brother whom he suspects of being there to intercept his going to the Jew. When Barabas in the last scene dies in his own trap, it would be but a light task for the scene-painter to find some effective substitute for the hot caldron, in which he dies cursing the Christians.   As for the false-floor business, that would be in precise accordance with the latest humour for " sensation" plunges; while the advantage on the side of the old play would be that, from first to last, with incidents even more highly spiced, there is the poet's energy of thought supplanting the bald slipshod English of a modern melodrama.   Nay, taking a yet more extreme case, we may go back even to the first English comedy, and find in *Ralph Roister Doister* a prototype of Lord Dundreary.   Were that play skilfully condensed into three acts, and represented with all due vivacity by players who could make the rhyme run merrily, we might have even Udall again setting the house in a roar; Mr. Sothern might be the vainglorious suitor laying siege to the heart of Mistress Christian Custance ; Mr. Compton might be the dry humourist Matthew Merrygreek, who fools him and sponges upon him.   And there would be no want, at the same theatre, of a comely Mistress Custance governing her garrison of maids, and a drily sedate Gavin Goodluck to come over the sea to her at pairing time, when the play ends.

I repeat that I am pointing here to some of those oldest of our dramas which appear to be least promising, not for the sake of recommending these particular works for revival, but for the sake of suggesting that, if even among those beginnings of our great dramatic literature there is good actable matter, how much more is to be said of the same literature in its strength !

Has Massinger written nothing but *A New Way to Pay Old Debts ?* Has Ben Jonson written only one play, *Every Man in his Humour ?* in which, by the way, Shakespeare acted. Beaumont and Fletcher, too, who might give a good theatre good matter to act for a dozen years together, why are they to be shelved that we may poison our English Thalia with a diet of translations of the works of MM. Péché and Bonbon ? Farquhar, Wycherley, and Congreve are cleaner than the playwrights of modern France, and in comparison of wit are as true salt to gravel. It is as easy to recast them to the modern taste as to clean out French impurities from the French dramas, and how much bright dramatic dialogue should we recover to its proper use ! Good English thought revived upon our stage would make itself at home again among the English people.

Let all who can make a voice heard join in asking for it, and the change may come. Whenever it does come we may be sure that the blockheads of the town, whose taste is catered for too much, will follow the new lead. They are born to follow a bellwether. Let such a change come, and actors with parts worth their best study will develop their best skill, as they now simply cannot ; while audiences, trained to some appreciation of the best dramatic writing, may recover to the stage the service of true poets, and regain for our dramatic literature its old place among the sunny pasture-grounds of English wit.

Here ends the prologue, and the curtain rises on the players.

May 1866.

THE JOURNAL

A LONDON PLAYGOER.

1851. *August* 30.—The discriminating Mr. Barnum has had reason to think that the English taste turns very much upon small things; and he now challenges for two miniature actors the success that attended his Tom Thumb. The "Bateman children" are little girls respectively of eight and six, who are both pretty and clever, but whose appearance in an act of *Richard the Third* (at the ST. JAMES'S THEATRE) is a nuisance by no means proportioned to the size of its perpetrators. No doubt there is talent shown in it; and it is curious to hear such small imps of the nursery speak so fluently, and, strutting about easily, repeat a well-taught lesson with such wonderful aptitude. But this is the feeling of a moment, and nothing is left but the wearisome absurdity of such big words in such little mouths.

The comic French piece, *The Young Couple* (written for the child Leontine Fay by M. Scribe), is another matter; and here the little girls are thoroughly amusing. They play a couple of children of the old French *noblesse*, married by order of the Court, who, without knowing what love is, are supposed to imitate in a pretty piquant childish way such of its symptoms as they have had an opportunity of watching in the case of their two grown-up cousins. The least of the children, who had strutted and stamped in Richard, plays the boy; and to see her, in a bag-wig and knee-breeches, and with a better sense of broad humour than she had shown of tragedy, represent a boy attempting little freedoms of the meaning of which he has not the remotest notion, which on the other hand are accepted or flirted off with equally innocent airs of determined coquetry by his small shrew of a mistress, is no doubt irresistibly comical. Though the younger actor has perhaps the more whimsical turn for comic and farcical display, the elder seems to be the better actress of the two. Her first scene (with the grown-up cousin) showed not a few of the qualities of impulsive and natural acting—even to the broad provincialisms of dialect which had been scrupulously suppressed in the absurd declamation of Richmond.

The audience enjoy the entertainment as far as it goes, but it must be confessed that this is not very far; and how many pieces are there like this of M. Scribe's which have been actually written for children? It is quite certain that repeated exhibitions such as that of the *Richard the Third* ought to be too much for public patience.

1852. *January* 17.—The readers of Mr. Dickens's pleasant book about Italy can hardly have forgotten his account of that famous company of Milanese puppets which he saw at Genoa engaged in the representation of *Napoleon at St. Helena*. One of his remarks upon a member of the company was particularly impressive. He is describing, as a triumph of art, a heavy father with grey hair, whom he saw sitting down on the regular conventional stage-bank blessing his daughter in the regular conventional way, and he observes that no one "would suppose it possible that anything short of a real man could be so tedious". I have sometimes wished to see that heavy father.

The secret of the pleasure derived from his exhibition of tediousness was no doubt the absence of what the philosopher calls *sham*. It was a stick passing for what it was; and not pretending to be anything else. Puppets have at various times, therefore, and in various countries, had a larger following than one might have thought fairly due to the merits of wooden actors in the abstract.   Wooden actors in the concrete (flesh and blood) have been so much worse. The puppets were as popular in Paris when Le Sage wrote for them, as in London when Addison and Steele wrote about them ; and who has forgotten those London puppets of a later date whom Burke and Goldsmith went to see at Panton Street in the Haymarket, on that memorable night when Goldsmith broke his shin after supper by attempting to exhibit to his friends how much better he could jump over a stick than the wooden actors?

Puppets, then, have a certain classical association with us, though living rivals in the histrionic art have of late years so dispossessed them that even their English name has departed. We must now call them Marionetti, and we are invited to a Royal Marionette Theatre.   This is all very good.   The only doubt is whether the selection for the opening per- formance of a subject in itself burlesque, such as *Bombastes Furioso*, was quite judicious.   The triumph of the whimsical one would suppose to consist in a contrast of intense gravity in the subject with helpless absurdity in the actor.   Thus when Mr. Dickens describes to us (in the Sir Hudson Lowe drama) Buonaparte's boots so wonderfully beyond his con- trol as to do marvellous things of their own accord—double themselves up, get under tables, dangle in the air, and at times even skate away with him out of all human knowledge —one source of the exquisite mirth inspired by these mis- chances must surely have been that " settled melancholy" which he at the same time tells us was depicted in the face of Napoleon.   A burlesque subject does not admit of this. Of course the "aspiring tendency" of the actors did not escape our great observer in Genoa.   When Napoleon was sick, he tells us, Doctor Antommarchi seemed to be hover- ing about the couch like a vulture, and giving medical opinions in the air.

February 7.—There is this great advantage which dis-
poses one to notice the efforts of the artists at the ROYAL
MARIONETTE THEATRE, that they are not thin-skinned. We
may praise puppet A without falling into mortal dislike with
puppet B, and need not fear to censure quite as freely as
we praise. They don't even know their own merits. Yet
the ingenious little actors of the Adelaide Street Theatre
perform with surprising accuracy the quaint romance of
The Bottle Imp, and afterwards, with consummate skill, go
through the principal movements of the old Italian harlequinade.

February 14.—There is not a play of Shakespeare's which
more admits or justifies a magnificent arrangement of scene
than the chronicle-play of *King John*. Its worthy presentation in an English theatre was one of the triumphs of Mr.
Macready's direction of DRURY LANE ten years ago, and
Mr. Charles Kean now follows that example in his revival
of the play at the PRINCESS'S with a devotion of care and
study as well as a lavish expenditure of scenic resource
which is entitled to the highest praise.

So mounted, we see in this play—what the great Marl-
borough saw nowhere else so satisfactorily—a solid frag-
ment of our English history. We see revived the rude
chivalric grandeur of the Middle Age, the woes and wars of
a half-barbarous time, in all its reckless splendour, selfish
cruelty, and gloomy suffering. In the latter features of the
picture the play of *John* stands apart among Shakespeare's
regal chronicles. The heart heaves and throbs beneath its
coat of mail. It has a state greater than the state of kings,
and a throne on which sits a higher sovereign. None of
the characters of the tragedy are cast in an unyielding
mould. John shrinks appalled and self-abased from the
guilt he has designed, the heated iron falls from the hand of
Hubert, and even Falconbridge becomes amazed, and fearful he should lose his way among the thorns and dangers of

this world. Mad world, mad kings, mad composition—yet, with good and evil blended in all, the many-toned wisdom of humanity vibrates through such history as this.

Mr. Kean plays John with an earnest resolve to make apparent to the audience his mean and vacillating nature, his allegiance to "that smooth-faced gentleman, tickling Commodity, Commodity, the Bias of the World", and the absence of dignity in his suffering. Mrs. Kean throws all her energy, and much true emotion, into Constance; and in Falconbridge Mr. Wigan makes a more sensible advance than we have yet had to record into the higher region of chivalric comedy. There is a clever child, too, in Arthur, a Miss Terry, and the minor parts are effectively presented.

June 5.—While a great French actress is filling the ST. JAMES'S THEATRE from floor to roof with audiences eager to see a good play for the sake of genius shown in the acting of it, Mr. Mitchell brings to the same theatre a German company to play for twelve nights on alternate evenings. The Germans also must win favour by good acting, or not at all, and they have Herr Emil Devrient for chief of their company.

The play chosen for the opening night was Göthe's tragedy of *Egmont*, begun at the time when his mind expressed itself through *Werther* and *Götz von Berlichingen*, occasionally continued, and finished in its first shape more than seven years after it was begun; but after another couple of years thoroughly revised and recast as a whole work of art, when Göthe was in Italy in 1787. How different this sort of work from the off-hand "adapting" of French plays that showed in their first inventors only a tact in recombining certain stage-effects and using surface-knowledge of society, while they give no scope to the actor for the exercise of all his powers, and reduce the practice of a noble art to a knack that can be acquired as readily by the quick-witted trifler as by the artist who has genius and will to work!

Egmont would perhaps scarcely pass muster as a tragedy
in England, where scenes are not accounted tragic if they do
not move the sensitive to tears.   Nor does it fulfil a chief
condition of good tragedy : there is too little dramatic
action.   The plot of the play is very simple.   It is laid at
Brussels, in the time when the Netherlands, tainted with
heresy, were beginning to give trouble to their rulers at the
Court of Spain.   Egmont, Prince of Gaure, a brave, free-
hearted chief of Netherlandish blood, is idolised by the
people, and, together with William of Orange and some
other chiefs, suspected by the Court.   Philip the Second
finally resolves to send his bloodthirsty general, the Duke of
Alva, with an army into Brussels, whither the duke accordingly betakes himself, and where, according to a preconcerted
plan, having superseded the regency of Margaret of Parma,
he invites Egmont and Orange to the palace with a
treacherous intent.   Orange, with accustomed shrewdness,
had foreseen the plot against them, and warned Egmont
to withdraw himself in time.   Egmont, frank and generous, refuses to mistrust his king, and will not think precau-
tion necessary.   He therefore, of course, visits his enemy
when summoned, Orange prudently remaining absent.
Egmont, invited by Duke Alva to give counsel for the
pacification of the Netherlands, talks of the rights of the
people and the duty of respecting them.   Meanwhile troops
are encircling the palace, and when he has spoken his
mind Egmont is carried to a dungeon, whence he goes out
the next day to be beheaded.   But before his execution he
learns in a vision that his death will lead to the liberation of
the Netherlands.

With these public events is interwoven an amour between
Egmont and Clärchen, a simple cottage girl, who dotes
upon the hero, falls into simple admiration over his embroi-
dery, raves in the street when he is imprisoned, and takes
poison on the morning of his death, being supported through

the latter scenes by a discarded lover of her own station in life. Clärchen is another version of the same ideal so familiar to all in the Margaret of *Faust*.

The merit of the play itself—which was written in prose—lies in its masterly depiction of character, in its terse energetic writing, and in the wonderful skill with which it reproduces the results of a shrewd study of human society. The ignorant and unstable multitude is represented in a series of scenes which contain some of the best writing in the drama. The groups in which the shopkeeper, the tailor, the carpenter, and soapboiler are prominent, form town-scenes elaborated with the utmost care, and through the person of Vansen, a decayed, dissipated clerk, and public agitator, Göthe represents the way in which men who have nothing to lose endeavour to stir up a tumult out of which there may be something to gain. The personation of this public agitator by Herr Birnstill was full of humour. The decayed, dissipated, jaunty air, the gold ring, probably mosaic, still upon the finger, and the affectation of a cane—the glibness of speech, the infinite variety and energy of action, which gave to the whole man a sense of slipperiness, the absence of all sensibility to shame, were harmonised into a bright and clear dramatic study. The voiceless men in the crowd, each listening to the orations of Vansen with feelings especially his own, displayed an amount of intelligence in the performance of inferior parts which we are not used to see in English theatres. Herr Denk, as Jetter the Tailor, entered with very great unction into the humour of his part, and would have shone as an especial star, had he not been surrounded by a group of minor actors scarcely less efficient. One of the especial facts to be noted in connection with this German company is the efficiency of all its members, and the complete and even representation which they consequently give of the good play submitted to their treatment.

Complete, as far as they go; but *Egmont*, being a long

drama, was shortened by omission of two characters. So
far as mere plot is concerned, a quarter of the play suffices
to narrate it; but as a poem, though the play gains something of the required predominance of thought in action
which is the soul of a good drama, the original design is spoilt
by every curtailment.

A ferocious make-up according to approved tradition, the
impatient military walk while giving orders, and all other
fitting accessories duly supplied, with a very good delivery of
all he had to say, made Herr Kühn's Alva an extremely
satisfactory performance. The sordid, querulous old woman,
Clärchen's mother, was very well represented by Frau
Froitzheim. Clärchen herself seemed to be a character
in which Frau Stolte was not able to do perfect justice to her
powers. It was acted very well, and there was much pathos
in the street scene where Clärchen, after the arrest of
Egmont, is wildly endeavouring to excite the good tailor
and shopkeeper and carpenter to make some effort for the
rescue of their friend. Frau Stolte claimed a portion of the
honours of the night, but it seemed likely that she would
appear to much greater advantage in future characters.

The acting of Herr Emil Devrient as Egmont was the
great triumph of the evening, and established thoroughly in
London his title to the honours accorded to him on the
German stage. In his conception of the character of
Egmont there was more dignity and somewhat more reserve
than was designed by Göthe in his sketch of the free-
hearted Prince. This, doubtless, was meant to meet half-
way the objection of Schiller, that in Göthe's Egmont we
are told of the heroism but shown the weakness. As far
as the actor could, he sought to modify that character of
the dramatic poem which has been thought to impair its
interest as an acted play. Herr Devrient has, it should be
said, a handsome figure, which aids him in the personation
of a youthful hero. As Egmont he first appears upon

the stage during a tumult which his popularity enables him to still, and in this very brief scene wholly assumed the dignity of bearing which, as I have said, clashed with my previous conceptions. His next scenes with his secretary and with William of Orange modified and refined that first impression. The love-scenes in *Egmont* are exquisite specimens of Göthe's manner of conceiving such affairs. The scene between Alva and Egmont, at the end of which Egmont is to be betrayed, contains fine opportunities for noble acting, of which Herr Devrient made ample use.

June 12.—Schiller's *Kabale und Liebe* (Intrigue and Love) is one of his first three plays, and shares with *The Robbers* a good deal of admiration for "Titanic" qualities. It was written in the full ferment of youth, and the difference of taste is vast between the mind of Schiller when it was ripening and the same mind when it was ripe. In Southey, who resembled Schiller in the one respect that in his mature life he was among the most pure-minded of poets, there was a long literary interval between *Wat Tyler* and *Roderick*. In Schiller there is an equal interval between such works as *The Robbers* or *Kabale und Liebe*, and such works as *Don Karlos* or *Wallenstein*. One must not be suspected, however, of a comparison between *Wat Tyler* and Schiller's early plays. In this *Kabale und Liebe*, written while smarting under the sting of persecution, the young poet declaimed in a way that would have made his work immortal were it only as a sample of rude German energy.

Very German, in the worst as well as best sense of the word ; abounding in absurdity and outrages on good taste, from which nobody in later life removed himself more utterly than Schiller—nevertheless, it is a play to go and see. Except the coolness of some men who plot outrageous villainy (the heads of the "Intrigue"), there is not a scene in the play that does not glow with red-hot passion. Every-

body in every moment of every scene is in a most
enormously excited state of mind ; and here, in what
follows, is the gist of the domestic tale that is developed.

A terrible duke, in any grand duchy you please, robs,
burns, and plunders subjects, as a matter of course. He
does not appear upon the scene. His prime minister,
President Von Walter, is the most heartless villain who
ever existed, with the single exception of his secretary,
Wurm. Wurm is not to be compared with men, he is a
devil. President Von Walter got his presidency by
murdering (if not something worse than murdering) his
predecessor, and by any number you like to suppose of
other crimes. Wurm (worm) helped him ; Kalb (calf), the
baron, had a hand in it ; the virtuous son knows all about
it. The very virtuous son, Ferdinand, is the handsomest,
the most generous, the most high-minded of creatures, with
the pardonable failing, if it be a failing, that he is furiously
hot, horribly enthusiastic. Love never equalled his devotion to Louisa, the simple, artless, inexpressibly sentimental
and devoted daughter of that incarnation of rude virtue,
Miller the musician, and the good soul his wife.

Wurm wants Louisa, and Louisa, in white muslin, loves
the Major, and the good talkative soul of a wife causes
Wurm to know that the Major, Ferdinand, loves Louisa.
That furnishes the Love. Wurm goes to the Major's father,
and the Secretary and the President make the Intrigue.
The President tells his son to marry the Duke's mistress,
Lady Milford, and stirs up a hurricane of virtue. The son
goes to Lady Milford to abuse her, and finds that she is a
high British dame of the house of Howard, Joanna of
Norfolk, who, after the unhappy decapitation of her father,
was walking about, aged-fourteen, in the streets of Holland,
when she met the wicked Grand Duke, who offered her
love, and she became his mistress, and her whole care has
been to keep him out of wickedness, and she loves

Ferdinand and means to marry him. Ferdinand runs gasping to Louisa. To them comes his father, with Wurm, to imprison or hang Miller and his wife, and put Louisa in the pillory. The son foams at the father, the father sneers at the son. Everybody is gunpowder, and they are all going off together. The whole scene, though utterly absurd, is magnificent in its effect, for the wild power with which it is worked up. Finally the son, who has tried all means to move his obdurate father in vain, closes the dispute by coming to his ear and telling him in a voice agitated by the intensest imaginable passion, that he may proceed, but that he is going out to tell the world—how a president's place is sometimes to be gained.

The manner in which Herr Emil Devrient uttered this last threat, with which an act is closed, raised the whole theatre to instantaneous enthusiasm. The curtain fell before a greater tumult of applause than is often to be heard within the walls of the St. James's Theatre. Herr Devrient appeared, retired, and was immediately summoned by fresh plaudits to appear again. Herr Devrient embodies the ideal Ferdinand, full of passion in his tones and gestures. Fräulein Schäfer, young and pretty enough to look like Schiller's own Louisa, acts with quiet intelligence, and supplies all the sentiment and suffering required in an extremely arduous part, which ends between the unhappy lovers with a poisoning. Old Miller the musician, with his warm heart and boiling temper, was excellently represented by Herr Birnstill, the same who so well personated Vansen in the *Egmont*. Herr Kühn, late Duke of Alva, performed Wurm with the care of an accomplished artist. His by-play was all weighed with nicety, and was made to express so perfectly the cold black-coated and white-neckclothed Mephistopheles, that one looks forward with great curiosity to his appearance as the Mephistopheles of Göthe's *Faust*. A Herr Schrader, as the Baron von Kalb, represented the exquisite of a small German court with as much obvious care and study as was to be noted in the well-considered movements of Herr Kühn; but the effect of the study was attained in a performance of the richest comedy, scarcely a word or gesture from the Baron failing to excite mirth.

A German comedy—*Der Majoratserbe* (the *Heir-at-Law*)—by the Duchess Amelia of Saxony, is written with much pleasant tact, in four acts, on a slender plot. The comedy was written to display the powers of Herr Devrient, and is an outline which it is left wholly to the actor to fill up. Count Paul Scharfeneck, the hero, has been educated in the country, and spoilt as an only son and heir. He has come into possession of a large estate, and is plighted to a certain Countess Bertha.

On a certain day, and at a certain hour, he is to appear at the house of a lady whom he has not previously seen, and offer marriage. Bertha starts forth for a ride upon the morning of that day, and, being overtaken by a heavy shower, comes into an inn for shelter. Here the play opens. While Bertha is changing her wet riding-dress for dry clothes belonging to the people of the inn, Count Paul, with his cousin Otto, the next heir to Scharfeneck, make their appearance, accompanied by Paul's favourite old servant, Barmann. Paul is restless, full of whims and humours, demanding service of everyone; and although behind the time at which he was expected by his friends at the castle, in no great hurry to proceed. Bertha, making her appearance in a peasant's dress, soon finds herself called upon to bestir herself in the service of the impatient Paul; who treats her with so much fidgety rudeness, and talks with so much indifference of his business at the castle, that she vows to herself, when the act closes, that she will never marry him.

In the next act, Paul and his cousin Otto are in the

dwelling of the lady, where Count Lauerfeld, the papa, suffers much at the hands of the respected heir. He is kept politely standing because Paul forgets to sit. He is tumbled over. He is requested to change his dinner-hour because Paul is not hungry. Paul has been down into the kitchen to exhort the cooks not to put onions in anything. He has brought two great dogs from the country with him, and they bark and bite in the courtyard. He has arranged his room to his own humour, and to the horror of good housekeepers. He practises duets upon the violin in his bedroom with his dear old servant Barmann, and is always, in his impatience, some quarter of an hour in advance as to the time. And now Bertha receives Paul in the most chilling way, and adds a sting to her reception by affecting the most cordial manner to his cousin Otto, whom she had met some seasons before at the baths, and with whom she had flirted.

Up to this point Devrient's acting was a piece of unmixed comedy. His spoilt nobleman was not a lout—he was a nobleman in the midst of his ill manners. His movements were all followed by laughter ; and it was not because he made his Paul a person to be laughed at, but a man whose whims and oddities were amusing ; he was what the Germans commonly call *launig*, not ridiculous. But the coldness of the lady, and the warmth of good-will awakened in him by her presence, work a change in the Count's manner ; and when the father, having found that his daughter regards her intended husband as " insufferable", warns him before he leaves them together not yet to speak of marriage, Paul wonders, and begins to manifest his sense that things are not proceeding smoothly with him. He talks to the lady, first of his cousin, with whom she had appeared to be so agreeably intimate, and (for it is to be understood that Paul is at heart a miracle of generosity and goodness) praises Otto heartily—Otto, as the lady remembers, who had not

long before been ridiculing him. The Count discourses
then of country pleasures, and dwells with good-humoured
gusto on the pleasures of the country in the winter; pictures,
in delicate words, Bertha with a husband looking out from
his castle window upon a country winter scene; so delicately,
however, as not to overstep the spirit of her father's warning.
Then he talks of his country rounds among the people;
whereupon Bertha compares, disparagingly, the mad rounds
he would run, with the deed of a certain Count S—— who
had been talked about lately in all the papers for the risking
of his life to save a family. Paul irritates the lady by pro-
nouncing the whole story stupid nonsense; she is loud in
praise of Count S——; till it presently appears that the S.
stood for Scharfeneck. Finally, Paul leaves the lady overcome with a sense of his goodness, but by no means reconciled to 'his odd ways; and in leaving, he begs her to
remember what he said about the castle window in the
winter—that he has his reasons, etc. The parting words
are nothing in themselves, but the acting of Herr Devrient
converts them into phrases that imply and do not tell his
love. The exquisite delicacy with which the natural heart
speaks in this part of the story contrasts admirably with the
external rudeness which from the first was clearly marked
as an acquired way, and not as an expression of the character. In the rest of the story, the troubles of Paul's course
of love, which I need not relate, give opportunity for
numerous diversities of light and shade. The movements
of a noble soul, and the true feelings of a generous and
good man, begin to be more and more perceptible through
the mere accidents of education. Paul is refused by Bertha,
though she loves him, on the ground that she would not
like to be his partner in society; that, good as he is, "a
woman would rather be unhappy and envied, than happy
and laughed at by the world". He retires with manly
dignity, although in grief. Being made afterwards to

believe that the cause of his refusal is Bertha's love for
Otto, Paul pleads for his cousin with the old Count, who
swears that his daughter shall marry no one but the heir of
Scharfeneck. Paul then determines to give up his birth-
right and deprive himself of all, that he may not stand
between the happiness of the two. Of course, things do
not come to this ; for Bertha (who found a lively and agreeable representative in Fräulein Stromeyer) decides joyfully
at last to get into the arms of a good husband, though in the
world's eyes he may be an oddity.

It will be seen from this sketch of the main business,
that in Count Paul the German actor is provided with a
part which none but a great actor could succeed in at all,
and which a great actor can create for himself into first-rate
importance. There is no single part in which Herr Devrient
has yet appeared affording him equal opportunity of displaying in a few hours the wide range of his talent.

From the whimsical Paul Scharfeneck to Hamlet was a
great step. ' Herr Devrient's Hamlet differs in a great many
respects from the Hamlets of the English stage. He has
applied his own genius to the play, and develops his part
according to his own conception. German acting does not
rely at all upon "points", and many passages which on our
own stage are especially made to stand out, of course fell
back into the ranks on Thursday night. Every line by
every actor is studied with an equal care. This conscientious rendering makes it almost as difficult to extract from
the actor as from the author any one-sided theory of
Hamlet's character. Herr Devrient marked very strongly
Hamlet's natural affection for his mother. When being
instructed by his father's ghost of her part in the crime, he
expressed finely, with his cloak thrown over his face, the
climax of his horror. That this crime of his mother has
spread a blot over his faith in the whole world, was the
impression which his subsequent acting frequently con-

veyed. For the crime of his mother, he lost faith in woman's continence, and saw no virtue for Ophelia out of a nunnery. In the scene with his mother after the play, his passion was mingled with affection, and, after his father's ghost had vanished from the chamber, his words to her were all spoken with endearments and embraces.

Devrient's Hamlet was weakened by the inevitable dilution with German of that large number of terse lines which have passed out of this play into common English speech. The *Hamlet* of A. W. Schlegel is a wonderful translation, but the terse philosophy of Shakespeare is not to be fully translated. Again, there are some points of stage-business familiar to the English, handed down by tradition from actor to actor, which the Germans have not been able to discover for themselves, which really are good points, and which we miss. On the other hand, we have our bad traditions, and from these the Germans find it advantageous to be free. As a whole, Devrient's performance of Hamlet was most acceptable; he was followed throughout with hearty applause, in which many English actors and many of his German fellow-actors, not occupied in the business of the evening, warmly joined. He was recalled between every act, and his countrymen present were proud of him, as they had fair reason to be. "The man is in his part," said one of them; "I do not believe he knows that he is acting."

The other characters in the play were filled with the even excellence characteristic of the German company. The Ophelia was well acted by Fräulein Schäfer, but, as she speaks the songs, singing only here and there a word or two, she acted well in vain.

Herr Kühn has appeared as the Master in *Die Glocke*— Schiller's "Song of the Bell", snipped into a drama by being apportioned to speakers, and illustrated by a scene representing the business of the foundry. Stage-furnaces and

painted bells rather retard than help the fancy ; and as we
are still looking at a canvas furnace while we should also
follow the fancy of the poet to homesteads, towns, burials,
and other scenes, the retardation is still more complete.
The scene was well managed, the grouping of the workmen
perfect, and the recitation admirable. But there was no
reason at all in art why it should be recited by more than
one person, or at most by two ; and there are half-a-dozen
reasons why it should not be divided among seven. Herr
Kühn's " make-up" as the Master was astounding. This
actor is a master of costume. When one sees him as the
founder of the Bell, and looks back upon his Duke of Alva
and his Wurm, it is difficult to conceive that these three
characteristic figures are all personated by one man.

June 26.—Last Saturday evening Herr Devrient performed
the insignificant part of Count Appiani in *Emilia Galotti.*
His Faust on Tuesday evening was as good a Faust as one
could wish to see, but Faust himself in Göthe's play is not
an effective dramatic character. The play, however, in its
compressed form acts well ; and is made to include in the
grouping the realisation of a good many of Retzsch's outlines. In Schiller's *Robbers* the part of Charles Moor was
transferred to Herr Wisthaler. The last week has been,
therefore, a week of special prominence for Herr Kühn,
who has been personating three stage-demons, Marinelli,
Mephistopheles, and Francis Moor. Of the Marinelli I can
say nothing, because I did not see it. The Mephistopheles
more than made good the prediction which most people
ventured who saw the human Wurm represented by the
same actor in *Kabale und Liebe.* It is paying him a high
compliment to say that Herr Kühn is possibly the greatest
villain on the European stage. For assuming a malignant
tone and face and gesture, for the most elaborate, artistic
painting of anything in the way of cold-blooded rascality,
and from thence up through all the passions of ferocious

exultation or of hatred, agonies of cowardice or of despair, there is no abler man than Herr Kühn in the range of living English experience ; though, no doubt, he is in his home a very mild and philosophic personage.

At any rate, he has thought calmly and philosophised much over his Mephistopheles. One sees in him the fiend who walks about and scarcely can abstain from gratifying his desire to make a spring upon this victim or that, while there is also abundant indication of the largeness which belongs to any great conception of a demon. In the chamber of Faust, one of Kühn's most effective attitudes is to recline carelessly, with his arm spread about a large terrestrial globe. The ironical vein of humour in the evil spirit is at the same time strongly marked. Mephistopheles will doubtless be remembered as Herr Kühn's greatest performance on the London stage ; and the character, good in itself—a mature poetical conception—is much better worth elaborating than, for example, such a mere daub of pitch as Francis Moor in *The Robbers.*

Schiller, writing at the age of about eighteen, out of a hot youth, heaped one revolting thing upon another to make out of Francis Moor a perfect villain. All Herr Kühn's power of depicting villainy was brought to bear upon this nightmare character. The scene of terror and despair in which Francis rushes in, in his night-dress, from a dream of the Last Day, was sickening in its perfection. An atrocious stage-alteration at this point drags out his tortures by not suffering him to strangle himself at the end of the scene, as in the printed play. He is carried alive to his brother, crouches and shrieks before him in the insanity of despair, and is buried alive in the tower to which he had consigned his father. The acting of Herr Kühn realised this revolting scene only too well. Among other stage-alterations to which the play is subject, the love-passages between Charles and Amelia, and sundry parts which in the printed play mingle some taste and delicacy with the wilder mass, have been omitted. The repulsive features of the production being thus at the same time exaggerated in the text and brought into strong relief by the acting, the whole result is anything but pleasant.

Herr Kühn took occasion, when recalled before the last act, to make a small speech to the London public. That, he said, was the last important part in which he could at present appear before them, owing to the limited nature of the *répertoire* during a short engagement. He regretted that he had not been able to present some other of his favourite characters, but the kind applause he had met with among us would, he suggested, cause him to appear again upon the stage of London at a future day.

Sustaining characters which exhibit an abundant versatility of power, equally at home in Tragedy or Comedy, Herr Emil Devrient has confirmed for himself easily, in England, the reputation that he had acquired in Germany. Admirers of spasms may not always appreciate his purity of taste, and may miss some points because they are not prodded into them. I do not know what characters remain behind in Herr Kühn's *répertoire*, but he has been seen during the last month shining exclusively in characters of one especial class. In these his study is elaborate, and his acting perfect of its kind : but his range may possibly be very limited.

June 19.—If there be truth in the old adage, that " when things are at the worst they must mend", the bettering of Spectral Melodrama is not distant ; for it has reached the extreme point of inanity in the new piece which was produced on Monday at the PRINCESS'S THEATRE, under the attractive title of *The Vampire.*

Its plot is chiefly copied from a piece which some years ago turned the Lyceum into a Chamber of Horrors ; but it has been spun out into three parts, facetiously described as "Three Dramas": the little period of a century has been in-

terposed between each part ; and, in order that the outrage
on the possible shall be complete, the third part is projected
forward into the year that will be 1860 ! By this ingenious
arrangement, the resuscitation of the original *Vampire* has
been enabled to supply the lovers of the revolting at the
Princess's with three acts of murder—that is, two consum-
mated, and one attempted ; but, as the delicate process of
vampirical killing is exactly after the same pattern in each
case, the horror is quite worn out before the career of the
creature terminates.   Nothing but tedious trash remains.

To "an honest ghost" one has no objection ; but an animated corpse which goes about in Christian attire, and
although never known to eat, or drink, or shake hands, is
allowed to sit at good men's feasts ; which renews its odious
life every hundred years by sucking a young lady's blood,
after fascinating her by motions which resemble mesmerism
burlesqued ; and which, notwithstanding its well-purchased
longevity, is capable of being killed during its term in order
that it may be revived by moonbeams— such a ghost as this
passes all bounds of toleration.

The monster of absurdity was personated by its reviver,
Mr. Boucicault, with due paleness of visage, stealthiness
of pace, and solemnity of tone ; the scenery, especially a
moonlit ridge amidst the heights of Snowdon, was beautiful,
and the costumes were prettily diversified ; but the dreary
repetition of fantastical horror almost exhausted even the
patience which a benefit enjoins.   Unfortunately, the mischief of such a piece, produced at a respectable theatre,
does not end with the weariness of the spectators, who come
to shudder and remain to yawn ; for it is not only "beside
the purpose of playing", but directly contravenes it ; and
though it may be too dull to pervert the tastes of those who
witness its vapid extravagances, it has power to bring discredit on the most genial of arts.

July 27.—Spohr's opera of *Faust*, produced at the ROYAL

ITALIAN OPERA on Thursday night, under the direction of the composer, was one of the most perfect performances ever seen even upon that carefully appointed stage. The opera will live for all time as a classical work full of fine music with a somewhat tedious general effect, and based upon a version of the old legend of Dr. Faustus which must be pronounced bad even for a libretto. Signor Ronconi was Faust, Herr Formes Mephistopheles, Mdlle. Anna Zerr Rosina, and Madame Castellan Cunegonda. Tamberlik as Count Ugo, on his way to rescue his Cunegonda from the power of the demon-in-human-flesh, Gulf, sang a spirited air, " Ah non temer", set in a chorus of breastplated soldiers, which produced a most vociferous encore, the only encore of the evening.

At the end of the first act Dr. Spohr received a merited ovation. The last half of the first act contains some of the most effective music in the opera, but the extreme stupidity of the libretto, and the solidity of Dr. Spohr's style, caused the delight in some scenes of the work to be confined entirely to musicians. The whole of the concerted music at the end of the last act is very beautiful.

November 27.—The new play at the HAYMARKET wants the scope and proportions of a regular English comedy, being in outline and structure of a French cast; but in character it is English, in sentiment thoroughly so, and its language and expression, whether of seriousness or humour, have the tone at once easy and earnest which truth gives to scholarship and wit.

The acting, too, is unusually good. There is a poor poet who doubles the scanty callings of painter and player, and whom Goldsmith could not have better described, or Leslie painted, than Mr. Webster acts him. The delicacy and strength of this performance took us by surprise. The humour and pathos closely neighbouring each other, smiles playing about the tears, and the mirth always trembling into

sadness, belonged to most real art. And it was full of
minute touches which showed the discrimination of the actor.
For instance—that absurd air of helplessness which the
habit of incessant failure gives to a man. The poor starving
author cannot hold even a couple of his own rejected tragedies in his hands without dropping one of them, nor pick
up the straggler till its companion has tumbled after it.

The title of the comedy is *Masks and Faces, or Before and
Behind the Curtain.* Its heroine is Garrick's favourite, Peg
Woffington ; whose attractive sprightliness, spirited independence, good understanding, and thoroughly good nature,
distinguished her so favourably among the dames of the
English theatre in the old days of the Sir Harry Wildairs
and Lady Betty Modishes, and while yet the Iphigenias wore
cherry-coloured silk over their large hoop petticoats. The
drift of the little comedy is to show the good heart of the
actress shining out through the disadvantage of her position
and her calling, and rebuking the better fortune of those
who have to struggle with no such temptations. There
appears to be just now a great run upon such subjects with
our French neighbours. Shut out by the censorship from
most topics that trench upon the real world, French playwrights have betaken themselves in despair to the world of
unreality, and now find their most popular subjects behind
the scenes. They have just invented a model English actor
at the Français, who by all sorts of nobility and propriety of
conduct breaks down the most inveterate prejudices of caste ;
and at the Variétés they have reproduced a scamp of an
actor of the infamous days of the Regency, who turns out
to be after all the most interesting and fine-hearted rogue
conceivable. In short, the Parisian spirit of the day, in these
matters, is pretty much expressed in what one of our own
wits used to be fond of contrasting in the fortunes of the two
Duchesses of Bolton.. The poor high-born lady, educated in
solitude with choice of all good books, with a saintlike

governess, and fairly crammed with virtue—what did it all come to? her husband despised her and the public laughed at her. Whereas the frank and fearless Polly, bred in an alehouse and produced on the stage, obtained not only wealth and title, but found the way to be esteemed, so that her husband respected and loved her, as the public had done before him.

The authors of *Masks and Faces* (for there are two, Mr. Tom Taylor and Mr. Charles Reade) do not quite fall into this vein, however. They rather follow the example of the enthusiastic bishop, who, on hearing an actress of doubtful reputation sing divinely at an oratorio, suddenly and loudly cried out, "Woman, thy sins be forgiven thee!" They do not suppress the sins of Mrs. Woffington, in the act of exhibiting what virtues as well as sorrows neighboured them; and, while they represent her with a touching sense of her own degradation, they have yet the courage to show her accepted for her virtues by the innocent and pure, and not disqualified by her vices to put conventional morality to shame. In a word, it is a very manly and right-minded little comedy; with matter of just reflection in it, as well as much mirth and amusement.

That is a charming scene where Peg visits the poor poet in his garret, while his ailing wife and starving children are sadly interrupting the flow of its comic muse. Nothing here was lost in Mr. Webster's hands—the angry fretfulness followed by instant remorse, the efforts of self-restraint which are but efforts in vain, the energy that fitfully breaks out and then pitifully breaks down, and the final loss of hope, even of faith in a better providence which is to set right all that misery and wrong—the picture was complete, and set forth with its immemorial Grub Street appendages of no shirt and ragged but ample ruffles. An excellent touch, too, it was in this scene, when the poor, patient, sickly wife, nicely looked and played by Mrs. Leigh Murray, after rebuking her hus-

band for his little outbreak of distrust in Providence, cannot
help showing her own little jealousies and fellow-actress's
distrust of Mrs. Woffington. But Peg plays the part of
Providence in the miserable garret, and in doing it Mrs.
Stirling threw off all her too conscious airs and was really
hearty and delightful. She gave the pathetic passages with
genuine feeling, the mirthful with cordial enjoyment; and
several heightening touches in both marked the personal
sympathy and emotion with which the character appeared to
have affected her.

The critics introduced are poor enough, and this part of
the piece is here and there too long. Mr. Bland, moreover,
who played Quin, exaggerated a mistake for which the
writers had given him too much excuse, and made a mere
loud, coarse, vulgar epicure of him. Quin was a gentleman
and a man of wit. We remember him always as the patron
as well as friend of the poet Thomson, and as the author
of some of the very best things on record. Generally, however, the acting was very good. There was a little sketch of
old Colley Cibber, by Mr. Lambert, particularly worth mention as observant and faithful.

On Monday, *March 14th*, 1853, Mr. Webster delivered
his farewell address as manager of the HAYMARKET THEATRE,
which has since that time been under the management of
Mr. Buckstone, as the ADELPHI has also since that time
been under Mr. Webster's management. The following
sentences from Mr. Webster's address contribute something
to the current history of the stage :—

"To authors I find I have paid nearly £30,000, if not more.
'Tis said, 'Uneasy lies the head that wears a crown'; but far more
uneasiness has the head begirt with the tinsel crown of theatrical
sovereignty, where every popular favourite is a viceroy over him,
and where the ways and means are not compulsory, but solely
dependent on the will and pleasure of our sovereign the public.
However, if my labour in the cause of the drama, which has

been a labour of love, has met with the approval of you, my tried and valued friends, it will not have been *Love's Labour Lost*. Those who remember this theatre when I first took it, sixteen years ago—of course I exclude the ladies from so long a remembrance—must perceive the extensive alterations, and I think I may venture to say improvements, that I have accomplished during my tenancy. Abrupt angles have given way to curves, and my circles, especially from their present occupancy, appear graceful in the extreme. I have backed the pit, and could in another sense—for respectability—against any pit in London. I have stalled off what was originally the orchestra, sometimes discoursing sweet sounds, though sweeter music to my ear has supplied its place in the audible approbations of my exertions as, to quote the words of Triplet, 'author, manager, and actor, too'. The proscenium I have widened eleven feet, and entirely remodelled it, and introduced gas for the fee of £500 a year, and the presentation of the centre chandelier to the proprietors; and behind the curtain money has not been spared to render the stage as perfect for dramatic representation as its limited means will furnish ; in fact, I have expended, with no ultimate advantage to myself, on this property over £12,000 besides paying more than £60,000 in rent."

July 9.—At the OLYMPIC a new and very smart travestie of *The Merchant of Venice* draws a crowded house every night. The piece is full of undeniable cleverness, and also deserves mention as giving scope to a new and remarkable burlesque actor. Mr. F. Robson is a downright good actor—a new performer who, notwithstanding the unpromising material he at present works in, promises to be a solid acquisition to the stage. And it is odd enough that, at a time when all serious acting is tending to the burlesque and unreal, a burlesque actor should start up with a real and very serious power in him. The only regret in observing his execution of Mr. Talfourd's Shylock is that he had not made trial of Shakespeare's in preference. But there is no doubt that we shall have other and higher things to report of a performer who begins his career by showing himself really in earnest.

On the stage it is the secret of success in everything—even burlesque. It does not do to play at acting.

October 22.—Mr. Alfred Wigan, in assuming the management of the OLYMPIC, has the good wishes of all who still care for the better and more agreeable entertainments of the stage, and who do not think that vulgarity and bad taste have reached their millennium because they happen to attract temporary crowds of barren spectators and noisy applauders. Mr. Wigan has been for many years quietly and steadily advancing in the public esteem as a careful and conscientious actor, who understands the art to be an intellectual one, and so pursues it; we are glad to see an artist of his quality take upon himself the direction of a theatre to which it is proposed to attract favour by the legitimate resources of good writing and good acting, as far as these may yet be procurable.

Criticism of the "occasional" piece or prologue, *The Camp at the Olympic*, which opens the career of the new management, would be out of place. It might have had greater freshness in its design, but, being written by Mr. Planché, of course it has its points of merit, its ready and fluent verse, its jokes regulated by good taste, its happy allusions to incidents of the day, and its pleasant parodies of popular airs to which the beautiful voice of Miss P. Horton gave singular spirit and charm.

The success of the night was undoubtedly the assumption of a serious part by the burlesque actor, Mr. Robson. That there would be other and higher things to report of a performer who, while other people were burlesquing reality, could put such a startling reality into burlesque, was not to be doubted. But one hardly expected it so soon. The part he plays in *Plot and Passion* (a drama of which the central figure is Fouché, its characters being the agents or objects of his villainy, and its catastrophe his disgrace) is that of a mean, double-faced, fawning, cunning, treacherous tool, in whom the sordid passions have nevertheless not wholly extinguished others that place him finally at the mercy of his victims. Here the actor's opportunity is that of a constant and quick transition within the limited range of the emotions expressed; and from meanness to malice, from cringing humility to the most malignant hate, from a cat-like watchfulness to occasional bursts of passion that seemed to defy control, Mr. Robson passed with a keen power and ready self-possession that never missed the effect intended to be produced. If this was not always natural, the fault was more with the feeling to be expressed than with the actor's mode of expressing it. In truth, the character is greatly overstrained, and the mixing up of its fiendish qualities with what was meant to be a strong and self-exalting emotion has the usual result of detracting from both.

Mr. Robson's great quality is the downright earnestness by which he makes others feel what he very evidently feels himself. He has defects of voice and person of the gravest kind, but some part of that which made " Pritchard genteel and Garrick six feet high" has descended to him. The sort of character in which he is likely to excel may always lie within the narrowest range, but by the strength and intensity he puts into it he will never fail to attract an audience. He wants finish, refinement, relief—fifty things which will come with experience and study, if he has a proper regard for his calling and for himself; but already, with none of these things, he is a genuine actor, and everyone feels it. The drama had been but a short while opened on Monday night when the general interest fixed itself on that ill-dressed, meagre, dwarfish figure, and, whoever else might occupy the scene, the eye still sought him out. For the present, therefore, the little man is undoubtedly the great fact at the OLYMPIC.

Yet Mr. Wigan and Mrs. Stirling played also with

excellent feeling and truth in parts much the reverse
of attractive. Mr. Emery wanted delicacy and tact in
Fouché.

September 10.—DRURY LANE has reopened, and Mr.
G. V. Brooke is for the present its chief attraction. It is
a pity that he should prefer to act Shakespeare—for which
he is as little qualified as the company engaged to support
him—rather than a good, ranting, roaring melodrama, which
he would play admirably. This would be infinitely better
than making a melodrama of *Othello;* but in this as in
other things there is no accounting for tastes, and, to judge
by the noise they made, the taste of the crowds who filled
the theatre goes very decisively against our own.

October 29.—That "unparalleled tragedian, Mr. Brooke",*
having departed from DRURY LANE, "Tom Barry, the deathless and renowned clown", succeeds; and there is no reason
why the ingenious lessee, declared on high authority to be
a mirror of managers, should not make the second B as
profitable as the first. "His name and fame are enough,"
pursues the enthusiastic Mr. E. T. Smith; backing him up
at the same time, like a wary tactician as he is, with "a
galaxy of equestrian talent never before assembled con-
junctively in even this the metropolis of nations." A galaxy
assembled individually might, perhaps, have been more
novel, but to so sagacious a manager as Mr. Smith the hint
is offered with much deference. Indeed, it particularly

---

* Mr. G. V. Brooke is said by all who knew him to have
been most amiable and generous. He was drowned in the
wreck of the *London* (Jan. 11, 1866), after distinguishing himself in the last hours of danger and despair by higher qualities
than actors have been often called upon to show. None
laboured more strenuously to avert the deadly issue; which none
bore, when it became inevitable, with more tranquil fortitude
than he. Though he could not act Shakespeare, he must have
been a noble fellow.

becomes the critic to handle with tenderness a conjunctive galaxy of this sort, in which " not only has no expense been spared, but, in making arrangements, a wise discretion, *the result of a deliberative council in science*, has been observed". Besides, is not Mr. E. T. Smith careful to add that " fortuitous *but* accidental circumstances have thrown" the galaxy together " for a short season, *but* other American and European engagements will prevent a continuance of the exalted scientific compact"?

In such fortuitous *but* accidental circumstances, then, what better can either critic or playgoer do than seize the opportunity of the minute, and catch ere they fly the Cynthias of this exalted and scientific, but, alas ! too fleeting compact? Though Mr. Smith has preferred a conjunctive to an individual galaxy, he does his best to supply even the latter want by presenting the youthful Hernandez as " the very constellation in the hippodramatic hemisphere". There also is Eaton Stone, " confronting in a marvellous manner the wild horse of the prairies". James Newsome is also there, " reflecting a glory on the sports of Old England". And there is Madame Pauline Newsome, whose two horses " *stand* unequalled in the Spanish and cadenced *steps*, and will perform with wonderful precision the same movements as if guided by the power of electricity". And there, for a climax, is the " champion vaulter of all the world", Arthur Barnes, " who has accomplished the unprecedented feat of throwing ninety-one somersaults in succession"; attended by " that renowned American artiste", Mr. W. O. Dale, the thrower of eighty-one. From the great American Dale, by four somersaults only, the greater English Barnes snatched the crown ! It will surely be worth the whole price of admission to see this American hero, mighty even in defeat, by the side of his mightier vanquisher, the new Arthur of England.

Mr. E. T. Smith is not the first manager who has played

the part of his own critic, and he really tops the part so magnificently that it would be a pity to take it from him. But, absurdity apart, his company of horses and riders, of vaulters and tumblers and self-suspenders, of dancers on decanters, balancers on poles, and tossers of tubs and children, is not a bad one; and if he would but introduce a few more of the lighter female graces, and stop the mouth of the deathless Tom Barry, it would be a first-rate entertainment of its own very small kind.

October 15.—Every reader of Shakespeare is disposed to regard the *Midsummer Night's Dream* as the most essentially unactable of all his plays. It is a dramatic poem of the utmost grace and delicacy; its characters are creatures of the poet's fancy that no flesh and blood can properly present—fairies who "creep into acorn-cups", or mortals who are but dim abstractions, persons of a dream. The words they speak are so completely spiritual that they are best felt when they are not spoken. Their exquisite beauty is like that of sunset colours which no mortal artist can interpret faithfully. The device of the clowns in the play to present Moonshine seems but a fair expression of the kind of success that might be achieved by the best actors who should attempt to present the *Midsummer Night's Dream* on the stage. It was, therefore, properly avoided by managers as lying beside and above their art; nor was there reason to be disappointed when the play some years ago furnished Madame Vestris with a spectacle that altogether wanted the Shakespearean spirit.

In some measure there is reason for a different opinion on these matters in the *Midsummer Night's Dream* as produced at SADLER'S WELLS by Mr. Phelps. Though stage-fairies cannot ride on blue-bells, and the members of no theatrical company now in existence can speak such poetry as that of the *Midsummer Night's Dream* otherwise than most imperfectly, yet it is proved that there remains in the power of the manager who goes with pure taste and right feeling to his work, enough for the establishment of this play as a most charming entertainment of the stage.

Mr. Phelps has never for a minute lost sight of the main idea which governs the whole play, and this is the great secret of his success in the presentation of it. He knew that he was to present merely shadows; that spectators, as Puck reminds them in the epilogue, are to think they have slumbered on their seats, and that what appeared before them have been visions. Everything has been subdued as far as possible at SADLER'S WELLS to this ruling idea. The scenery is very beautiful, but wholly free from the meretricious glitter now in favour; it is not so remarkable for costliness as for the pure taste in which it and all the stage-arrangements have been planned. There is no ordinary scene-shifting; but, as in dreams, one scene is made to glide insensibly into another. We follow the lovers and the fairies through the wood from glade to glade, now among trees, now with a broad view of the sea and Athens in the distance, carefully but not at all obtrusively set forth. And not only do the scenes melt dream-like one into another, but over all the fairy portion of the play there is a haze thrown by a curtain of green gauze placed between the actors and the audience, and maintained there during the whole of the second, third, and fourth acts. This gauze curtain is so well spread that there are very few parts of the house from which its presence can be detected, but its influence is every-where felt; it subdues the flesh and blood of the actors into something more nearly resembling dream-figures, and incorporates more completely the actors with the scenes, throwing the same green fairy tinge, and the same mist over all. A like idea has also dictated certain contrivances of dress, especially in the case of the fairies.

Very good taste has been shown in the establishment of a harmony between the scenery and the poem. The main

feature—the Midsummer Night—was marked by one scene
so elaborated as to impress it upon all as the central picture
of the group. The moon was just so much exaggerated as
to give it the required prominence. The change, again, of
this Midsummer Night into morning, when Theseus and
Hippolyta come to the wood with horn and hound, was
exquisitely presented. And in the last scene, when the
fairies, coming at night into the hall of Theseus, "each
several chamber bless", the Midsummer moon is again seen
shining on the palace as the curtains are drawn that admit
the fairy throng. Ten times as much money might have
been spent on a very much worse setting of the *Midsummer
Night's Dream.* It is the poetical feeling prompting a judicious but not extravagant outlay, by aid of which Mr. Phelps
has produced a stage-spectacle more refined and intellectual,
and far more absolutely satisfactory, than anything I can
remember to have seen since Mr. Macready was a manager.

That the flesh and blood presentments of the dream-
figures which constitute the persons of the play should be
always in harmony with this true feeling, was scarcely to be
expected. A great deal of the poetry is injured in the
speaking. Unless each actor were a man who combined
with elocutionary power a very high degree of sensibility and
genius, it could hardly be otherwise. Yet it cannot be said
even here that the poet's effects entirely failed. The *Midsummer Night's Dream* abounds in the most delicate passages of Shakespeare's verse; the SADLER'S WELLS pit has a
keen enjoyment for them; and pit and gallery were crowded
to the farthest wall on Saturday night with a most earnest
audience, among whom many a subdued hush arose, not
during but just before, the delivery of the most charming
passages. If the crowd at DRURY LANE is a gross discredit
to the public taste, the crowd at SADLER'S WELLS more
than neutralises any ill opinion that may on that score be
formed of playgoers. The SADLER'S WELLS gallery, indeed,

appeared to be not wholly unconscious of the contrast, for, when Bottom volunteered to roar high or roar low, a voice from the gallery desired to know whether he could "roar like Brooke". Even the gallery at this theatre, however, resents an interruption, and the unexpected sally was not well received.

A remarkably quick-witted little boy, Master F. Artis, plays Puck, and really plays it with faithfulness and spirit as it has been conceived for him by Mr. Phelps. His training has evidently been most elaborate. We see at once that his acts and gestures are too perfect and mature to be his own imaginings, but he has been quick-witted enough to adopt them as his own, and give them not a little of the charm of independent and spontaneous production. By this thoughtfulness there is secured for the character on the stage something of the same prominence that it has in the mind of closet-readers of the play.

Of Miss Cooper's Helena we cannot honestly say very much. In that as in most of the other characters the spirit of the play was missed, because the arguing and quarrelling and blundering that should have been playful, dreamlike, and poetical, was much too loud and real. The men and women could not fancy themselves shadows. Were it possible so far to subdue the energy of the whole body of actors as to soften the tones of the scenes between Theseus, Hippolyta, Lysander, Demetrius, Hermia, and Helena, the latter character even on the stage might surely have something of the effect intended by the poem. It is an exquisite abstraction, a pitiful and moving picture of a gentle maid forlorn, playfully developed as beseems the fantastic texture of the poem, but not at all meant to excite mirth; and there was a very great mistake made when the dream was so worked out into hard literalness as to create constant laughter during those scenes in which Helena, bewildered by the change of mood among the lovers, shrinks and com-

plains, "Wherefore was I to this keen mockery born?"
The merriment which Shakespeare connected with those
scenes was but a little of the poet's sunlight meant to glitter
among tears.

It remains for us only to speak of the success of Mr.
Phelps as Bottom, whom he presented from the first with
remarkable subtlety and spirit, as a man seen in a dream.
In his first scene, before we know what his conception is,
or in what spirit he means the whole play to be received,
we are puzzled by it. We miss the humour, and get a
strange, elaborate, and uncouth dream-figure, a clown restless with vanity, marked by a score of little movements, and
speaking ponderously with the uncouth gesticulation of an
unreal thing, a grotesque nightmare character. But that,
we find, is precisely what the actor had intended to present,
and we soon perceive that he was right. Throughout the
fairy scenes there is a mist thrown over Bottom by the
actor's art. The violent gesticulation becomes stillness, and
the hands are fixed on the breast. They are busy with the
unperceived business of managing the movements of the
ass's head, but it is not for that reason they are so perfectly
still. The change of manner is a part of the conception.
The dream-figure is dreaming, there is dream within dream,
Bottom is quiet, his humour becomes more unctuous, but
Bottom is translated. He accepts all that happens, quietly
as dreamers do ; and the ass's head we also accept quietly,
for we too are in the middle of our dream, and it does not
create surprise. Not a touch of comedy was missed in this
capital piece of acting, yet Bottom was completely incor-
porated with the *Midsummer Night's Dream*, made an
essential part of it, as unsubstantial, as airy and refined as
all the rest. Quite masterly was the delivery by Mr. Phelps
of the speech of Bottom on awakening. He was still a man
subdued, but subdued by the sudden plunge into a state of
unfathomable wonder. His dream clings about him, he

cannot sever the real from the unreal, and still we are made
to feel that his reality itself is but a fiction.   The preoccupation continues to be manifest during his next scene
with the players, and his parting " No more words ; away ;
go away", was in the tone of a man who had lived with
spirits and was not yet perfectly returned into the flesh.
Nor did the refinement of this conception, if we except the
first scene, abate a jot of the laughter that the character of
Bottom was intended to excite.   The mock-play at the end
was intensely ludicrous in the presentment, yet nowhere
farcical.   It was the dream.   Bottom as Pyramus was more
perfectly a dream-figure than ever.   The contrast between
the shadowy actor and his part, between Bottom and
Pyramus, was marked intensely ; and the result was as
quaint a phantom as could easily be figured by real flesh.
Mr. Ray's Quince was very good indeed, and all the other
clowns were reasonably well presented.

It is very doubtful whether the *Midsummer Night's
Dream* has yet, since it was first written, been put upon the
stage with so nice an interpretation of its meaning.   It is
pleasant beyond measure to think that an entertainment so
refined can draw such a throng of playgoers as I saw last
Saturday sitting before it silent and reverent at SADLER'S
WELLS.

November 19.—At the LYCEUM Mr. Tom Taylor has provided the clever manager with a piece that may with
advantage to the general mirth retain its place upon the
stage as long as there can be found two actors so perfectly
able to support it as those upon whom its weight now rests.
Mr. Charles Mathews and Mr. Frank Matthews appear as
the heads of *The Nice Firm*.   This is the firm of Moon and
Messiter, solicitors, and is composed of Mr. Moon, who is
not a mere Midsummer moon, but is for ever mooning; and
of Mr. Messiter, who has for his planet not the moon but
Mercury, if it be Mercury that rules the admixture of quick-

silver with legal blood. The visitors to the LYCEUM are
indulged with a peep at a day's "business" perpetrated by
this highly respectable firm, of which the respectability
among clients out of doors is maintained by the quiet intervention of a sensible chief-clerk. The clients know nothing
about that, but the whole anatomy of the office is now made
public and open to the ridicule of men and gods. The
story is contrived loosely enough, as the vehicle for display
of a very loose system of conducting business; and the
rambling character of the work done by the two partners
while their head is out, though it keeps the house incessantly alive with laughter, is just so much too true to
nature as to require rendering a little more compact. Mr.
Charles Mathews represented the mercurial attorney as
nobody else now can do it. Mr. Frank Matthews gave an
elaborate study of the mooning partner, finished in every
detail, and amazingly effective. Mrs. F. Matthews was a
female client competent to try the patience of much
stronger legal minds than those which she was doomed
to test.

At the ADELPHI there has been a farce of the broadest
and most laughable school (in terse and expressive play-
bill language, an "Adelphi screamer"), in which Mr. Keeley
finding himself in a perpetual state of mystery and amazement, the audience as a matter of course are in a perpetual
roar. Certainly it would be difficult to name an actor,
from the stage past or present, whose comic efforts are so
natural and unstrained as those of Mr. Keeley. His touch
is so easy that under it extravagance itself loses the air of
unreality. He never grimaces, he never winks at the
audience, he never takes anybody but himself into his confidence—yet what a never-tiring figure of fun he is, how
unconscious he seems of the laughter he provokes, and
what a solidity he appears to give to the most trivial expres-
sions! Not, however, that the dialogue of this farce is

altogether trivial, for it is really above the average of things of the kind ; and it introduced a new and promising actor, Mr. Garden, to the always good-natured appreciation of the audience at the ADELPHI.

Another new piece at the LYCEUM, being a clever and well-constructed adaptation from the French, promises to have a long and most successful run. It suits the company exactly, is excellently played by everyone engaged in it, and not only gives scope for the best acting of Mr. Charles Mathews in his ordinary manner, but carries him into ground where he may establish fresh claims to the liking of his audiences. The character is that of a young ruined scapegrace and adventurer in whom a good heart has not wholly been extinguished, and who, under an unexpected temptation to do good, finds himself suddenly and very heartily giving way to it, and rises into happiness and wins esteem. The piece offers also to the public favour, in the person of Miss F. Hughes, a very nice and clever little *débutante.*

December 10.—One of the most distinguished and respected of our actresses, who has for years maintained her family by her exertions, was the other day subjected to the distress of appearing, through her husband, in the Insolvent Debtors' Court. It appeared that for some time she had been afflicted by the growth of a most painful disease, in spite of which, while strength remained, she laboured actively in her profession. Compelled at last to desist, the pains of poverty might have been felt not less sharply than the pains of sickness, had not friends been at hand to deprive them of their sting. The proceedings in the Debtors' Court disclosed only truths that come home to us all. They told us that an intellectual and high-spirited woman had supported herself and her children by laborious exertion in the highest department of dramatic art—that by the rapid growth of a terrible disease she had been checked in her career—and that this deprived her, as it would deprive any one among the millions of her countrymen or country-women, of the means of fulfilling the moderate and reasonable engagements formed in days of health. All that it told us more than that was of the human sympathies awakened by the case. We cannot say of such a reverse that it suggests charity, using the word in its cold modern sense. But it arouses sympathies, and it enables those who stand about to claim a privilege of ministering by kind offices to a most sacred grief.

Kind offices, thus done in secret, have, through the investigation in the Insolvent Court, been forced into publicity. We should not speak of them, if we had not been made to see that there was one gentle hand among those ready to smooth the pillow of the sinking actress, which Englishmen are always proud to recognise, and never yet have found stretched out for any evil work. Not only have fellow-artists gathered about Mrs. Warner, but some others who, as the world knows, are never absent when a kind word is to be said or a kindly act done, and by accident the Queen's name slipped into the narrative. Among other indications of the great respect in which the sick lady is held, it appeared that her Majesty had not been content with simply subscribing towards the support required by Mrs. Warner's family, now that its prop fails—but that, having learnt the importance of carriage-exercise to the patient, with a woman's delicacy at once found the kindest way to render service, by herself hiring a carriage which she has caused, and causes still, to be placed daily at Mrs. Warner's disposal.

It is properly in the nature of acts like this to remain unknown to the world, and it is with reserve and misgiving one gives to so graceful a private action more publicity than it already has. Yet surely gentle qualities which no possessor would parade, we are bound to recognise, and are entitled to admire, in one another. Her Majesty makes few state visits to the English theatres. Chance has disclosed, however, how the actor's art may be more surely honoured by a courtesy more womanly and quite as royal.

December 17.—Mr. Albert Smith has for the present season very much improved and amplified his entertainment. The public now sits to be amused, if it will think so, among the houses of a Swiss village, their fronts modelled of life-size, flanking the central point, the stage, upon which Switzerland appears through the scenes of Mr. Beverley. Beside Switzerland stands London, in the person of Mr. Albert Smith, a gentleman to whom justice will not be done if, after the next European war and partition of territory, Mont Blanc is not assigned to him as his just share. It is of no special use to any other potentate, but to him it is a little realm, and one, too, in which the financial condition, as a necessary consequence of the first-rate character of his budget, is in the finest order. The budget for this year is better than ever, and is developed in an address which it would tax greatly the powers of Mr. Gladstone to deliver.

Soberly speaking, Mr. Smith has every faculty that is required for the effective execution of an enterprise like that in which he is engaged. He has great ability, a good ready sense of fun, abundant power as a mimic, willingness to spare no personal exertion on the perfecting of his entertainment, and a great deal of the most serviceable tact. He tells his stories always with good taste, obtruding none of his jokes, good or bad, but leaving all to find their friends out for themselves. He breaks off every song, and every story, a full minute before there is any possibility of any-one beginning to think that it is tedious. And he contrives to fill two hours and a half with an entertainment, during which he is incessantly before his audience, sometimes grave, but chiefly provoking mirth, without leaving at the

end the recollection of one ill-humoured word, or of a
syllable that could be construed into undue egotism or
impertinence.   Some of the new bits of character are among
the very best.   The remarkably wise English engineer who
talks over his pipe, down· in the engine-room of a boat on
the Lago Maggiore, is one of the best and truest reproduc-
tions of character that can be met with in our day.

Hearty praise of this entertainment should not close without a reference to the great pains taken by Mr. Albert Smith
in the regulation of his room, and in the abolishing of every
usage that interferes in places of amusement with the good-
temper of the audience.   There are no fees levied for anything, and there is no unpunctuality.   The lecture begins true
to " electric time", and the intervals between the parts are
confined to a most exact five minutes.

December 31.—In his Christmas fairy spectacle of *Once
upon a Time there were Two Kings*, Mr. Planché develops
one of the Countess d'Aunois' tales into a drama with
enough plot to amuse, and enough sparkle in the dialogue
to scintillate agreeably throughout the piece, without any
impertinent obtrusiveness.   He has abstained almost wholly,
and might as well have abstained altogether, from political
allusions, for there is no connection between corn-laws,
foreign wars, cab-strikes, and fairy-land ; and it is quite right
that Mr. Planché should deny practically their existence.
Allusions to current events are the life of a pantomime ; but
they are the death of a fairy spectacle, presented in good,
earnest, fairy style.

How people dressed in the times of the fairies, even Mr.
Planché does not appear to know.   He has therefore used
an excellent discretion in supposing that the characters of
his tale dressed as its first readers would suppose them
dressed, and accordingly we have shepherds with blue satin
body-suits, ruffs and crooks, kings, gentlemen, and ladies, in
the style proper to the days of Louis Quatorze.   A very

elegant effect is produced by the use of this quaint and
picturesque Louis Quatorze costume, and the actors do
their business with an air and grace that would have charmed
the great monarch himself and all his court.

Fairy stories never were more elegantly acted, ridiculous
things never were elevated with more grace and finish into
an ideal region, than when intrusted to the hands of the
Lyceum company. As for Mr. Beverley's scenery, our admiration of it makes it difficult to describe. Perhaps it will
be enough to say that it is worthy of his reputation, and that
in the final scene of the piece a fairy effect has been created
of the completest kind, by lengthening the silver skirts of
damsels who appear to hover in the air, grouping them into
festoons, and giving to their beauty something of a fantastic
unearthly character. [Nowadays, 1866, one of the com-
monest forms of stage-decoration in a Christmas piece.]
This perhaps is the crowning triumph of the theatre so far as
mere spectacle is concerned. Madame Vestris appeared as
the wife of the shepherd-monarch, acting with consummate
ease and good-sense, as she always did and does, and singing with the beauty of voice and articulation which clings to
her still.

Though tolerably early in my visit to DRURY LANE, I was
afraid, by the aspect of business on the stage, that the pantomime was begun. There was a lady in black going
through a series of decidedly comical pantomimic gestures,
apparently directed to a gentleman in white trousers, with a
very broad black shining belt round an extremely narrow
waist, a Byron collar, a jacket almost indiscernible through
its crowd of glittering buttons, and, tumbling over the front
of the shining belt in the direction of his knees, an expanse
of shirt that in the streets would have been so alarming as to
call for the police to tuck it in. However, it appeared that
the lady was Mrs. Lewis as a heroine of domestic life, gone
mad in a colour which is against all the established rules,

and that the gentleman was Mr. Belton in the character of her lover and a true British tar.

The pantomime, which followed duly, seemed to give great pleasure to all the eager young critics present, and this of course is the merit of a pantomime. To the juvenile world indeed the Drury Lane manager more peculiarly addresses himself, the monarch of the introductory burlesque being no other than an enormous humming-top, and his kingdom the land of toys. There is a prince who suffers from low-spirits, and he is restored to bliss by marbles, foot-ball, hop-scotch, and other such youthful felicities. Of the harlequinade I cannot reasonably say much, but there was one good change; there was plenty of thieving by the clown; there was some table-talking; and there was a great deal of very clever and not at all disagreeable posturing, by a family called Ethair, which must be a corruption of I' th' air, for this volatile family is evidently much more at home in the air than on the ground.

1854, *February* 11.—*Guy Mannering* is very nicely pro-duced at the HAYMARKET. The scenery is new, the grouping is effective, the cast is tolerably good, and there is one piece of acting in it of an excellent and very striking kind. Miss Cushman's melodramatic Meg Merrilies has quite as indis-putably the attributes of genius about it as any piece of poetry or tragedy could have. Such is her power over the intention and feeling of the part that the mere words of it be-come a secondary matter. It is the figure, the gait, the look, the gesture, the tone, by which she puts beauty and passion into language the most indifferent. When these mere arti-fices are continued through a series of scenes, a certain strain becomes apparent, and the effect is not wholly agreeable. Nevertheless it is something to see what the unassisted resources of acting may achieve with the mere idea of a fine part, stripped of fine language, unclothed as it were in words. The human tenderness blending with that Eastern pictur-

esqueness of gesture, the refined sentiment breaking out
from beneath that heavy feebleness and clumsiness of rude
old age, are wonderfully startling.   Mr. Compton is a good
Dominie Sampson, and Miss Harland looks and sings very
pleasingly in Lucy Bertram.   Mr. Howe is not enough of the
ruffian in Dirk Hatteraick.   He looks rather an honest fellow;
and though he might have been as innocently fond of a
garden of tulips as Scott makes his Dutch smuggler, he
would not have plundered and murdered on all sides simply
to get at that source of natural enjoyment.

How quaint and pretty the introduction to the pantomime
at this theatre is, and what a nice little dancer and actress is
Miss Lydia Thompson, the heroine of the three bears, Little
Silver Hair !   She is a true heroine for a nursery-story,
dancing, and talking, and laughing, as if she meant never to
grow bigger, or more foolish, or less cheerful.

March 25.—At the ADELPHI, Messrs. Tom Taylor and
Charles Reade, authors of *Masks and Faces*, have produced
another drama, *Two Loves and a Life*, which will much
confirm their credit as well-coupled no less than accomplished authors.   There has not been for years a better
thing of its kind upon the stage than *Masks and Faces*, and
here we have another play which also of its kind is excellent.   Its kind is that which is best expressed to playgoers
by the phrase "Adelphi drama".   It is the Adelphi drama
spiritualised, and in that sense a perfect study.   The
authors have evidently determined that they would deprive
the Adelphi audience of not one of its usual delights.
There should be in their drama, mystery, villainy, comic
business, smugglers, caves, crossing of swords, firing of
guns, lost daughters, mysteriously recovered, shrieking
their way into their fathers' arms, hair-breadth perils, exe-
cutions, reprieves.   Mr. O. Smith should be a villain ; Mr.
Keeley should have his comic genius, especially in the
depiction of mortal terror, well brought out ; Mr. Webster

should have a part to make a study of quite in his own vein ; Mr. Leigh Murray should have a gentleman's part ; Madame Celeste should have something melodramatic and picturesque which would enable her to display all the great power that is in her ; and Miss Woolgar should be enabled also to bring into play nearly the whole range of her skill. Other actors were to be equally well-fitted—and all this has been done wonderfully.

There is the Adelphi audience fitted to perfection with its play, and every actor fitted to perfection with his or her part ; yet, after all, nothing is displayed more perfectly than the true power of the authors of the entertainment. We may imagine how we are indebted, now to Mr. Reade's power of expressing passion, now to Mr. Tom Taylor's constructive skill, everywhere to the skill which both gentlemen have as polished writers, and a quick sense both of humour and of pathos. Thus it happens that we have here all the vulgar elements of an Adelphi drama, lifted far above the regions of vulgarity, the oldest tricks of the stage being made new and striking by some touch which sets the stamp of genius upon them. Old as the material all is, this story of Jacobite plots and perils, and of two village women rivalling each other in struggles to save the life of him whom they both love—he is saved at last by the one whose love he does not return—is constructed with a plot so full of matter, and so artfully developed, that the interest of the most practised playgoer is sustained firmly to the end. It abounds in finely conceived situations, which not only satisfy the intellect, but are (speaking in a popular sense) of the most effective kind. Mr. Webster's character of a Jesuit disguised, who is also a man disguised, concealing tender feelings and hot passion under a hard and cold manner, was so personated as to form one of the best pieces of acting that can now be seen. Madame Celeste never displayed more energy and spirit, more power of depicting half-untutored passion, than in the part which she here sustains. Mr. Keeley, as a meddling schoolmaster, undergoes many troubles ; his part belonging wholly to the story, for there is no under-plot. And when he is ordered by a shaggy ruffian to walk twenty paces before a loaded pistol in an unconcerned way, with the information that he will be shot if he betrays any emotion, his attempt to walk like a gentleman at ease is an absurdity that steps across to the sublime.

April 22.—It is well that opera-frequenters should be allowed an opportunity of hearing such a work as *Matilde di Shabran*, just revived at COVENT GARDEN, for whoever has heard it knows Rossini better than before. In a greater effort, the master comes to us with the direct purpose of compelling our respect and admiration ; in a piece like this, recklessly dashed off as it was, in a few days, to please the good-tempered public that enjoys itself over the humours of the Carnival, the composer does not stand upon his guard, and the familiar view we get of him thus causes us to understand him as we understand a friend. Perhaps a fourth part of this opera was written in bed— Rossini, I think, wrote in bed sometimes—it is certainly not composed ambitiously ; strains that had been used by himself in former operas were welcome to appear again, if they recurred to him again ; and though the libretto was atrociously absurd, that did not matter. The beauty Matilde was to subdue the beast Corradino, and the beast's was to be "a part to tear a cat in". Rossini has no taste for tearing cats, and cared as little for the tremendous situations furnished to his pen as the public, before so ridiculous a story, could be supposed likely to care. He toned the plot all down by his treatment of it to a conventional level, and made out of the heaviest libretto in existence a light entertainment full of airy strains of playfulness and delicacy.

To hear *Matilde di Shabran* is to hear Rossini at ease,

making music as if for his own amusement, sometimes
starting a fresh strain, and sometimes remembering himself,
but always displaying naturally the most characteristic
features of his genius. It is an opera chiefly remarkable
for the number and great beauty of its concerted pieces for
from four to eight voices ; it also contains one or two
charming duets, not many solos. The pleasure of the
music is enlivened by the humours of one of those buffo
characters—a wandering *improvisatore*, a true carnival personage—for which none ever knew better than Rossini how
to provide hints in his music, and which no man knows
better than Ronconi how to sing and act.

Matilde di Shabran was revived before a full house,
which at first listened coldly, but, as the business went
on, the force of a good company singing its best began
to tell upon the audience, the beauty of the concerted
pieces was felt, and long before the end of the first act
it had been warmed more than once to a complete enthusiasm. It enabled Mdlle. Bosio to achieve one of her
highest triumphs, and has, in one night, done more to make
the public acquainted with her merits than might otherwise have been effected in a month or two.

This opera, sung and acted as it is, may prove more
attractive than its antecedent failures might induce us to
suppose. When it was last produced in London, and supported by Madame Persiani, by Rubini, Tamburini, and
Lablache, all that is best in the second act, including a
duet which is now one of the triumphs of the night, was
omitted, and a long scene was retained that spoiled by
ridiculous excess the comic part. This is now very judiciously cut out. In other respects, also, the opera, when it
was last produced, was altered in a way which must have
helped greatly to assure its failure.

April 29.—Two or three lines shall record a performance of *L'Elisir d'Amore*, in justice to Mdlle. Bosio, whose

growing success with the public calls for record. This is the opera in which she first appeared before a London audience, and the very great advance she has made is too remarkable to pass unnoticed. As a singer in the pure Italian style, and as both singer and actor in all parts that require no more acting than the expression of natural grace, and of the little charms that belong properly to a woman, she bids fair to become perfect. Of Ronconi's Dulcamara nothing remains to be said.

The event of the week at COVENT GARDEN was the appearance of Mdlle. Cruvelli in *Otello*. The lady was nervous, and perhaps the opera was not well selected, for it was one in which it might have been foretold that the chief honours would be all carried off by Signor Tamberlik. The one great enthusiasm that is excited by the performance arises out of the scene between Ronconi and Tamberlik, wound up with a duet which produces Signor Tamberlik's wonderful chest-note. Mdlle. Cruvelli had a courteous but not a genial reception.

May 6.—The best of operas, Beethoven's *Fidelio*, is now assured a place on the Italian stage. Mdlle. Cruvelli has of old shown occasional want of reverence for operas of lower mark, which in her hands have suffered mutilation. Her Leonora is not only the sole passable Leonora now to be had, but is a conscientious and most accurate performance. But, admirably as she sings her part, Mdlle. Cruvelli does not act it. She appears on all occasions to perform rather with all her head than with all her heart. The parts assumed by her are always declaimed well, sometimes with great spirit and vivacity, but they are not, in any high sense of the term, acted.

May 27.—Verdi's *Rigoletto* has attracted two full houses. The music is tolerable, the melodrama which forms the basis of the libretto, Victor Hugo's *Le Roi s'amuse*, is highly spiced and has many striking points, the stage-appointments are of the very best, the singing is good, and the fool's tragedy is driven home to the heart by Ronconi's acting as the ill-fated jester Rigoletto, that being his finest tragic part.

The new drama of *The Marble Heart*, translated from the French and played at the ADELPHI THEATRE on Monday night, is chiefly to be noticed for a very striking piece of acting by Mr. Leigh Murray. He plays a young sculptor whom the seductions of a Parisian fine lady have enticed from the labours of his studio and the enjoyments of his home, and whose sensitive heart, after frenzied alternations of hope, triumph, misgivings, and despair, is finally shattered against the lady's heart of marble. There is a scene in the fourth act where he learns his fate, struggles against it, will not submit to it, tries every vain expedient of indignation and reproach, and is by turns defiant to the highest pitch and abject to the lowest and most pitiable, while the lady sits all the while calm and unmoved against the passion thus foaming and dashing itself against her, which is as good a piece of natural tragic acting as has been seen for a long time.

Its only defect marks strongly the defect of the whole piece. It was too much prolonged. The scenes never stopped where they ought to have stopped. In every case, no matter how good the thing was, we had too much of the good thing. The best passages in the fourth act were twice as long as they should have been, and the whole of the first and the whole of the fifth act might have been spared altogether. The first was a kind of allegory or dream, in which the actors, who afterwards figure in modern Paris, present themselves as denizens of ancient Greece—a poor labouring girl as a slave, a newspaper editor as Diogenes, and so forth—but the drift of it all was not clear, the performance not remarkable, and the connection with the subsequent drama very imperfectly made out. The last act, being entirely occupied by the death of the young sculptor, had only the effect of weakening, to the full extent of its continuance, the very tragical and affecting picture of his despair.

June 3.—The uncertainty which has attached to Signor Mario's voice, since what we suppose we may therefore call his disastrous Russian campaign, was curiously exemplified on Tuesday night. His first air in the *Puritani, A te O cara*, was given beautifully, and all went well until towards the conclusion of the act, when there was an evident abatement of the rare sweetness of his tones. At last the voice flickered and went out suddenly, as a gaslight, at the close of the scene with Henrietta, during the somewhat trying outburst of musical affection, *Non parlar di lei*. In the second act Arturo does not appear, but the third depends mainly upon him, and of the third therefore the audience was disappointed. It was found necessary to substitute a portion of another opera.

On Monday night Mdlle. Cruvelli made her last appearance, and that was before the audience of an extra night. Her services had been confined latterly to extra nights. It was only by accident that she had been brought before the subscribers on the previous Saturday, when, on account of the illness of Signor Tagliafico, *Don Giovanni* was given as a substitute for two acts of *Masaniello* and *L'Elisir d'Amore*. The audience that went to hear Auber and Donizetti absolutely grumbled to itself at being put off with —Mozart! In cold justice, a certain amount of admiration will be always accorded to Mdlle. Cruvelli's powers; but while she sings like a musical instrument endowed with locomotion, and acts, even in her few energetic bursts, like an ingenious automaton, she never will excite that sense of personal sympathy, that idea of hearty mutual goodwill, which, rightly or wrongly, an English audience always wishes to establish with its entertainers.

June 17.—Three of Madame Grisi's farewell nights have now been devoted to the performance of *Lucrezia Borgia ;* and the first three nights of Madame Viardot—who, to the great joy of the public, reappears at length upon the stage —have been occupied by the *Prophète.*   Both operas have drawn overflowing houses.

Apart from all appreciation of good acting, we might wonder very much at the attractive power of the merely pretty music—to be sure, the utmost he could furnish—with which Donizetti has beset, in the case of the first-named opera, an extremely powerful libretto ; but the truth is, that Madame Grisi's Lucrezia Borgia cannot be thought of apart from the fine acting by which she has created it into one of her best personations.

Of the *Prophète,* and of Madame Viardot's Fides, it is enough to say that they have lost in this year's representation none of their old sterling value.   Madame Viardot, the most subtle and spiritual of our actress singers, is to Grisi what Ronconi is to Lablache, not so much less or greater, but in such manner differing.

July 1.—Madame Viardot has materially strengthened the cast of *Don Giovanni* by taking the part of Donna Anna, which was intrusted in the earlier part of the season, to Mdlle. Cruvelli.   Except in the one air *Or sai chi l' onore,* which had the benefit of all Mdlle. Cruvelli's physical power, and was one of the few fine " bits" in her acting, there is no part of the character in which comparison can be instituted between the two performers that does not make one heartily glad of the change.

The *Prophète* has been repeated, and Madame Grisi has been singing in *The Huguenots.*   The heroines of Meyerbeer are unsuited to Madame Grisi's genius, and Valentine is but the least unsuccessful of her personation of them. Her scene with Raoul in the third act is indeed magnificent, but it is reached only through two acts and a half of com parative failure. I do not mean real failure, for that could scarcely be ; but there are characters, and this is one of them, in which the breadth of style and boldness of effect which render Madame Grisi's performances perhaps the most popular on the Italian stage, have not fair play. Just in the same way there are other characters—such as Norma, or Lucrezia Borgia—that would be represented ill by the subtle play of light and shade, the accumulation of effects minutely studied, in which lies the charm of Madame Viardot's acting. Daguerreotype Madame Viardot suddenly at any moment during her personation of Fides, and, though she may be only passing at that moment from one gesture to another, you will fix upon the plate a picturesque and expressive figure, which is moreover a figure indicating in its face and in its attitude that precise feeling which belonged to the story at the moment chosen. A personation of this kind is required for the perfection of the part of Valentine, a part in which the special gifts of Madame Grisi are only once or twice brought into use.

July 15.—Signor Lablache brings with him to COVENT GARDEN the means not only of greatly strengthening old casts, but also of producing several operas to the success of which he is indispensable. Almost a part of this artist's personal and inalienable property is the character of the maestro in the few merry scenes that are all man endures of Gnecco's three-act *Prova d' un Opera Seria.* But the opera-goer who enjoyed that musical farce, interlude, or afterpiece, when Lablache made its whole glory in the Haymarket, now finds the enjoyment of it trebled by the addition to his genial humour of Ronconi's more than Buckstonian drolleries as the poor poet, and of Madame Viardot's piquancy as the perverse prima donna. On Tuesday evening this piece of fun was performed after no more than a portion of an opera, in order that Her Majesty might have an opportunity of seeing it without waiting till midnight ;—denial to spectators of a decent hour of bedtime being the great drawback upon its performance in the usual manner as an afterpiece.

August 12.—*Le Comte Ory* is wonderfully pretty, and if it should fail to hold its place upon our stage it will fail only by reason of its libretto, which is not merely stupid, but detestably immoral.   The count is a libidinous young scamp, who, hearing of a castle full of ladies, plots to get among them with his knights, and to do so uses the cloak of religion. Twice an attempt is made to excite laughter by a comic use of prayer.

That music so charming as that of *Le Comte Ory* should be set to the most abominable of libretti is surely great pity. Would it not be worth while to write another book for it? The task could not be difficult, and no wrong would be done to Rossini, since the music was not originally written for the book that is now used, and the notes therefore are not by any means wedded to the incidents of the existing story.

September 23.—At the ADELPHI the revival of Mr. Morris Barnett's *Monsieur Jacques* for a few nights, coming in aid of old Adelphi pieces, fills the house as it should.   It is some time since Monsieur Jacques with his darling opera, and his monomania touching the return of Mariane, left the stage in the person of Mr. Morris Barnett.   That gentleman re-appears now for twelve nights.

October 21.—*Pericles, Prince of Tyre*, that Eastern romance upon which Shakespeare spent some master-touches as a dramatist, and which he may have re-adapted to the stage even while yet a prentice to his art, has been produced at SADLER'S WELLS by Mr. Phelps, with the care due to a work especially of interest to all students of Shakespeare, and with the splendour proper to an Eastern spectacle.

The story was an old one ; there is a version of it even in Anglo-Saxon.   Gower had made it the longest story in his *Confessio Amantis*, and the one told with the greatest care ;

and the dramatist in using it made use of Gower. The story was a popular one of an Eastern prince whose life is spent upon a sea of trouble. Everywhere he is pursued by misfortune. He seeks a beautiful wife at the risk of death, through the good old Eastern plan of earning her by answering a riddle. She proves a miracle of lust. He flies from her, and is pursued by the strong wrath of her father. To avoid this he is forced to become an exile from his house and people. He sails to Tharsus, where he brings liberal relief to a great famine, and is hailed as a saviour ; but to Tharsus he is pursued by warning of the coming wrath of his great enemy. Again he becomes a fugitive across the sea. The sea is pitiless, and tosses him from coast to coast until it throws him ashore, the only man saved from the wreck of his vessel near Pentapolis. But in Pentapolis reigns a good king, whose daughter—still in the true fashion of a story-book—is to be courted by a tourney between rival princes. Pericles would take part in such ambition, and the sea casts him up a suit of armour. He strives, and is victor. He excels all in the tourney, in the song, and in the dance ; the king is generous and the daughter kind. But the shadow of his evil fate is still over Pericles. He distrusts a thing so strange as happy fortune, and thinks of it only "'tis the king's subtlety to have my life". Fortune is, however, for once really on his side. He marries the Princess Thaisa, and, being afterwards informed that his great enemy is dead and that his own subjcts rebel against his continued absence, he sets sail with her from Tyre.

The good gifts seem, however, only to have been granted by Fortune that she might increase his wretchedness tenfold by taking them away. The sea again " washes heaven and hell" when his ship is fairly launched upon it, and in a storm so terrible that

> " the seaman's whistle
> Is as a whisper in the ears of death,
> Unheard,

the nurse brings on deck to Pericles a new-born infant, with
the tidings that its mother Thaisa is dead. The sailors,
believing that a corpse on board maintains the storm about
the ship, demand that the dead queen be thrown into the
sea. Most wretched queen! mourns the more wretched
prince,

> "A terrible childbed hast thou had, my dear;
> No light, no fire : the unfriendly elements
> Forgot thee utterly ; nor have I time
> To give thee hallowed to thy grave, but straight
> Must cast thee, scarcely coffined, in the ooze ;
> Where, for a monument upon thy bones,
> And aye-remaining lamps, the belching whale
> And humming water must o'erwhelm thy corpse,
> Lying with simple shells."

Being at this time near Tharsus, however, and remembering that Tharsus owes to him a debt of gratitude, Pericles
makes for Tharsus, in order that he may place his infant with
the least possible delay upon sure ground and under tender
nursing.

The daughter there grows up under her father's evil star.
"This world to me", she says, "is like a lasting storm, whir-
ring me from my friends." The Queen of Tharsus becomes
jealous and resolves to murder her. It is by the sea-shore
that the deed is to be done. When Pericles comes for his
child her tomb is shown to him, and under his last woe his
mind breaks down. He puts to sea again with his wrecked
spirit, and, though the sea again afflicts him with its storms,
he rides them out.

I have not told the familiar story thus far for the sake of
telling it, but for the sake of showing in the most convenient way what is really the true spirit of the play. At
this point of the tale the fortune of Pericles suddenly
changes. A storm of unexpected happiness breaks with
immense force upon him. The sea and the tomb seem to

give up their dead, and from the lowest depths of prostration the spirit of the prince is exalted to the topmost height, in scenes which form most worthily the climax of the drama. "O Helicanus," he then cries,

> " O Helicanus, strike me, honoured sir ;
> Give me a gash, put me to present pain ;
> Lest this great sea of joys, rushing upon me,
> O'erbear the shores of my mortality,
> And drown me with their sweetness."

In telling such a story as this, Shakespeare felt—and young as he may have been, his judgment decided rightly—that it should be shown distinctly as a tale such as

> " Hath been sung at festivals,
> On Ember eves and holy ales" ;

and he therefore brought forward Gower himself very much in the character of an Eastern story-teller to begin the narrative and to carry it on to the end, subject to the large interruption of five acts of dramatic illustration. A tale was being told ; every person was to feel that, although much of it would be told to the eye. But in the revival of the play, Mr. Phelps was left to choose between two difficulties. The omission of Gower would be a loss to the play, in an artistic sense, yet the introduction of Gower before every act would very probably endanger its effect in a theatrical sense, unless the part were spoken by an actor of unusual power. The former plan was taken ; and in adding to certain scenes in the drama passages of his own writing, strictly confined to the explanation of those parts of the story which Shakespeare represents Gower as narrating between the acts, Mr. Phelps may have used his best judgment as a manager. Certainly, unless he could have been himself the Gower as well as the Pericles of the piece, the frequent introduction of a story-telling gentleman in a long coat and long curls would have been an extremely hazardous experiment, even before such an earnest audience as that at SADLER'S WELLS.

The change did inevitably, to a certain extent, disturb the poetical effect of the story ; but assuming its necessity, it was effected modestly and well. The other changes also were in no case superfluous, and were made with considerable judgment. The two scenes at Mitylene, which present Marina pure as an ermine that no filth can touch, were compressed into one ; and although the plot of the drama was not compromised by a false delicacy, there remained not a syllable at which true delicacy could have conceived offence. The calling of Blount and his Mistress was covered in the pure language of Marina with so hearty a contempt, that the scene was really one in which the purest minds might be those which would take the most especial pleasure.

The conception of the character of Pericles by Mr. Phelps seemed to accord exactly with the view just taken of the play. He was the Prince pursued by evil fate. A melancholy that could not be shaken off oppressed him even in the midst of the gay court of King Simonides, and the hand of Thaisa was received with only the rapture of a love that dared not feel assured of its good fortune. Mr. Phelps represented the Prince sinking gradually under the successive blows of fate, with an unostentatious truthfulness ; but in that one scene which calls forth all the strength of the artist, the recognition of Marina and the sudden lifting of the Prince's bruised and fallen spirit to an ecstasy of joy, there was an opportunity for one of the most effective displays of the power of an actor that the stage, as it now is, affords. With immense energy, yet with a true feeling for the pathos of the situation that had the most genuine effect, Mr. Phelps achieved in this passage a triumph marked by plaudit after plaudit. They do not applaud rant at SADLER'S WELLS. The scene was presented truly by the actor and felt fully by his audience.

The youthful voice and person, and the quiet acting of Miss Edith Heraud, who made her *début* as Marina, greatly helped to set forth the beauty of that scene. The other parts had also been judiciously allotted, so that each actor did what he or she was best able to do, and did it up to the full measure of the ability of each. Miss Cooper gave much effect to the scene of the recovery of Thaisa, which was not less well felt by those who provided the appointments of the stage, and who marked that portion of the drama by many delicacies of detail.

Of the scenery indeed it is to be said that so much splendour of decoration is rarely governed by so pure a taste. The play, of which the text is instability of fortune, has its characteristic place of action on the sea. Pericles is perpetually shown (literally as well as metaphorically) tempest-tost, or in the immediate vicinity of the treacherous water; and this idea is most happily enforced at SADLER'S WELLS by scene-painter and machinist. They reproduce the rolling of the billows and the whistling of the winds when Pericles lies senseless, a wrecked man on a shore. When he is shown on board ship in the storm during the birth of Marina, the ship tosses vigorously. When he sails at last to the temple of Diana of the Ephesians, rowers take their places on their banks, the vessel seems to glide along the coast, an admirably-painted panorama slides before the eye, and the whole theatre seems to be in the course of actual transportation to the temple at Ephesus, which is the crowning scenic glory of the play. The dresses, too, are brilliant. As beseems an Eastern story, the events all pass among princes. Now the spectator has a scene presented to him occupied by characters who appear to have stepped out of a Greek vase; and presently he looks into an Assyrian

palace and sees figures that have come to life and colour
from the stones of Nineveh. There are noble banquets
and glittering processions, and in the banquet-hall of King
Simonides there is a dance which is a marvel of glitter,
combinations of colour, and quaint picturesque effect.
There are splendid trains of courtiers, there are shining
rows of vestal virgins, and there is Diana herself in the sky.

We are told that the play of *Pericles* enjoyed, for its own
sake, when it first appeared, a run of popularity that excited
the surprise and envy of some playwrights, and became
almost proverbial. It ceased to be acted in the days of
Queen Anne ; and whether it would attract now as a mere
acted play, in spite of the slight put upon it by our fathers
and grandfathers, it is impossible to say, since the *Pericles*
of SADLER'S WELLS may be said to succeed only because it
is a spectacle.

October 28.—At the OLYMPIC THEATRE a new two-act
drama, called *The Trustee*, introduces Mr. A. Wigan in the
character of a high-minded old Frenchman, intrusted during
war-times with a large sum by a friend who falls in battle.
The care of the money in an unsettled district overrun by
plunderers, and one especial terror, having reduced the old
man to a state of great nervous prostration, he removes the
money to a new hiding-place while in a state of somnam-
bulism, and afterwards forgets what he has done. The
consequence is that, when his daughter's bridegroom and
his friend's heir arrive on the same day, he believes his
trust-money to be lost, and feels bound in honour to replace
it with the dowry that was to have secured his daughter's
happiness. All ends well, but in the course of the tale Mr.
Wigan has opportunities of expressing many shades of
character and changes of emotion, which he does with so
much fidelity to nature, as well as to the highest rules of
art, that he gives attractiveness to a little drama possessing
in itself but slender merit.

December 2.—The ADELPHI is indebted to Mr. Mark Lemon for another most successful farce, *The Railway Belle*, which keeps the house ringing with laughter. Mr. James Rogers, as a waiter desperately mad with love for the belle of the refreshment station, distinguishes himself greatly in this piece of genuine mirth; Mr. Selby is also very amusing; and Miss Wyndham, who is the belle in dispute between the waiter, the station-master, and Mr. Samuel Greenhorne the passenger, forms a delightful centre of confusion.

Three years ago Mr. Lemon had two pieces of mark in course of performance at two theatres. At the ADELPHI *Sea and Land*, with a fine part for Mrs. Keeley, of a generous nature half brutalised by ill-usage, slow of intellect, and quick of feeling. When that was produced there was being acted at the HAYMARKET a new play of Mr. Lemon's, entitled *Mind Your Own Business*, a tale of English life a hundred years ago, but embodying the character and sentiment which belongs to every day. The nominal hero was a good-natured meddler, whimsically played by Mr. Buckstone, who involved the plot by attending to everybody's business but his own. The real hero was a country squire, whose despair on finding himself rejected by the damsel upon whose consent he had too confidently built, carried him to the dissipations of town life, drinking and dicing, from which he was rescued by the sister of the girl to whom his addresses had been paid— that sister to whom he found in the end that his devotion was more properly due. This was a part in which Mr. Webster shone. The change from buoyant eagerness, tempered by a certain manly shyness, into a dull drunken debasement, through which gleams of a better nature are still strongly visible, was a piece of that true acting in which transitions apparently the most extreme are kept within probability and nature. Miss Reynolds and Mrs Stirling gave interest to the two sisters. The underplot was chiefly sustained by Mr. Keeley in the character of a lucky and unlucky footman, happy in an eccentric nabob's large legacy, and miserable in having been married for it by a vulgar widow, whose magnificent airs and fine company he nevertheless sadly mortified by always unconsciously resuming the plush in his speech, and at last more deliberately reassuming it on his person.

December 9.—Mr. Charles Mathews has achieved fresh success at the LYCEUM, and again sustains the credit of his theatre mainly by the force of his own talents. His last farce-comedy, adapted from the French, and entitled *Aggravating Sam*, is one of the merriest possible of those pieces of absurdity in which the best acting is above all things essential, and of which all the burthen therefore falls on himself. Mr. Sam Naggins finds an exquisite delight in aggravating all people with whom he comes in contact. For the sore points in his fellow-creatures he seeks carefully, and when he has found them rubs at them with an impish malice. The farce contains many characters, of whom all and each are brought into a high state of excitement by the contrivances of Aggravating Sam. It would be idle to tell the plot. Mr. Charles Mathews, as the man with the propensity to mischief, is the soul of it. He feels his way into every bright scheme for the aggravation of a fellow-creature with a serious carefulness, and a philosophical and curious forecasting of results, which is wonderfully ludicrous. When he has carried out a plan of annoyance, he watches for its effect with the relish of a scapegrace boy waiting the explosion of a cracker tied to some unsuspecting creature's tail. Finally, when the explosion does take place, he becomes radiant with triumph at the consequences, and his success of course is welcomed with incessant laughter.

December 16.—At the ADELPHI a new drama has been produced, of which Madame Dudevant is the author, and the adapter Mr. Boucicault. It is called *Pierre the Found-ling*, and is, in fact, an idyllic representation of the rural life of Brittany. Its story is unexaggerated and brief, being employed only for the eliciting of a picture of manners. Mr. Webster is a noble-minded Breton peasant, protected in childhood by and devoted in youth to Madame Celeste, a gentle widow, suffering much from the persecution of Miss Cuthbert, a cruel dame, her neighbour, who for a long time threatens her with a false claim by which she can be ruined. Miss Woolgar is the widow's sister-in-law, a rustic coquette of Brittany; Mr. Keeley is a right-hearted peasant, through whose stupidity flash gleams of shrewdness; and Mrs. Keeley is a sturdy Breton serving-maid, devoted to the fortunes of her mistress.

December 30.—What English author was it who, being in a country town at which he had been a schoolboy, ordered the host at his inn to get him some of the works of a certain pieman that he had once thought exquisitely delicate? The pies were brought to table and disgusted him. It is not so with us in keeping Christmas at the theatre. It is not so with the pie in which four-and-twenty blackbirds were baked, now being served up at DRURY LANE. That remains a pretty dish to set before a king, a judge, or a prime minister. Nobody is dignified or wise enough to make a wry face at it. One is disposed, indeed, to bring to book the author, and on behalf of all children to request that he will show us his authorities for considering the history of the four-and-twenty blackbirds as a necessary sequel to the accidents of Jack and Jill. No doubt he is justified by diligent research among the nurseries of England in asserting that Jill was so far wanting in domestic education as to be unable to make a pie, that this was the cause of her misfortune, that the making of a pie was its remedy, and that the pie she made was the well-known pie of blackbirds mentioned in the Song of Sixpence. But we must take all this for granted,

for the author has himself taken for granted whatever he
pleased, and whatever has pleased him must please us and
all spectators of his pantomime. We are busied among
visions of good things, jams of all sorts, sauces, spices,
pickles, and we are refreshed in a temple of salad; but we
do not know what we see, nor do we care to understand
anything more than that it is all reasonably good, that it
gratifies the eye, tickles the ear, and vivifies the fancy. The
DRURY LANE pantomime is like one of the sauces represented in it, an inscrutable compound, but not without relish.
In the pantomime proper there is a profusion of harlequinade, there are feats of strength by "the Italian brothers"
and others, and the fun attempted is brisk enough. The
martial feelings of the nation are also effectively appealed
to at DRURY LANE as at many other theatres.

The ADELPHI, indeed, in its Christmas entertainment,
appeals almost exclusively to our interest in the Crimean
War. It is entitled *Zigzag, or the Adventures of the Danube
and the Pruth in search of Truth*, the rivers being imper-
sonated by Mrs. Keeley and Miss Woolgar. It has little
story, being chiefly a vehicle for the introduction of effective
scenery, views in the Baltic and Black Seas, in Wallachia,
Constantinople, St. Petersburg, etc., and of such effective
business as belongs to a dramatic enforcement of the
popular opinions about the Russians, and a putting of them
down, so far as it lies in the power of an enterprising playhouse manager to do it. The piece is received with full
applause, and a French dance, *La Flotte*, now extremely
popular in Paris, has been introduced with success. I cannot say that I find much wit, and certainly I see no grace,
in the representation of a naval combat by the dancing of
ladies and gentlemen with ships on their heads.

At the PRINCESS'S THEATRE there is also *La Flotte* introduced into the pantomime, which is on the subject of *Blue*

Beard, and is written by Mr. J. M. Morton, the author of some of our funniest farces. His pantomime, however, so far from being particularly funny, is remarkably dull, in its introductory part ; neither is there anything at all striking in the tricks or transformations of the harlequinade. The most effective thing is a concluding scene that represents the quarter-deck of a man-of-war (for here, too, we are warriors as well as Christmas merrymakers) on the eve of an action, and in action. The manœuvres are cleverly gone through by a group of children ; and the use of children to represent the officers and sailors, providing a small scale of comparison, magnifies the entire scene, and makes the illusion excellent.

Little Bopeep who Lost her Sheep is the heroine of the HAYMARKET pantomime, and the introductory burlesque is a neat little story very elegantly put upon the stage, with Arcadian shepherd scenery, and bursts of fairy splendour. The succeeding pantomime is not too lively, but it is carefully and handsomely got up, is well worked, and, without omitting all allusion to the war, contains less reference to it than occurs in many other houses, a reserve which perhaps we owe to the mishap that befell a piece here called *The Sentinel of the Alma*. Señora Perea Nena, the popular Spanish dancer, who shakes her petticoats and observes curiously the twinkling of her swift, impatient toes, has left us, and the manager of the HAYMARKET has brought back the young lady who so delightfully imitated her at the ST. JAMES'S THEATRE, Miss Lydia Thompson, the little Silver-hair of last year's Haymarket pantomime. A better representative of Little Bopeep could scarcely have been found. The best performer in the harlequinade was the pantaloon, Mr. Barnes, a name honoured of pantomime. The scenery throughout was excellent, and one particular transformation, of a party in a ball-room, with couches and chairs, into the same party accommodated with a coach and horses, was the cleverest thing of its kind done at our theatres in Christmas, 1854.

Mr. Planché's burlesque is to be found, not at the Lyceum, but at the OLYMPIC. The subject is *The Yellow Dwarf*, a good story, followed throughout with that conscientious resolve to enter heart and soul into the spirit of fairy-lore which makes this writer's Christmas pieces always so delightful. The story has been chosen evidently with a view to providing a character in which Mr. Robson might display his rare power of combining tragic passion and real hints of the terrible with ludicrous burlesque, and seldom has that clever actor been so neatly fitted with a part. As a piece—on the score of literary merit—Mr. Planché's *Yellow Dwarf* is more complete than any other holiday performance, and Mr. Robson's Yellow Dwarf we should take to be the best specimen now to be seen of burlesque acting.

January 20, 1855.—At the ST. JAMES'S THEATRE an entertainment has been provided from one of the most perfect and touching of Greek legends. *Alcestis* is a lyrical play, adapted by Mr. Henry Spicer from the French of another adapter of Euripides, M. Hippolyte Lucas ; and set off by a careful performance of some of the music which Glück wedded to the subject, and by the good classical acting of Miss Vandenhoff. The simple beauty of the fable itself, breaking through all disguise, asserts itself to every heart. It is a story for all time, typical of woman's love and of man's friendship. Alcestis gives her own life for her husband's, and the man, more selfish than the woman, can accept the sacrifice. The husband's selfishness, again, is the first motive of his grief, when he has lost so noble a possession as a wife like this. The other part of the fable touches on another of the best and simplest feelings of humanity. The guest of Admetus, before whom the grief of the heart must be concealed, and of whom

the pleasure must be set before our pain, comes more
than once in a lifetime to us all. It is not always a
Hercules. It may be the little child left to a widower,
whose smiles must be awakened, and whose laughter must
be echoed, even while a wound is bleeding in the father's
heart. It may be the chance friend who calls upon us at a
time when we are occupied by sorrow, before whom we
take care to come with dry eyes, and in whose presence we
put aside our griefs to do the courtesies belonging to fit
welcome. Such hospitalities, such acts of self-forgetfulness,
are, it is true, sacrifices far less difficult than was that of
Alcestis. Admetus, who could rise to one, could not rise
to the other. But they are honest sacrifices that by no
means ceased with the noble line of Pheræ. To the end
of time Admetus will have guests, though he may never
have another guest like Hercules, to bring him the Alcestis
that his heart desires.

Mainly, then, to the eternal truth and beauty of the fable
—to the perfectness of its appeal to every heart—is the
success of *Alcestis* at this theatre to be attributed. Such
good fortune is largely aided by the musical accompaniment, selected from Glück's choruses, and arranged by Sir
Henry Bishop, who presides over the orchestra. But
neither plot nor music could have secured the success
desired had not the Alcestis of Miss Vandenhoff expressed
not unworthily both the classical form and the pathetic
reality of the story. The second act, which is by far the
best, comprises that scene of farewell between Alcestis, her
husband, and her children, upon which Euripides has dwelt
so largely. Little departure is here made from the Greek
text, and the sustained beauty of the situation becomes
irresistible.

February 10.—Miss Fanny Kemble's reading of the
Midsummer Night's Dream, backed by a performance of
Mendelssohn's exquisite music to the play, has filled

EXETER HALL. The great beauty of the reading is the
charm˙which Miss Kemble throws over the characters of
Hermia and Helena, the clearness with which she distinguishes between them, and the completeness of her
success in bringing out the character of Helena as something true and womanly.

There is a new drama by Mr. Boucicault at the ADELPHI.
It is a little too long, and its interest, which is very great,
is here and there too painful to pass under the name of
entertainment; but it is unusually clever, and throughout
very original in treatment. The drama is entitled *Janet
Pride*, and is in five acts—two said to be acts of prologue,
three said to be acts of drama. The action all turns on the
sin and misery that follow an inveterate addiction to drink.
Richard Pride, unable to break himself of drunken habits,
becomes a forger, and escapes with a young wife to Paris,
where she suffers cruel deprivation, and her infant is perish-
ing. He steals for drink-money the means of buying
medicine, at the last moment when medicine can be of use;
and his starved wife totters with her dying infant to the
Foundling Hospital one winter's night, yields it up to the
hands of strangers, and perishes in the agony of that hard
sacrifice. She dies in the street, and there her drunken
husband finds her. The story from this point takes many
ingenious and interesting turns.

Richard, returned to England after many years under a
false name, lives in the family of an old French watchmaker
who had owed debts of gratitude to Richard's wife, and for
her sake had taken her child from the hospital to live in his
house as friend and housekeeper and manager (a very
bustling manager) of all affairs. This daughter, Janet, is,
of course, the heroine of the drama. How she, an innocent
girl, is brought to the dock of the Old Bailey for a crime
committed by her father, and how she is saved only by his
making the discovery in court that he was on the point of

crushing his own daughter, as he had already crushed his wife, the drama most effectively sets forth.

Madame Celeste performs with her best skill the part of mother in the prologue, and of daughter in the play itself. The drunken airs and variations in the temper—the half-sober efforts to stare down suspicion and to hide fear when in the presence of one who may detect a crime—the faint strugglings of a naturally gentle heart, overpowered by the curses that come in the train of drunkenness—are marked by Mr. Webster in his part of Richard with peculiar refinement. The simple-hearted old French watchmaker had in Mr. Selby a most admirable representative ; and Mr. Keeley, as the watchmaker's apprentice, spoiling clocks and loving Janet with a devotion by far more pathetic than ridiculous, enjoys not a merely ludicrous part, but a real character in which his power as an actor is displayed to excellent advantage.

The scenery, too, with which the stage is furnished for this clever piece is of a striking kind. The scene which shows the outside of the Foundling Hospital at Paris is remarkably well managed, and the reproduction in the last act of the Central Criminal Court, with all the forms and furnishings of an Old Bailey trial, wonderfully accurate as it is, will be remembered among the dexterous feats of stage-appointment for which our theatres in these days are remarkable.

At the MARYLEBONE our old friend the Man in the Iron Mask is made the hero of a play by Mr. Bayle Bernard. Mr. Bernard's *Leon of the Iron Mask* is written with the taste and skill that might have been expected from so clever and experienced a dramatist. The original story, and all tales or dramas founded upon it, Mr. Bernard has used as much or as little as he pleased, and he has produced out of them a piece which takes with it the sympathies of its spectators. The demand made by it on the powers of the leading actor,

Mr. Wallack, is great, for its story extends over a long period of time, and its hero is shown not only at different periods of life, but also under circumstances of the most contrasted kind. The demand thus made upon his skill Mr. Wallack meets in a way that has added much to his credit, which Mrs. Wallack shares, too, as the heroine. At the MARYLEBONE, as elsewhere, stage-appointments and effects are studied carefully. The manager boasts that, though his theatre is small, his stage is one of the longest in the world, and to make the best possible use of this advantage is always a problem for the decorator. Such use is made in the play of *Leon*, where a capital scenic effect is obtained in a representation of the interior of the Louvre.

March 17.—At the HAYMARKET Mr. Stirling Coyne has taken the idea of a German play, *The Secret Agent*, and worked it up into a brief half-farcical comedy. A young prince whose government is infested by his mother and her favourite ministers, Messrs. Buckstone and Compton, takes a young lady's advice, and alarms his perplexers by announcing the arrival of a secret agent who is at the bottom of everything. Messrs. Buckstone and Compton, who have snug places, are terrified out of their wits at the mysterious scrutiny with which they are threatened, and out of their perplexities the chief fun of the piece springs. The merriment is the greater as they appear during a part of the time at a masked ball, Mr. Buckstone with feminine airs as a lady, and the other as Mephistopheles, duly diabolical.

At the ADELPHI Mrs. Keeley is in force as Betty Martin, the distressed maid of a choleric major. She has broken the house-clock, and inflicts tortures on Major Mohawk not only by her terrors at the catastrophe, but by her ingenious efforts to prevent its discovery. The farce is adapted from a piece by Madame Girardin, but as played at the ADELPHI it belongs entirely to Mrs. Keeley.

Will the Fielding Club be engaged to fight a campaign in the Crimea and retrieve the honour of Great Britain by capturing Sebastopol? Do we want a Ministry of unexampled power and aptitude for office? Of gentlemen who can on demand become the best of harlequins, clowns, acrobats, and pantaloons, anything may henceforward be suspected. Hitherto it has certainly been supposed that the business of harlequin or clown was one that required long and painful training from youth up, and a continual devotion of all faculties to the achievement of the final object of ambition. But perhaps society has been under a delusion on this head. After one's experience of last Saturday, one will really not know of whom not to suspect that he is a gentleman addicted to flying about his house, and taking leaps or turning summersaults in the retirement of his study.

The affliction of a clever writer, the desire to assist whom has already produced an admirable lecture from Mr. Thackeray, produced last Saturday night an amateur performance at the OLYMPIC THEATRE, which was witnessed by an audience including no small part of all the aristocracies we boast about in England.

The Fielding Club's conception of a pantomime—which it is able perfectly to execute—aims at a height unattainable by the most practised harlequins and clowns. It adds to all the professional elasticity of body more than the professional elasticity of mind; it throws a glow of wit and humour over the leaps and contortions of the scene; and it asserts in no ineffective way the dignity of nonsense.

Before the pantomime a prologue, written with much tact and feeling by Mr. Tom Taylor, was delivered, and then the curtain rose on *Harlequin Guy Fawkes.* Mr. Albert Smith, as Catesby, opened the entertainment with one of those wonderfully rapid songs with which he is continually pleasing the town. Presently Mr. Holmes, as Guy Fawkes, made his bow to the audience, and in so doing dropped his head between his feet, as though he had been without a backbone. But Mr. Holmes did far more surprising things than even this, and his burlesque singing was of the highest order. We had also a " terrific combat" between this gentleman and Mr. Albert Smith, which would have doubled the receipts of any provincial or transpontine manager.

The introductory burlesque was in one scene only, but this was worth half-a-dozen of the ordinary sort ; and thereafter appeared Mr. Bidwell as an amateur harlequin, Mr. Arthur Smith as an amateur pantaloon, Mr. J. Robins as an amateur clown, and Mr. Edmund Yates as a burlesque lover ; the best, most sprightly, and most cheerful of columbines, Miss Rosina Wright, giving her professional help to the enterprises of these gentlemen.   How Mr. Bidwell leapt, how he leapt in his spangles, how he leapt as a *danseuse* in expansive satins, how he disappeared through windows as if all his life he had been doing nothing else ; how Mr. Arthur Smith tumbled in slippery shoes, and Mr. Yates used his eyeglass and performed on imaginary tight-ropes, and Mr. Robins responded to the call for "Hot Codlins" ; how Messrs. Ibbetson, Holmes, and Hallett convulsed the audience with their performance as acrobats, in the scene of Epsom Downs; how, in fact, the whole pantomime carried one's thoughts back to the days of Grimaldi, and showed how dead the art as an art is now, by letting us see what it is like when life and strength are put into it by such amateurs as these—and above all, we must add with much emphasis, how curiously the grace and ease of the gentleman was mixed, throughout and uniformly, with evolutions that shirked nothing of the full measure of clown's, or pantaloon's, or burlesquer's extravagance—they only can tell who saw this wonderful performance.

An entertainment, entitled *Illustrative Gatherings*, was

given last Monday at the St. Martin's Hall, by Miss P. Horton. The lady who by this name- is so widely known as a public favourite is the wife of a skilful musician and composer, Mr. T. German Reed, who assists in the entertainment. Mainly it consists, however, of those characteristic songs and personations by which Miss P. Horton won her reputation on the stage. In one of the latter she admirably represents a dialogue between two old women, being differently dressed on either side so as to put each vividly in turn before her audience. Another of her characters is a singing, laughing dandy, in ringlets and moustache, whose *méthode* as a dandy singer is hit off with exquisite skill. And throughout it is delightful to hear her fine voice, and observe her free, cordial, unaffected manner.

April 28.—Mdlle. Jenny Ney has made her *début* in *Fidelio*, and lost none of the good report she brought with her from Vienna. She has youth in her face and voice, and, without appearing to be a great actress, is surely a good one. She brought back to *Fidelio* much of the pathos that Mdlle. Cruvelli so completely took away, and showed throughout occupation with her part, and a delicate sense of its feeling.

June 9.—Once upon a time—long ago—twenty or thirty years, indeed, before the rising of the curtain, there was a Spanish Count who had two infant sons. And as it fell upon a day, there was an old gipsy, "an inauspicious and ghastly woman", found in the morning by the cradle of the second-born, who stated herself to be engaged about its horoscope, but who was considered to be looking at it with the evil-eye. The baby awoke screaming—"he arose with piercing lamentation, the effect of incantation. The hideous sorceress was then arrested, and doomed to perish in tormenting fire." I quote from the libretto of the *Trovatore.*

The poor old gipsy may have visited the Count de Luna only for his spoons ; at any rate, it was a cruel thing to burn

her, and so thought her daughter Azucena, a most sensitive
and loving woman, the young mother of an infant child.
She followed her own mother, child in arms, to the place
of execution, saw her pricked forward by the sword-points
of the soldiers, was tossed back when she would struggle
through them for a last embrace, and heard through their
jeers nothing but the old woman's wail, *Mi vendica*—" Be
my avenger."   Directly afterwards she saw her mother burnt
alive, watched her tortures, and was filled by the sight with
a mad passion that ran through her after-life.   The old
woman's wail, *Mi vendica*, never again died from her
ears, and her own voice learnt to repeat its boding note.
Of course she resolved on vengeance, and at once began it,
in true gipsy style, by stealing the child which her mother
had been burnt for looking at.   She would burn that alive
on the place of her mother's execution : but when the fire
was lighted, and she took the child to thrown it in, its
infant cry touched all the woman in her.   In a passion of
grief she put it aside, until, before long, the passion of grief
changed to another passion, as the scene of her mother's
execution rose upon her memory.   With averted eyes she
completed the horrid purpose ; but no sooner began to look
at what she was about, than she found that she had not
burnt the right baby.   She had destroyed her own ; and,
therefore, whether to satisfy her vengeance or her love I
cannot tell, adopted little Master Garzia de Luna for her
son Manrico.   Now, Manrico is Il Trovatore, or the
Troubadour.

The old de Luna died.   He had believed and not believed
in Garzia's death, when " of a young child, scattered
around, still stained with blood, the bones were found".
But he had a presentiment that the boy lived ; and dying,
he bequeathed to his eldest son the task of hunting for his
brother.   So, he being dead, his eldest son was Count de
Luna in his stead, and grew to be a fine grandee of Spain,

while Garzia became known as Manrico, the proscribed chief of a horde of gipsies in the mountains of Biscay, a man with a decided taste for music.

Now there was a certain fair lady of whom nothing is known beyond the fact that she was called Leonora, that she lived in a good house with a great deal of attached garden-ground, and that she is to be identified with Mdlle. Jenny Ney. The Count de Luna loved this lady, and was much annoyed at the attentions paid to her by Il Trovatore, a mysterious troubadour. This troubadour is Signor Tamberlik, the proscribed gipsy, and the lady has been won by his singing. The brothers, who do not know that they are brothers, thus become rivals in love. As these facts are developed very clumsily in the course of the libretto, it is advisable that the audience should have discovered them before the rising of the curtain.

In the first scene a bit of the preceding story is sung by Signor Tagliafico, as Ferrando, the Count's confidential friend, to a noisy chorus of domestics, early in the morning, near his lordship's bedroom-door. The music, which is meant to give the audience the horrors, is well executed, but fails of its purpose. The next scene is by moonlight in Leonora's garden. The Troubadour sings a love-song off the stage. The lady is lured out by it, the Count (who is the new singer, Signor Graziani) comes, cat-like, to the garden courting, and the lady, perplexed by a cloudy night, mistaking him for the Troubadour, is led to put her arm about the neck of the wrong lover. Enter the other Tom, who becomes wild at what a gleam of moonlight shows him. The lady explains her mistake and corrects it, whereat the Count in his turn becomes wild, and the two brothers, of whom nobody knows that they are brothers, rush out with drawn swords to fight a duel.

It is important for the audience now to understand that a great battle is fought behind the curtain. The duel has expanded privately into the battle of Pellilla between the troops of the Count and the gipsies under Manrico. In the course of that battle the Count's life is in Manrico's power, but a mysterious fraternal instinct stays his hand. He is, nevertheless, defeated, scored with wounds upon the bosom, and left for dead upon the battle-field. His gipsy mother, Azucena, makes search for his body, finds life in it, nurses him, and saves him from the grave. Only the gipsies know that he is living.

The second act opens among the mountains of Biscay with a rather effective gipsy chorus, which Madame Viardot, as Azucena, interrupts with a wild Moorish chant, containing some part of the story of her mother's death. Now for the first time the attention of the audience is fixed. The genius of the great actress-singer puts a spell upon the house. The very defects of Verdi's music are wrested to the purpose of the artist, and serve to give dramatic colour to the fitful spirit of the gipsy. The wailing echo of her mother's cry, *Mi vendica*, the fierce hold taken upon her imagination by the horrible spectacle of her mother's execution, which she presently relates, the maddening horror with which she reverts to her infant son, thrown by her own hands alive into the fire, give opportunity to Madame Viardot for displaying her powers in a dramatic scene of the most effective kind. It is unluckily allowed to run into an anti-climax. Enters a gipsy messenger, whose story Azucena, though she is present, is bound by the necessities of the story not to hear. Ruiz, a gipsy chief, has seized the town of Castellor. Near the town is a nunnery, in which Leonora, who believes Manrico to be dead, proposes that same evening to take the veil. She must be carried off before she does so. Manrico instantly demands a horse, and departs, after a scene of wild expostulation from Azucena —out of which Madame Viardot does her best in vain to make something. He does not tell where he is going, and her only fear is lest horse exercise may cause his recent wounds to bleed afresh. The scene then changes to the convent. The Count also has made up his mind to steal the lady. He and his men are first upon the spot. When he is about to achieve his purpose, Manrico appears suddenly as from the grave. Afterwards the gipsies rush in, and, in the midst of a good deal of noisy music, carry Leonora off, a willing prisoner.

The third act opens in the camp of the Count de Luna, who is besieging Castellor, determined to fetch Leonora out of the same fortress. No time is supposed to have elapsed, and it had better be supposed to be any distance or no distance from Biscay to Castellor. Azucena, wandering in search of her adopted son, has been caught prowling round the Count de Luna's camp, seized, bound, and dragged before him. There she learns into whose power she has fallen, is recognised as the fiend who destroyed the infant, and devoted to the stake. Her roving, melancholy, gipsy spirit, and her abject crouching fear, bursting out suddenly into a flash of wild defiance, are finely acted and most expressively sung by Madame Viardot. She is dragged off, and her adopted son Manrico is next shown to us within the walls of Castellor, upon the point of leading his bride to the altar. The martial chorus which succeeds the interruption of the wedding by the news of Azucena's capture brings the third act to a close with some effective music.

By the omission of a weak scene between the Count and Leonora, the fourth act, as presented now at COVENT GARDEN, will do more for Verdi's reputation than anything of his that the English public has yet heard. Manrico, who has been taken in an unsuccessful sally, is shut up with Azucena in a tower. Leonora, coming in search of her Troubadour, hears his voice as she stands under the window of the prison. Signor Tamberlik in his dungeon,

Mdlle. Jenny Ney upon the stage, backed by a chorus of unseen priests chanting the *Miserere* for a parting soul, give fine effect to the music of the first half of this act. The last scene is within the dungeon. Azucena—who is exhausted by her trials and her passions, and who shudders at the dreadful image of the stake—after a good duet with Manrico, falls asleep, with the desire to end her days in peace among the mountains of Biscay, and a low melody to this effect, murmured by her in her sleep, backs a passionate interview between Manrico and Leonora. The lady has given herself to the Count in return for the life of the Troubadour, who spurns her for the purchase. It was only her dead body that she meant to give, for she has taken poison, and the Count enters in time to see her die of the effect of it. He immediately orders the Troubadour out to the scaffold. Then Azucena wakes, stumbles upon the body of a woman, and asks for Manrico. The Count draws a curtain from before an extensive grating, and shows her the scene of execution, the headsman wiping his axe, and Manrico in his coffin. Suddenly, then, she is awakened from the first pang of despair by noticing that the cry of her mother has been answered. She explains to the Count that he has chopped off his lost brother's head, and falls with the cry, *Sei vendicata, o madre !*

And so the curtain falls upon *Il Trovatore.*

June 30.—The accidents of a small cast, and of the subsequent long survival of each member of it on the stage, can concur in the case of few new operas. Possibly, therefore, the performance of *Don Pasquale* at COVENT GARDEN on Thursday night, by the same artists for whom it was composed twelve years ago, is an accident far from likely to occur hereafter in the case of any other work. Of the four singers by whom *Don Pasquale* is performed, one, Signor Mario, was—for that night at any rate—more than his old self. Signor Lablache was in his most farcical mood, and in good voice. Madame Grisi proved herself, as she always does in the part of Norina, a consummate actress, and gave less reason than usual to regret the decadence of her voice. Signor Tamburini's presence on the stage is at all times agreeable, and if his voice were merely gone one might be happy ; but it is not gone merely, a something has come in the place of it which prompts unpleasant thoughts. After the fossil opera had been produced there was a fossil ballet to be seen, Cerito again in *La Vivandière*.

July 14.—On Tuesday evening, at Campden House, Kensington, the residence of Colonel Waugh, semi-private theatricals were given, with a charitable purpose, and with striking success, under the management of Mr. Charles Dickens.

At Campden House there is a miniature theatre, complete with pit and boxes, stage and footlights. For the benefit of the funds of the Bournemouth Sanatorium for Consumptive Patients, the amateurs performed in this little theatre, before a crowded audience composed principally of ladies, a new two-act play by Mr. Wilkie Collins, and a two-act farce. The play was called *The Lighthouse*, and told a tale of Eddystone in the old times. An exquisite picture (for such it is, and not a mere ordinary scene) of Eddystone as it stood in those days, from the pencil of Mr. Stanfield, was the drop-scene, and the actors were exhibited throughout as shut up in a little room within the lighthouse, also of Mr. Stanfield's painting, which, from its nature, could with the best possible effect be set up in a private drawing-room, or on a miniature stage. Similar exigencies appear also to have been consulted in the manner of developing the plot of the play; the crime, the wreck, and all the events upon which hangs the passion of the story, not being produced upon the scene, but breaking out from the narration of the actors. None of the leading incidents are shown actually, but their workings on the minds of the three lighthouse-men who are the chief performers, and of the few other persons introduced into the story, contribute interest enough to sustain an earnest attention throughout. The little piece told upon the audience admirably.

But it had rare advantages. It was, in its principal parts, acted by distinguished writers, with whose artistic skill upon the stage the public has been for some time familiar. The three lighthouse-men are at first shown cut off by a month's storms from the mainland. They are an old man and his son, together with the father of the young man's sweetheart. The old man's memory is haunted by what he believes to have been his passive consent to a most foul murder. Weakened by starvation, his brain becomes wholly possessed by dread of this crime. The spectre of the supposed murdered lady seems to stand at his bedside and bid him speak. He does speak, and, possessed with a wild horror at all he recollects, reveals to his son his shame. Upon the acting of this character depends the whole force of the story, as presented to the audience, and it is in the hands of a master. He is a rough man, whose face has been familiar for years with wind and spray, haggard and wild just now, and something light-headed, oppressed not more by conscience than by hunger. He tells his tale, and his son turns from him, shrinks from his touch, struck down by horror of the crime and the humiliation to himself involved in it. Relief comes to the party soon after this ; they are fed, and the physical depression is removed. Eager then to regain his son's esteem, and cancel the disclosure of his secret, the old lighthouse-man changes in manner. By innumerable master-touches on the part of the actor, we are shown what his rugged ways have been of hiding up the knowledge that stirs actively within his conscience ; but his effort to be bold produces only nervous bluster, and his frantic desire to recover his son's respect, though he may take him by the throat to extort it from him, is still mixed up with a horrible sense of blood-guiltiness, wonderfully expressed by little instinctive actions. I will not follow the story to its last impressive moment of rough, nervous, seaman's prayer, in which the old man stands erect, with his hands joined over his head, overpowered by the sudden removal of the load that has so long weighed upon his heart.   But to the last that piece of the truest acting was watched with minute attention by the company assembled; and rarely has acting on a public stage better rewarded scrutiny.

July 21.—The success of Meyerbeer's *L'Etoile du Nord*, properly produced for the first time in this country on Thursday night under the personal direction of the composer, who appeared before the curtain to receive the plaudits of the English public, has been of course great.

The story of the opera, such as it is, can be told very briefly.   Giorgio Savoronsky and his sister Catterina (Mdlle. Bosio) are orphans. Their mother was a gipsy of the Ukraine, who said on her deathbed that her daughter's star shone with a bright radiance over the North, and that some one coming thence would blend with hers his mighty fortune.   The brother and sister came to settle at a village in the neighbourhood of the docks at Wyborg, on the Gulf of Finland, where George played the flute and Catterina sold wine to the workmen. There the Czar Peter, disguised as a workman, fell in love with Catterina.   He played the flute with her brother for the sake of being near her, received from her useful advice against his habits of anger and hard drinking, and was finally accepted as her suitor when she found that he had been born at Moscow, on condition that he would become a soldier, earn some glory, and so make good the prediction of her mother.   He agreed to that.   At about the same time a party of Calmucks, headed by a comic Calmuck Tartar (Signor Lablache), entered the village.   There was a conscription of young men, and Catterina's brother, in the very hour appointed for his marriage with Prascovia, was to be taken as a recruit if he could not promptly find a substitute.

Catterina, because she pitied the bride, and was strong-minded, and it had been given in charge to her to watch over her brother, assured to Prascovia a substitute for fifteen days; and, while the Finland wedding ceremonies were proceeding, set off in male attire, after a benediction of her brother, from the jetty.   The dying of her voice in the distance, as the boat was supposed to row towards the ship, were the last sweet notes of the voice of Mdlle. Bosio to which the drop-scene fell upon the first act of the opera.

In the second act we are introduced to the camp of Peter the Great, adjoining the hostile Swedish army.   There is a revolt among the troops, which Peter, coming suddenly in disguise, desires to quell.   A tent is pitched for him, and Catterina placed as one of the three sentinels outside.   She peeps, and recognises first his favourite, Danilowitz, formerly a pastrycook at Wyborg, and then himself, supposing him to be her Peter, rapidly become a captain.   Peter gets drunk, and scandalises Catterina by the liberties he takes with two vivandières.   While irritated at what she is seeing, the comic Calmuck, now a corporal of Grenadiers, comes to relieve the guard.   She will not be removed, and when he presses her departure, boxes his ears.   Hubbub arises, and a complaint is brought before the drunken Czar, who orders the recruit to be immediately shot.   Catterina makes an effort to recall Peter to his senses, and is dragged away.   Her voice has, however, penetrated through his drunkenness; he sobers himself by an effort, and demands that the prisoner shall be brought back into his presence.   While they are bringing her she adroitly escapes, swims across a river, and is wounded in the water by a musket-ball.   The revolt then occupies the scene.   Peter quells it by his personal influence ; and the Russian army prepares in a magnificent *finale*, magnificent both as a piece of music and as a spectacle, for instant engagement with the Swedes.

In the third and last act the Czar is unhappy in his palace.

Catterina has been found, maddened by her wound and by grief. She is brought to the palace, where a vision of her Finland village is constructed mechanically from the design of Peter; her fellow-villagers, who have been brought to Moscow, repeat the songs of Finland; and George and Prascovia, who have come on foot from Finland to Moscow in fifteen days, to relieve the substitute, are made to enact over again the wedding scene, that Catterina may be thus recalled to her old self. Finally her lover Peter plays his old tune on the flute. Her voice instinctively keeps time to it, and the result of the device is a sudden cure. She is at once dressed in Imperial robes, the Finland village scenery gives place to the magnificence of the Imperial court, and Catterina's star, that shone so brightly over the North, is proved to have been no false prophet.

The part taken by Signor Lablache, though in the libretto utterly silly, is in the opera of great importance. Some of the finest music is connected with it, and not only did Signor Lablache do perfect justice to this, but he contrived also to lift the character a little out of the depth of absurdity in which it was conceived. But the great vocal triumph of the evening was that of Mdlle. Bosio, who sustained a long and arduous part in a way that left no doubt on any mind as to the position she means to take on the Italian lyric stage. When, as Catterina, she emphatically taught her friend Peter that to will is to do—*voler e poter*—it was impossible not to reflect that she herself had proved the doctrine. She has willed perfection as a vocalist, and has astonished the public by the rapidity of her advance towards it. She is now also willing to herself a fair share of skill as an actress—a thing of which she was at one time wholly destitute—and is equally on the way towards that. *Voler e poter.*

The ovation to M. Meyerbeer has not been the only stirring incident during the past week within the walls of a

playhouse.   On Monday evening Mr. Farren took leave of.
the public at the HAYMARKET THEATRE, the scene of all his
later triumphs, supported by his friends and many veterans
of the profession, after having acted once more, and for the
last time, a short scene from *The Clandestine Marriage.*
Every living actor seems to have been anxious to do
something on the occasion, and by performing fragments
room was made for the loving help of a great many ; even a
corner was made for Mr. Albert Smith, who sang one of his
songs.   The unrestrained cordiality with which Farewell was
said by the public to one of the most finished actors by whom
the stage has been adorned during the present century, could
not fail to excite emotion even in bystanders, and how much
more in the person of the artist towards whom all that warm
feeling was expressed.   Mr. Farren was unable to speak his
own good-bye.   All had to be felt, and there was nothing
to be said.

   August 4.—Mdlle. Rachel, on her way to America, gives
sudden life to playgoers in London by appearing at this
theatre in four of her greatest characters.   At one time
The Examiner stood almost alone in the endeavour to
describe in detail these remarkable performances.   Over
and over again have we expressed our wonder and admiration of the sublimity and beauty infused into the old French
drama by the genius of this great actress.*   Before she
taught us how they might be filled with every passion,
how a life of woe might find expression in a sentence, we
were apt to weary over the cold heroics of those famous
French tragedies.   But presented by her, they amaze us
with grand conceptions.   Awe, pity, terror, are awakened as
we look and listen, and nothing remains for our self-respect
as critics but to attribute half the poetry and passion, as

---

   * The criticisms of Rachel in *The Examiner* were from a
better hand than mine.

well as all the expression they receive, to the actress herself.

October 13.—The great Egyptian spectacle, *Nitocris,* turns out to be a spectacle and nothing more, the literary part of the work having been found incompatible with the magnificence and show tacked on to it. The result is one upon which the manager did not exactly calculate, though it might have been easily enough foreseen. The success of spectacle in these days is no doubt an obvious fact, but successful spectacles, it is not less certain, have generally been associated with some matter that the public thought worth hearing. To connect spectacle with one of Shakespeare's plays ensures a certain degree of success. Even to connect it with a telling melodrama, which, though it appeals to a low taste, still appeals to a taste quite apart from the mere dazzling of the eye, will always prevent any downright failure. But though, when allied to Mr. Planché's wit, few things have been more successful than the LYCEUM spectacles, others at the same theatre have had a different fate ; and the best scenery, as Mr. Charles Mathews might have warned the DRURY LANE manager, will not draw houses in connection with a play which contains nothing to interest the public. In spite, then, of a great outlay, of a striking stage-effect, representing the rush of the Nile into a grotto and the drowning of conspirators, in spite of all the gods of Egypt carried in procession through the length of a whole act, the gods of DRURY LANE inexorably hissed, and *Nitocris* has fallen to the level of an afterpiece. It would be a kindness to Miss Glyn, fitted with a part so much below her powers, to convert the spectacle into pantomime, by getting rid entirely of the spoken words.

December 29.—Of one of the pantomimes of this year, by a system of puffery little short of the marvellous, the highest expectation had been raised. The greater the expectation,

the greater the disappointment. It is but too likely that
the public will soon have to settle down to the conviction
that the COVENT GARDEN pantomime, " *The* pantomime of
1855-6", as it is modestly called, is the dullest that has anywhere been seen in London for a good many seasons past.
On the first night the audience was highly discontented,
but the fault was laid upon the fact that it *was* a first night,
and things were to go better afterwards. It was my lot to
suffer the infliction of it on the second night, and the sole
relief to its weariness was the sense of indignation begotten
among respectable visitors at the monstrous system of
puffery by which they had been brought together. There
is a contempt of the public intellect implied in the coarse-
ness of the stimulants to curiosity thus employed, and in
the midst of it all a personal obtrusion that appears
singularly distasteful. When the public applauds the one
scene of this pantomime by Mr. Beverley, which is supposed to be a justification for the announcement that the
scenery is " by Mr. Beverley and numerous assistants", the
" Wizard" comes forward upon the stage to take the
plaudits. Upon the harlequinade a scene is foisted, of
which the " Wizard" is the hero, in which a colossal plaster
bust of "the Professor" is brought forward, and out of
which a miniature " Professor" steps. When all is done, the
same wizard or professor comes forward arm-in-arm with the
clown to share even his honours, and in so doing flirts like
a prima donna over the acceptance of a solitary nosegay.

All this might be tolerated if in other respects faith were
kept, and the public had no reason to consider itself fooled.
But it has only too much reason for discontent. Let us
take one illustration of the whole. A vast posting-bill upon
the hoardings, addressed " to tall young women", had been
prepared to stimulate public attention, by requiring " two
hundred young women, none under the height of six feet
two, for the pantomime at Covent Garden". This results

in the appearance in the burlesque introduction of four masks as chambermaids, with high clogs and caps, who are styled Normandy peasants " six feet two in their clogs", and who perform some exceedingly stupid business with warming-pans. The " dioramas" are two small and bad transparencies. The great tournament after Holbein is a lump or two of armour upon hobbyhorses. There are, in fact, only two or three good scenes.

To the pantomime itself it can hardly be a reproach that the tricks often worked badly, for they were so pointless that they were not worth working well. They were poor in design, and destitute of any power to awaken mirth. The best clown and the best pantaloon in London, Mr. Flexmore and Mr. Barnes, with a graceful columbine, Miss Emma Horne, laboured, indeed, not always in vain to extract mirth and pleasure out of the most unpromising materials ; but, work as they might, the general desire among the audience seemed to be to get at the last scene, and be put of their pain as soon as possible. The last display was pretty, but not in any degree remarkable for splendour. The best transformation (and that really a very striking one) was the fall of the scene representing the wizard's laboratory on the heads of the actors, as if by a mishap, resulting in a complete change of the stage, and the spreading out of a cornfield before the palace of Balmoral.

Let me not pass from the COVENT GARDEN pantomime without commenting also upon the bad taste of the curtain provided for it, which is not in the least intended for the pleasure of the public eye, but is a mass of advertisements collected from Moses and Son and other well-known advertisers. This, in a place meant for refreshment and amusement, pains the eye with a reproduction of the nuisance of a hoarding, or of a ticket-bedaubed second-class carriage on the railway.

January 19, 1856.—War has broken out between the

powers that rule over DRURY LANE and COVENT GARDEN. A pleasant quiz upon the conjurings and claptraps of the "Wizard of the North", in a piece called *The Great Gun Trick*, written for Mr. Charles Mathews, also late of the LYCEUM and Wizard of the South-South-West-by-East, has for the last week or two preceded the pantomime at DRURY LANE; and as the caricature upon the conjuring threatens to prove a little more amusing than the conjuring itself, the COVENT GARDEN Wizard is in arms. Hitherto he has carried on the war by means of posters, or cartels, but a direct attack is now threatened in the shape of a farce courteously entitled *Twenty Minutes with an Impudent Puppy*. Meanwhile the smallest theatre in London, the STRAND, laughs at the two largest, in a farce called *A Plague on Both your Houses*.

The pantomime at DRURY LANE has maintained its attractions, and indeed all the theatres are prospering with their Christmas entertainments. At COVENT GARDEN the Wizard is doing his best to cast his former conjuring into the shade by drawing audiences to *Rob Roy* as acted without a morsel of curtailment, with himself for a vociferous hero. He explodes his asides defiantly into the faces of the people who are not to hear them, and "looks", says the critic of the *Times*, "as if he could thrash the other *dramatis personæ* all round without any fatigue to his muscles".

February 16.—The pantomimes at all the theatres have had a surprising success, still maintain their ground, and are to this day to be seen in full force and enjoyment. At DRURY LANE, Mr. Charles Mathews still makes merry as the Wizard of the South-South-West-by-East; and at COVENT GARDEN, the Wizard of the North has given up the attempt to retaliate with a small squib that would not go off satisfactorily. The public threw so much cold water on it, that after a little hissing it went out; and the great Professor resumed the career of actor upon which he had entered. Having enacted Rob Roy, he appears now as Black-eyed Susan—no, as William in that drama—and other novelties are in preparation. There are still three characters in which I trust that the Professor will not forget to appear— Juliet, King Lear, and Timour the Tartar. [Mr. Anderson's management ended w'th the burning down of the theatre at the close of a *bal masqué* on the morning of Wednesday the 6th of March.]

April 19.—The burnt-out singers have made a home of the LYCEUM, which theatre, having been throughout cleaned and retouched, reminds one again of the days when Madame Vestris made its elegance so notable. The delayed season opened on Tuesday last, before Queen, Court, and a brilliant little audience, with Verdi's *Trovatore*. As the opera is noisy, it at once put to the severest test the question of a change of house, as it affected the performances. The result was a strong impression of the skill with which actors and orchestra were able to accommodate themselves to altered circumstances ; but the opera itself, apart entirely from all question of performance, did not come altogether well out of the ordeal. Without the most extensive adventitious help, and, above all, without the acting of Viardot to add to its musical attraction, Verdi's best opera cannot be said to be relished keenly by the public.

May 17.—A new drama called *Retribution*, put together, it is understood, by so many hands that there is somebody in town who calls it *Contribution*, has been offered this week to the public, and—to a certain extent only—thankfully received. The plot is stupid enough, but the writing is throughout clever, and the acting of Mr. Wigan as one of those demoniacal avengers, cold without and hot within, familiar to the readers of French novels—a splinter of iced fire, impossible to find though startling to conceive—the acting of Mr. Wigan in this character of Count Priuli is so good, that the piece will probably have a successful run by reason of it. In the drama there appears also a *débutante*, Miss Herbert, who achieves no mean success.

May 31.—Mdlle. Piccolomini proves to be an artist young and spiritual, after the manner of Madame Viardot or Signor Ronconi. As an actress on the lyric stage she may live to display rare perfection ; and her voice is at least sufficient for her purpose. It is good inasmuch as it is sub-servient to her genius, and sufficient to maintain her due position in an opera, but, as in the case of the two artists just named, it is rather from a peculiarity of genius than of throat that the supremacy arises. We have now, in Signor Ronconi, Madame Viardot, and Mdlle. Piccolomini, three fine dramatic artists upon the Italian lyric stage. Madame Grisi I assume to have retired, and moreover should reckon as an artist rather bold than fine ; her acting was marked in each part by certain broad effects, obvious to every capacity and admirable in the eyes of all ; but much more rarely by that refined subtlety of conception, which gives meaning to every glance, every posture, every tone, every stirring of a finger. Mdlle. Piccolomini is an actress of the latter class ; and her reception at HER MAJESTY'S THEATRE, which has been most enthusiastic, she happens to have earned as an actress almost solely.

For of *La Traviata*, the opera with which she has con-nected her success, I must say candidly that it is the worst opera by Verdi that has found its way to England, while his very best is, on its own score, barely tolerable to the ears of any well-trained London audience. Generally, too, in each of Verdi's operas there is some one thing that, if not good, may pass for good among the many ; there is the *Donna e Mobile* in *Rigoletto*, the *Balen del suo sorriso* in the *Trovatore*, or the *Ernani involami* in *Ernani*. In the *Traviata* there is absolutely nothing. Grant a decent prettiness to the brindisi, *Libiamo*, and the utmost has been said for an opera very far inferior in value to the worst of Mr. Balfe's. Where the voice of the singer is forced into discords of the composer's making, and the ear is tortured throughout by sounds which the wise man will struggle not to hear, it is obviously impossible to judge fairly of the vocal powers of the prima donna.

In spite of bad music, and in spite of a detestable libretto which suggests positions for her scarcely calculated to awaken honest sympathy, in spite of the necessity of labouring with actors who, as actors, can make—and no wonder— nothing at all genuine out of their parts, Mdlle. Piccolomini creates and obtains the strongest interest for a Traviata of her own. Out of impurity she produces something exquisitely pure, and out of absurdity a pathos irresistible. We see her labouring through her most touching scenes, absorbing all attention as an actress, and drawing tears, while she is being acted up to by a gentleman who sings well and can act tolerably when he sees his way, but, as the heavy father of the piece, falls throughout into the richest burlesque manner of Mr. Paul Bedford, except once when he runs off the stage after the manner of Mr. Wright in *Paul Pry*. It does not matter. Mdlle. Piccolomini is the beginning, middle, and end of the opera, and it is her Traviata that the public goes to see. Her Traviata conquers the libretto to itself; and to a wonderful degree succeeds also in conquering the music, and in impressing its own stamp on very much of it.

Of the libretto I need say little. It consists of three acts. In the first act the Traviata, the lost one, the girl gone astray, otherwise the Parisian *lorette*, is shown holding an after midnight revel, and attracted by the offer of a something like true love from one of her adorers. In the second act she has carried this adorer to a country house, and lavishes her wealth upon him there as a kept man; but she gives him up at the request of a virtuous father for a virtu-

ous daughter's sake, and even leads him to suppose her tired
of him, as the sole way of ending the connection.   The
consequence of this proceeding is, that at the end of the
second act she is insulted by him at a ball given by another
lorette, and in the third act she dies elaborately of the insult,
and of a consumptive disease—the consequence of young
imprudences—which had been growing upon her from the
first.   Of course she does not die without a sentimental
parting from her friend.   This is the form of the libretto
founded upon the immoral drama *La Dame aux Camélias*.
Far different is the heroine for whom Mdlle. Piccolomini
engages all our sympathies.   Her Traviata is a girl fallen
into the nets of pleasure, and, with the hand of death upon
her, listening to the promptings of a pure and deep love;
lifted up by it out of all sin, developing all that is noblest in
woman, and repulsed by the rude hand of an unforgiving
world; but, though repulsed and tortured, and overcome by
mental anguish and her bodily disease, still dying at last
true to the high nature which had been once developed in
her.   She has a rare power of emotional utterances in song;
and in her power of expressing much by a few words and
their attendant gesture—as by the cry and the eager hurry
of her soul to meet the lover who returns to her too late,
the hurry of a soul that cannot drag the dying body after it
—she now and then reminds us of the special powers of
Rachel.

That Mdlle. Piccolomini is versatile, the range of emotion
taken by her Traviata, from a reckless joyousness to the
most sacred sorrow, fully testifies.   It is manifest also in her
mere aspect, which is in a remarkable degree indicative of a
quick nervous power.

June 7.—At HER MAJESTY'S THEATRE Madame Alboni
is singing the part of the gipsy Azucena.   Simply to hear
Madame Alboni's voice is a pleasure, for it has to an unusual degree a rich musical flow and a complete reliableness.

She has, what Madame Viardot has not, that rare gift of a natural quality of tone which skill alone can never reach; and there can be no doubt that the music of Azucena, which by chance is not a part to tear a cat in, never was so well sung in London as it is being now sung at HER MAJESTY'S THEATRE. Madame Alboni's acting also is much better than might have been expected from her, though in this respect she has in no degree approached the excellence of Madame Viardot.

In the midst of the din of Verdi—*Traviata* and *Trovatore* at the one house, *Rigoletto* at the other—the promise of a performance of Mozart's *chef-d'œuvre* broke upon the ear like the ripple of a spring in the desert. *Don Giovanni* was at one time announced for Thursday last, but we are not to have it yet. The opera which broke on Thursday last the reign of Verdi was the very familiar and weak result achieved by the Donizetti who would be a Meyerbeer, *La Favorita*. Why is it that English opera-goers are so much plagued by constant repetition of the worst and weakest music, when some of the best works of the best composers are within the *répertoire* of either house? No doubt *La Traviata* must draw crowds, because of the acting of Mdlle. Piccolomini; and *Rigoletto* must do the same, because of the acting of Signor Ronconi; and Signor Mario and Madame Grisi act and sing the last act of *La Favorita* in a way that makes it worth while to endure the others for the sake of it; but surely none of these artists are bound to persist in the connection of their talents rather with the poor operas than with the good ones.

June 14.—A charity has been benefited, and a large audience gratified, with a repetition of the display of talent by the clowns and harlequins of private life, who would have died and made no sign had not that great thought of the age, an Amateur Pantomime, come to maturity in our time.

The new harlequin proved himself even a more surprising jumper and dancer than his predecessor; and it is now therefore demonstrated that we are liable to meet in private life two gentlemen under whose broadcloth is a skin tattooed with spangles, and who may leap in at our windows nobody shall say why, when, or which end foremost. The clown and pantaloon were on Monday, as last year, Mr. Joseph Robins and Mr. Arthur Smith, both excellent. We had again also the surprising acrobats, and two gentlemen who very literally stooped to the presentment of a pair of dancing dogs.

June 21.—Mdlle. Johanna Wagner's voice is marvellously good, her figure is tall and shapely, her movements are graceful, her gestures and attitudes are in the highest degree picturesque, her acting is most carefully studied.

She has in the *Capuletti ed i Montecchi* a good acting-part, the libretto is not bad, and the notion of representing Romeo as a bit of a fire-eater as well as a lover was unquestionably good for lyric purposes. The music is, however, curiously poor. Bellini's mature works have a distinct place of their own in art, and have undoubtedly a soul of music in them; but this, his first crude effort, scarcely contained the promise of his future. It is less worth hearing than even *La Traviata*, and its dulness is exaggerated by division into four short acts, which implies the loss of some three-quarters of an hour's time in addition to that sacrificed over the music. Mdlle. Wagner's manner of acting rather aggravates than relieves the sense of tedium. It is clever, but very laboured; it is all the result of manifest and most praiseworthy care and pains. We see and admire the passage from one gesture to another; but we never for one instant forget that an actress is declaiming skilfully, or lose Mdlle. Johanna Wagner in her Romeo. She clothes herself too carefully, in fact, with her artist nature; it seems to be on her, and not in her, always.

July 5.—Mdlle. Piccolomini's *Figlia del Reggimento* exhilarates the audience. Last Thursday night I believe there was not one person in the crowded pit and stalls who did not rise to cheer the actress-singer. No doubt a great many who so applauded thought it was exquisite comic acting by which they had been stirred to much enthusiasm ; but the charm of the performance was something nobler and better. Mdlle. Piccolomini's Maria is not a comic character at all, and is not a pathetic character. It is essentially the character of a girl inspired by two of the best sentiments belonging to humanity, enjoyment of liberty and of love. She is the petted daughter of the regiment, no doubt, and the actress gives with exquisite piquancy all the little military ways of the *vivandière ;* but these lie only on the surface of the character, as she appears to have conceived it. Nursed under the roll of drum and sound of trumpet, these sounds have stirred her to high aspiration ; she has acquired not merely the free ways of the camp, but the whole spirit of freedom. Her gestures all point upward ; and throughout nearly the whole first act she makes herself felt in so high a sense as an impersonation of the Genius of Liberty, the chords she touches while she makes us merry music are so absolutely grave, that the conventional comic by-play of the soldiers (all very good and right) seems almost impertinent. The other sentiment is love ; and I do not know whether the most exquisite part of her whole performance as an actress be the sudden radiance that shines out of her when first the lover comes upon the scene, or the noble burst of patriotism in those lines which are the key to her peculiar reading of the entire character :

> " Evviva l' Italia !
> E i prodi guerrier ;
> Son dessi mia gioia,
> Mio solo pensier.

> Ad essi soltanto
> Aspira il mio cor ;
> Con essi ritrovo
> *La gloria, l'amor."*

The two passions of the new *Figlia del Reggimento*, then, are glory in the highest earthly sense, and love. All the other features in the representation are no more than the pleasant little accidents of sex and situation under which they lie. The episodical scene of practice in fine singing, which opens the second act, detaches itself from the rest of the performance as the one bit of·pure and simple comedy in the whole opera, and that is delicate and merry. Everything else is exhilarating. There is no stirring of laughter, no stirring of tears, but a stirring of the spirit as by roll of drum and trumpet-call.

As a singer of this part, Mdlle. Piccolomini is very far inferior to Madame Jenny Lind or Madame Sontag. The actual musical resources of her voice are small ; but her voice is yet good enough to sustain· her well in her position as a lyric actress, and for its shortcomings her quick instinct makes ample amends. Few singers have excelled her in the rare power of quickening with thought the sounds she utters ; and, as I have before observed, she seems to be one of those people who know what they cannot do, and take care never to attempt anything, however small, which lies beyond their compass.

The *Rosmunda* of Alfieri is a play worth seeing upon the stage for its own sake, and that on more accounts than one. In the first place, it is, I believe, the first of Alfieri's plays which has been represented in this country, and, although not one of the best works of that true poet, is a fair average example of his dramas. He was in his maturity when it was written, and it is designed according to the plan which he pretty uniformly followed. It exhibits that regard for the classical unities which was his invariable rule, yet at the

same time it differs essentially—and much for the better—
from that modification of the classic drama which was
found most germane to the genius of France. There is
more tragic passion and less explanation of passion. There
are no confidential friends and waiting-maids through whom
the public receives from the hero or the heroine miscel-
laneous information in a prosy and didactic form. More
of a magnificent gloom, more tragic passion, more of the
vague suggestion of great thoughts, more energy of conception, more intensity of expression, appeal to us in Alfieri,
than in Racine or Corneille. It is enough for an Italian
actress—to speak now only of actresses—to express worthily
the language of Alfieri ; but the French actress, to be tragical,
has mainly to express herself through the language of
Racine.

Without stopping to tell the plot, let us take the idea of
Rosmunda. It is a story of the savage days, when wild
Huns were abroad, and when kings' daughters, their fathers
being slain, became part of the spoil of the conqueror, and
might be called upon to drink out of their fathers' skulls.
Such a captive had Rosmunda been to Alboin, a savage to
whom she was wife and victim, who drove her spirit out into
a wild sea of hate, and made a wreck of it. A thirst for
vengeance, wild and unruly as the times in which it was
excited, becomes her torment. She has raised up an assassin
for Alboin. She has made a husband of the man who was a
traitor to his king, and, as a partner in crime, regarding him
as the only person with whom she can have a common tie of
love, she loves him—but the love, as Madame Ristori interprets it, has little root. Yet, when the man who had been
false to his king proves false to his wife also, the fury in
her, craving to work mischief, breaks out against him
into a wild and cruel jealousy. Him alone, until then, the
storms within her did not cover ; but against him, then, she
cries:

" Tu sola
Riedi, o vendetta, riedi ; e me riempi
Tutta di tutto 'l nume tuo ; s' io sempre
Per prima e sola deità mai t' ebbi."

She is driven upon action.   Words will not satisfy the tempest in her heart.   She does not know whither the passions broken loose will drive her.   Romilda, Alboin's daughter and her step-daughter, is her victim.   She hates her because she is of the blood of Alboin, and she will marry her to the fierce Alaric, who has already killed two wives, that Alboin's daughter may experience such wedlock as fell to the share of Alboin's captive wife.   She suspects at first, and finally discovers, that the partner of her throne and guilt, Almachilde, pursues Romilda with a guilty passion ; but with a brave soldier, Ildovaldo, young Romilda has exchanged honest affection, and when the Queen finds this she is content that they shall marry—although not even then content that Alboin's daughter shall be happy.   She consents to the marriage simply because her career of vengeance has been suddenly diverted towards Almachilde, and Ildovaldo is to rise against him to destroy him.   But he thinks of his love, when she would have him think only of her vengeance: and the fury turns again.   Romilda might have been his ; she could not tell—she knew not whither all was tending, except that there was before her blood, and only blood.

" Al ciel quai voti
Porgo ? . . Nol so. . . So che finor son tutti
Di sangue i voti miei ; nè sangue io veggo
Che ad appagarmi basti. . ."

While Almachilde and Ildovaldo should be battling, she grasps Romilda, and the issue of this struggle decides her fate.   Ildovaldo is content with having simply sent his soldiers against Almachilde, and is only eager to satisfy his love, having failed to satisfy Rosmunda's hate.   Almachilde afterwards enters victorious, whereupon Romilda dies by her stepmother s hand, and Ildovaldo kills himself. The wretched man and wife remain, and the curtain falls upon them. Two victims more, foes to the death, are left still treading their path of guilt, and the last word of each is a tremendous vow of vengeance on the other. Thus the play ends, after the dying cry of Ildovaldo to the king :

> " O tu, che resti . . .
>
> Fanne vendetta . . .
>
> *Almachilde.*   Io vendicarla giuro.
>
> *Rosmunda.*   Ho il ferro ancor ; trema : or principia appena
>
> La vendetta, che compiere in te giuro."

The conception of this close is, I think, one of the grandest features of the tragedy.

Now the play of which this is the main thought is, as to its action, carried out entirely by the four characters immediately concerned, and certainly three of the four demand high qualifications in the actor. Ildovaldo is not much more than a chivalrous young lover, but the king, Almachilde, and Alboin's daughter are characters developed with as much elaboration, and on which there has been lavished as much noble writing, as we find in that of Rosmunda. Almachilde is depicted as a man stout in bodily courage, but of a mean soul, yet there is good mixed with the baseness of his suit to Romilda ; and out of his very fear for Rosmunda comes the violence of his defiance of her, when he does come to defy. Romilda, too, is not a mere victim, but has the soul of a king's daughter, gentle and maidenly as she is. She dares to maintain her dignity in presence of her stepmother, and she royally maintains the bearing which is fit towards the assassin of her father. The tragedy demands imperatively four good actors, and it suffers much at the LYCEUM—and no doubt also in Italy as well—from being sustained only by one. Mdlle. Picchiottino is indeed a pleasant inoffensive actress, but the representatives of the two male characters have not even the good-sense to be quiet; they *will* act, and by their misspent energies they mar the effect of the play. The spectator must—in justice to Alfieri—remember that when he sees *Rosmunda* at the LYCEUM he sees only a fourth part of a four-character play; but for that fourth part's sake he may fairly be counselled to endure the rest.

Madame Ristori is a genuine actress. Her declamation is good, and in the early acts there is an effect of grandeur in the calm of her Rosmunda, disturbed only by flashes of that fire within which in the last act becomes irrepressible. Her way of coiling round the person of Romilda when the dagger has been drawn, terrible and graceful as a serpent that prepares to strike, is perfectly conceived. As an exception to this, we may say in England, that the usual Italian way of acting, not with the hands only, but even with the fingers, fails of effect; and even seems—not that it therefore is—ungraceful to a London audience. Like Madame Rachel, Madame Ristori creates out of certain lines, by unexpected gestures and tones, striking effects, but they are not so intense in expression, so subtle in conception, as the corresponding efforts of Madame Rachel.

July 19.— I have seen more of Mdlle. Wagner. But her Lucrezia more than confirms the impression made by her Romeo. The acting, although showy and much studied, wants the instinct of genius to make it good. For example, at the end of the prologue (or first act), the Lucrezia of this artist does not in a wild passion of rage and terror seek to fly from the insulting crowd of enemies who are abasing her before her son. The enemies depart and she remains, scornful, defiant. As the stage becomes cleared the curtain falls on Mdlle. Johanna Wagner striking an attitude. The second act ends with an attitude still less artistic in conception, though effective if taken apart from any sense. The close of the last act is marred by another attitude, which strangely interrupts the course of feeling just before Lucrezia's last interview with her dying son. The result of this kind of performance is that it leaves the audience half-satisfied and cold.

Madame Ristori's performance of Goldoni's *La Locandiera* supplies proof, if it were still needed, of the reality of her genius for tragedy. It is inevitable that whoever has the qualities essential to the genuine presentment of a tragic part should be able to present also true comedy ; the greater contains the less. Mere keenness of every-day observation may make a comedian, but the quick perception, the rare power of depicting all emotion, which belongs to the best tragic acting, must belong to comedy as well, and the tragedian is also in the best sense a comedian if his art be not merely a trick.

July 26.—Mdlle. Wagner takes leave of the London public as Tancredi. She does not act the part, and, considered as impersonation of a character, the errors are so manifest that probably no impersonation was intended. But the part is brilliantly dressed, after the child's *beau idéal* of a knight, the posturing is graceful and not once extravagant ; and the singing is her best.

August 9.—Mdlle. Piccolomini's Norina is very charming, but unsatisfactory. There is no deeper thought to be reached by genius of any sort than lies on the surface of *Don Pasquale ;* it is a farce opera with impossible incidents, and is best acted with farcical exaggeration. Signor Lablache, after all, is right in his way of performing it ; and Madame Grisi, the best of Norinas, is right also in the exaggerations she adopts, as in the interminable rising and bowing in the modesty scene before marriage. At HER MAJESTY'S THEATRE the Pasquale is Signor Rossi, who had shown before, as Don Magnifico in *Cenerentola,* that he can sing well and act with great humour and unction. His Pasquale is admirable, and its sole defect is very creditable to him. He acts it too well, as if the part were one of comedy and not of farce. That is the fault also inseparable from Mdlle. Piccolomini's Norina. She treats the whole plot as the romp of a quick-witted and light-hearted girl—a person perfectly answering to that description of herself which is the first thing Norina sings. The instant catching at the suggestion of a frolic, the impatience at being told details she has jumped at, her glee at the mischief, and her impatience to begin, are, in the Norina of this artist, as delightful a bit of comedy as anyone could hope to see. The trick once in hand, is carried through from first to last in a light spirit of happy fun ; but there is nothing in the plot to grasp. *Don Pasquale* being no more than a broad farce set to pleasant music, there is no true character to be eliminated out of it, no sentiment expressed through it ; and therefore the opera displays very much less perfectly than either of the others in which she has sung to us, Mdlle. Piccolomini's peculiar genius.

That in the two houses it should only have been possible for Londoners to hear Mozart twice, Rossini at most a dozen times—that they have been permitted to hear nothing whatever but the works of Bellini, Donizetti, and Verdi, and that the powers of Madame Ristori as an actress, such as they are, should have been expended chiefly upon worthless plays, *Medea*, *Camma*, and the like—all this is a marvel.

I am very glad to see that strong objection is now being urged against *La Traviata*, if we are to hope that it is the beginning of a stand against immoral opera libretti. It is not only upon *La Traviata* that we must found our complaint. Immorality in opera libretti is rather the rule than the exception. Rossini's *Comte Ory* is charming music, but the libretto is not only more licentious in its plot than *La Traviata*, but it is, moreover, in one or two parts, grossly profane. Let me not be misunderstood. I have no sym-

pathy with artificial decencies such as those which have
substituted for the words of Beethoven's sublime *Mount of
Olives* the words of *Engedi ;* but it would be easy to name
half-a-dozen of our best operas of which the interest and
value on the stage could be increased largely if a really able
man were asked to alter the libretto. There are not a few
which would gain, rather than suffer, if they were now linked
to something like true poetry in word and story. In the
essence of things it must be easier for a poet to set words to
music than for a musician to set music to words ; and there
is no reason why we should not have a revolution among
opera libretti. As literature, are there ten good enough to
save the entire class from condemnation ?

September 27.—Mr. Murdoch is a new actor at the
HAYMARKET who has come to us from the United States.
He begins his career in London as Young Mirabel, in a
discreetly-compressed version of Farquhar's comedy, *The
Inconstant ;* a comedy that for its wit's sake it is a joy to hear.
The London stage is at this time plagued with much bad
writing. There is Kotzebue's *Pizarro* at the Princess's; a
melodrama at the Lyceum with an ill-written burlesque ; an
ill-written burlesque at Drury Lane ; one of the most insane
dramas as to writing (though worth seeing for an actor's
sake) ever produced yet at the Adelphi : in the midst of all
this it is a great refreshment to hear one of Farquhar's comedies condensed into three acts of rapid incident and brilliant
dialogue. *The Inconstant* has by the adapter to the modern
stage been made quite fit not only for ears polite, but for pure
minds as well. It is free not only from immorality of speech,
but also from immorality of spirit. The Old and Young
Mirabel are both enacted by Americans. Mr. Chippendale
came over a year or two ago, and has seldom appeared to
more advantage than he now does as Old Mirabel. The
Young Mirabel is the new actor, Mr. Murdoch. Vigorous
without excess, lively and manly, his acting abounds in

shrewd and well-considered by-play. When he talks Bisarre down with Latin, it is with a genial rudeness that quite justifies the admiration of him joined to her vexation ; and it is without any exaggerated sentiment, but in a right honest way, that he expresses those twinges of emotion and repentance, at first short-lived and at last fixed, that show the sound heart in the midst of all his levity.

There are yet two more American actors to be named, Mr. and Mrs. Barney Williams, who have achieved a success that seems to have established them for a long time to come as favourites at the ADELPHI. Their sphere is farce. Mr. Barney Williams shines most as an American notion of an Irishman, and Mrs. Barney Williams delights London with the humours of the Yankee Girl. They have brought with them a wretchedly bad piece, called *The Middleman*, which has been performed with applause in America for several hundred nights, and which is having a run in London, solely because the new-comers act in it very cleverly, and dance in it, to the unbounded delight of every night's audience, an Irish jig. In farces suited to their humour these artists excel, and they have the rare merit of a complete absence of vulgarity. They know how to act broad farce with refinement. Of the two actors, the lady, as is fit, appears to be the better artist, and her whimsical songs, which are of a kind that any lady might sing who had but enough power of ludicrous expression, have already found their way into the London streets.

October 4.—The Belphegor of Mr. Charles Dillon merits distinct and emphatic commendation. It is much to win attention from the town in a part that has been made familiar in its perfection to one class of playgoers by the acting of Lemaître, and to another by a long run of the play at the ADELPHI. M. Frederick Lemaître, with a light French touch, depicted the vagabondage of the hero, and the pathos of the situations in which he is placed. Mr.

Dillon brings out all the pathos solidly and earnestly ; he makes it tell upon his audiences, but he is throughout so substantially earnest in his rendering, that the play now and then breaks down under him. We may compare the drama to bad ice, over which a light and rapid skater may pass, giving no one reason to suspect its unsafe condition, but which cracks at once under a man who treads with manifest deliberation. This criticism affects, certainly, the play rather than the actor. Mr. Charles Dillon displays in Belphegor powers of a high order as an English actor, and has achieved success before the London public.

October 18.—*Timon of Athens* has been reproduced again by Mr. Phelps, with even more pains than were bestowed upon his former revival of that play, which, when he first produced it, had been acted but a few times since the days of Shakespeare. As now performed it is exceedingly effective.

A main cause of the success of Mr. Phelps in his Shakespearean revivals is, that he shows in his author above all things the poet. Shakespeare's plays are always poems, as performed at SADLER'S WELLS. The scenery is always beautiful, but it is not allowed to draw attention from the poet, with whose whole conception it is made to blend in the most perfect harmony. The actors are content also to be subordinated to the play, learn doubtless at rehearsals how to subdue excesses of expression that by giving undue force to one part would destroy the balance of the whole, and blend their work in such a way as to produce everywhere the right emphasis. If Mr. Phelps takes upon himself the character which needs the most elaborate development, however carefully and perfectly he may produce his own impression of his part, he never by his acting drags it out of its place in the drama. He takes heed that every part, even the meanest, shall have in the acting as much prominence as Shakespeare gave it in his plan, and it is for this reason that with actors, many of whom are anything but "stars", the result most to be desired is really obtained. Shakespeare appears in his integrity, and his plays are found to affect audiences less as dramas in a common sense than as great poems.

This is the case especially with *Timon*. It may be that one cause of its long neglect, as potent as the complaint that it excites no interest by female characters, is the large number of *dramatis personæ*, to whom are assigned what many actors might consider parts of which they can make nothing, and who, being presented in a slovenly way, by a number of inferior performers, would leave only one part in the drama, and take all the power out of that. Such an objection has not, however, any weight at SADLER'S WELLS, where every member of the company is taught to regard the poetry he speaks according to its nature rather than its quantity. The personators of the poet and the painter in the first scene of the *Timon*, as now acted, manifestly say what Shakespeare has assigned to them to say with as much care, and as much certainty that it will be listened to with due respect, as if they were themselves Timons, Hamlets, or Macbeths. Nobody rants — it becomes his part that Alcibiades should be a little blustery—nothing is slurred ; a servant who has anything to say says it in earnest, making his words heard and their meaning felt ; and so it is that, although only in one or two cases we may have observed at SADLER'S WELLS originality of genius in the actor, we have nevertheless perceived something like the entire sense of one .of Shakespeare's plays, and have been raised above ourselves by the perception.

It is not because of anything peculiar in the air of Islington, or because an audience at Pentonville is made of men differing in nature from those who would form an audience in the Strand, that Shakespeare is listened to at SADLER'S WELLS with reverence not shown elsewhere. What

·has been done at Islington could, if the same means were employed, be done at Drury Lane. But Shakespeare is not fairly heard when he is made to speak from behind masses of theatrical upholstery, or when it is assumed that there is but one character in any of his plays, and that the others may be acted as incompetent performers please. If *The Messiah* were performed at EXETER HALL, with special care to intrust some of the chief solos to a good bass or con- tralto, the rest being left to chance, and members of the chorus allowed liberty to sing together in all keys, we should enjoy Handel much as we are sometimes asked to enjoy Shakespeare on the London stage. What Signor Costa will do for an orchestra, the manager must do for his com- pany, if he would present a work of genius in such a way as to procure for it a full appreciation.

Such thoughts are suggested by the effect which *Timon of Athens* is producing on the audiences at SADLER'S WELLS. The play is a poem to them. The false friends, of whom one declares, " The swallow follows not summer more willing than we your lordship", and upon whom *Timon* retorts, "Nor more willingly leaves winter," are as old as the institution of society. Since men had commerce first together to the present time the cry has been, " Such summer birds are men". The rush of a generous impulsive nature from one rash extreme into the other, the excesses of the man who never knew " the middle of humanity", is but another com- mon form of life; and when have men not hung—the poets, the philosophers, the lovers, the economists, men of all habits —over a contemplation of the contrast between that soft town-life represented by the luxury of Athens in its wealth and its effeminacy, and the life of a man who, like Timon before his cave's mouth, turns from gold because it is not eatable, and digs in the wood for roots? With a bold hand Shake- speare grasped the old fable of Timon, and moulded it into a form that expresses much of the perplexity and yearning

of our nature. He takes up Timon, a free-handed and
large-hearted lord, who, though "to Lacedæmon did his
lands extend", found them too little to content his restless
wish to pour himself all out in kindness to his fellows. He
leaves him dead by the shore of the mysterious eternal sea.

I do not dwell upon the play itself, for here the purpose
only is to show in what way it can be made, when fitly
represented—and is made at SADLER'S WELLS—to stir the
spirit as a poem. Mr. Phelps in his own acting of Timon
treats the character as an ideal, as the central figure in a
mystery. As the liberal Athenian lord, his gestures are large,
his movements free—out of himself everything pours, towards
himself he will draw nothing. As the disappointed Timon,
whose love of his kind is turned to hate, he sits on the
ground self-contained, but miserable in the isolation, from
first to last contrasting with Apemantus, whom "fortune's
tender arm never with favour clasped", who is a churl by the
original sourness of his nature, hugs himself in his own
ragged robe, and worships himself for his own ill manners.
Mr. Marston's Apemantus is well acted, and helps much to
secure a right understanding of the entire play.

October 25.—The beautiful mounting of the *Midsummer
Night's Dream* at the PRINCESS'S THEATRE attracts and
will attract for a long time crowded audiences. The words
of the play are spoken agreeably, some of the sweetest
passages charmingly, and much of Shakespeare's delicate
pleasantry is made to tell with good effect upon its hearers.
The *Midsummer Night's Dream* is full of passages that have
only to be reasonably well uttered to be enjoyed even by the
dull; and with so fair a Hermia as Miss Bufton, so whimsical a Bottom as Mr. Harley, who seems to have no
particular conception of the part, but nevertheless makes it
highly amusing—with a generally good delivery of words
and songs—the play speaks for itself in a great measure.

The one defect in the mounting of the *Midsummer*

Night's Dream is that which has lessened the value of many former efforts made at this house to produce Shakespeare with every accessory of scenic decoration. I do not think money ill spent upon stage-furniture, and certainly can only admire the exquisite scenery of the play now being presented at the Princess's; but there may be a defect of taste that mars the effect of the richest ornament, as can best be shown by one or two examples.

Shakespeare's direction for the opening scene of the *Midsummer Night's Dream* is: "Athens, a Room in the Palace of Theseus." For this, is read at the PRINCESS's THEATRE: "A Terrace adjoining the Palace of Theseus, overlooking the City of Athens"; and there is presented an elaborate and undoubtedly most beautiful bird's-eye view of Athens as it was in the time of Pericles. A great scenic effect is obtained, but it is, as far as it goes, damaging to the poem. Shakespeare took for his mortals people of heroic times, Duke Theseus and Hippolyta, and it suited his romance to call them Athenians; but the feeling of the play is marred when out of this suggestion of the antique mingled with the fairy world the scene-painter finds opportunity to bring into hard and jarring contrast the Athens of Pericles and our own world of Robin Goodfellow and all the woodland elves. "A Room in the House of Theseus", left that question of the where or when of the whole story to be touched as lightly as a poet might desire; the poetry was missed entirely by the painting of the scene, beautiful as it is, which illustrates the first act of the *Midsummer Night's Dream* at the PRINCESS's.

In the second act there is a dream-like moving of the wood, beautifully managed, and spoilt in effect by a trifling mistake easily corrected. Oberon stands before the scene waving his wand, as if he were exhibitor of the diorama, or a fairy conjurer causing the rocks and trees to move. Nobody, I believe, ever attributed to fairies any power of that sort. Oberon should either be off the stage or on it still as death, and it should be left for the spectators to feel the dreamy influence of wood and water slipping by their eyes unhindered and undistracted. This change leads to the disclosure of a fairy ring, a beautiful scenic effect, and what is called in large letters upon the play-bills, "Titania's Shadow Dance". Of all things in the world, a shadow dance of fairies! If anything in the way of an effect of light was especially desirable, it would have been such an arrange-ment as would have made the fairies appear to be dancing in a light so managed as to cast no shadow, and give them the true spiritual attribute. Elaborately to produce and present, as an especial attraction, fairies of large size, casting shadows made as black and distinct as possible, and offer-ing in dance to pick them up, as if even they also were solid, is as great a sacrifice of Shakespeare to the purposes of the ballet-master, as the view of Athens in its glory was a sacri-fice of poetry to the scene-painter. Enough has been said to show the direction in which improvement is necessary to make the stage-ornament at the PRINCESS'S THEATRE as perfect as it is beautiful. The Puck is a pretty little girl, belted and garlanded with flowers! From the third act we miss a portion of the poem most essential to its right effect —the quarrel between Hermia and Helena ; but we get, at the end, a ballet of fairies round a maypole that shoots up out of an aloe, after the way of a transformation in a panto-mime, and rains down garlands. Fairies, not airy beings of the colour of the greenwood, or the sky, or robed in misty white, but glittering in the most brilliant dresses, with a crust of bullion about their legs, cause the curtain to fall on a splendid ballet; and it is evidence enough of the depraved taste of the audience to say that the ballet is encored.

I make these comments in no censorious mood. It is a pleasure to see Shakespeare enjoyed by the large number of persons who are attracted to the PRINCESS'S THEATRE by the splendours for which it is famous. I do not wish the splendour less, or its attraction less, but only ask for more heed to the securing of a perfect harmony between the conceptions of the decorator and those of the poet.

At the OLYMPIC THEATRE a new drama, *Still Waters Run Deep*, has been produced. Its author, Mr. Tom Taylor, has obtained his plot from a French novel. The writing, which is easy and natural, and the dramatic construction of the piece, which has a somewhat lame conclusion, are his own. The still waters run deep in the person of a quiet husband, Mr. Wigan, who is taken for a fool by his wife and by others, but who contrives quietly to put down a swindling, rakish captain—acted by Mr. Vining— to protect his family from wrong and loss, and to assert his authority at home. The husband, Mr. Mildmay, affords Mr. Wigan an opportunity for his talent in a new character, which will rank with his most complete successes. Mr. Emery plays and makes up very effectively as an old man.

November 1.—At the OLYMPIC, Mr. Robson, after a season of illness, has reappeared, and there, following two little comedies perfectly well acted, may be seen again his wonderful burlesque of *Medea*, wherein he seems to have reached the climax of success in personating jealousy by a wild mingling of the terrible with the grotesque.

December 6.—The "Induction" to the *Taming of the Shrew* enables Mr. Phelps to represent, in Christopher Sly, Shakespeare's sketch of a man purely sensual and animal, brutish in appetite, and with a mind unleavened by fancy. Such a presentment would not suit the uses of the poet; it could excite only disgust; if it were not throughout as humorous as faithful. Mr. Phelps knows this; and perhaps the most interesting point to be noted in his Christopher Sly is that the uncompromising truth of his portraiture of the man buried and lost in his animal nature is throughout, by subtle touches easy to appreciate but hard to follow, made subservient to the laws of art, and the sketch, too, is clearly the more accurate for being humorous : throughout we laugh and understand.

Hamlet and Christopher Sly are at the two ends of Shakespeare's list of characters, and, with a singular skill, Mr. Phelps, who is the best Hamlet now upon the stage, banishes from his face every spark of intelligence while representing Sly. Partly he effects this by keeping the eyes out of court as witnesses of intelligence. The lids are drooped in the heavy slumberousness of a stupid nature ; there is no such thing as a glance of intelligence allowed to escape from under them ; the eyes are hidden almost entirely when they are not widely exposed in a stupid stare. The acting of this little sketch is, indeed, throughout most careful and elaborate. There is, as we have said, no flinching from the perfect and emphatical expression of the broader lights and shadows of the character. Christopher is, at first, sensually drunk ; and when, after his awakening in the lord's house, the page is introduced to him as his lady-wife, another chord of sensuality is touched, the brute hugs, and becomes amorous. Of the imagination that, even when there are offered to the sensual body new delights of the appetite, is yet unable to soar beyond the reach already attained, Mr. Phelps, in the details of his acting, gives a variety of well-conceived suggestions. Thus, to the invitation, "Will 't please your mightiness to wash your hands ?" Christopher, when he has grasped the fact that a basin is being held before him in which he must wash, enters upon such a wash as sooty hands of tinkers only can require, and, having made an end of washing and bespattering, lifts up instinctively the corner of his velvet robe to dry his hands upon.

The stupidity of Sly causes his disappearance from the stage in the most natural way after the play itself has warmed into full action. He has, of course, no fancy for it, is unable to follow it, stares at it, and falls asleep over it. The sport of imagination acts upon him as a sleeping-draught, and at the end of the first act he is so fast asleep that it becomes matter of course to carry him away. The *Induction* thus insensibly fades into the play, and all trace of it is lost by the time that a lively interest in the comedy itself has been excited.

December 13.—At the OLYMPIC, Mrs. Inchbald's *Wives as they were, and Maids as they are*, is a five-act play, which, being acted with vivacity, slips by as if it were a two-act comedietta. The play does not awaken any sort of violent emotion, but the audience is insensibly amused throughout, and quietly forgets the flight of time. In *Jones the Avenger*, which is a whimsical farce, adapted from the French, not very good in itself, Mr. Robson has one or two fine opportunities of burlesquing tragic passion. His terror in the thought that he has at last caused the death of his appointed victim by tempting him to swim over a canal with a heavy clock tied round his neck, and his fear of being ever more haunted by a ghost with a skeleton clock, are expressed in a soliloquy that awakens laughter, by combining ludicrous ideas with the display of a passion real as that in Macbeth's

> "Thou canst not say, I did it : never shake
> Thy gory locks at me."

1857, *January* 24.—For the past fortnight the four nights a week dedicated at SADLER'S WELLS to Shakespeare have been occupied by performances of *Twelfth Night*—last acted here five years ago—in which comedy the part of Malvolio is that sustained by Mr. Phelps. When but half-a-dozen more of these plays shall have been produced, it will become a subject of just pride to the manager of SADLER'S WELLS that he will have mounted on his little stage all the dramatic works of our great poet ; that—apart

from his own personations—he will have gathered round
him a small company of actors, zealous to perform them all
with a true sense of what they are about; and will have
taught an audience mainly composed of hard-working men,
who crowd a sixpenny gallery and shilling pit, heartily to
enjoy the sweetest and the noblest verse man ever wrote.

The aspect and behaviour of the pit and gallery at
SADLER'S WELLS during the performance of one of Shakespeare's plays cannot fail to impress most strongly every
visitor who is unaccustomed to the place.   There sit our
working-classes in a happy crowd, as orderly and reverent
as if they were at church, and yet as unrestrained in their
enjoyment as if listening to stories told them by their own
firesides.   Shakespeare spoke home to the heart of the
natural man, even in the same words that supply matter for
nice judgment by the intellect; he was as a cook, who, by
the same meat that feeds abundantly the hungry, tickles
with an exquisite delight the palate of the epicure.   It is
hard to say how much men who have had few advantages
of education must in their minds and characters be
strengthened and refined when they are made accustomed
to this kind of entertainment.

Upon a stage thus managed Mr. Phelps has of late years
been the personator of about thirty of the characters of
Shakespeare.   Great men or small, heroes or cowards,
sages or simpletons, sensual or spiritual men, he has taken
all as characters that Shakespeare painted, studied them
minutely, and embodied each in what he thinks to be a
true Shakespearean form.   Bottom the Weaver, Brutus,
Falstaff, Macbeth, Christopher Sly, are characters assumed
by the same man, not to display some special power in the
actor, but the range of power in the poet to whose illustration he devotes himself.   Good tragedian as he is, we suppose that it is in a sort of comedy, vaguely to be defined as
dry and intellectual, but in his hands always most diverting,

that Mr. Phelps finds the bent of his genius as an actor to be most favoured. Thus in Malvolio he would appear to have a part pretty exactly suited to his humour, none the less so because there is perhaps no character in which he is himself lost sight of so completely; substance vanishes, and shadow lives.

Malvolio lives at SADLER'S WELLS in bearing and attire modelled upon the fashion of the Spaniard, as impassive in his manner as a Spanish king should be. In one of the first sentences addressed to him we are told his character : " O, you are sick of self-love, Malvolio, and taste things with a distempered appetite." Such a man is the Malvolio we see. When in his tasting of Maria's letter he betrays his distempered appetite for greatness, we are not allowed to suppose for a moment that he loves his mistress. Seeing that, as Maria says, "it is his ground of faith that all that look on him love him", he accepts easily the hope of greatness thrust upon him, and his rejoicing is in the love of Olivia, not in the way of sympathy, but as a way to "sitting in his state, calling his officers about him in his branched velvet gown". Such a man, as Mr. Phelps represents him, walks not with a smirk and a light comic strut, but in the heaviness of grandeur, with a face grave through very emptiness of all expression. This Malvolio stalks blind about the world ; his eyes are very nearly covered with their heavy lids, for there is nothing in the world without that is worth noticing, it is enough for him to contemplate the excellence within ; walled up in his own temple of the flesh, he is his own adorer. If his ears are assailed with irreverences by the fool, he counts the fool as naught, and is moved therefore but to the expression of a passing shade of pity for his ignorance. Upon the debasement of Sir Toby and Sir Andrew he looks down with very calm disdain. When in the latter half of the play he has been bidden, as he thinks, by her who will thrust greatness upon him, to be opposite

with a kinsman, surly with servants, and, if he entertain her
love, to let it appear in his smiling; though he had been
practising behaviour to his shadow, all the smile he can
produce is one of intense satisfaction with himself, and all
the surliness but a more open expression of disdain for
those who do not pay him homage.   When locked up as a
madman he is sustained by his self-content, and by the honest
certainty that he has been notoriously abused; and when
at last he, for once, opens his eyes on learning how he has
been tricked, they close again in happy self-content, and he
is retiring in state without deigning a word to his tormentors,
when, as the fool had twitted him by noting how "the
whirligig of time brings in his revenges", he remembers
that the whirligig is still in motion.   Therefore, marching
back with as much increase of speed as is consistent with
magnificence, he threatens all—including now Olivia in his
contempt—" I'll be revenged on the whole pack of you ! "

Other Malvolios seen by the playgoers of this generation
have been more fantastical and caused more laughter—
although this one causes much—but the impression made
by them has been less deep.   Few who have seen or may
see at SADLER'S WELLS the Spanish-looking steward of
Countess Olivia, and laughed at the rise and fall of his
château en Espagne, will forget him speedily.   Like a quaint
portrait in which there are master-strokes, his figure may
dwell in the mind for years.

Madame Girardin's charming drama, *Une Femme qui
déteste son Mari,* has appeared this week at two of the
London theatres, and is to appear at yet another.   At the
HAYMARKET it is given nearly as the author wrote it, with
only such touches as belong of necessity to a clever stage-
translation, and is called *A Wicked Wife.*   At the OLYMPIC
Mr. Tom Taylor has adapted it, changing the scene from
France to England, and the title of the adaptation is *A Sheep
in Wolf's Clothing.*   Each version has its own merits;

both are most effective and successful. In the adaptation a great point was necessarily lost. The royalist husband whom the wife is concealing from the vengeance of the revolutionary tribunal, while affecting to be a hard-hearted republican, accepting the addresses of the friend of Robespierre, must needs be considered dead when the story is transferred to English soil. Easy divorce was not possible at any period of English history, and yet this topic yields some of the best points in the original drama. Mr. Tom Taylor, being compelled to give up this part of the story and to substitute weaker machinery, has taken pains to add one or two striking situations of his own invention to Madame Girardin's plot; thus there is on the whole, perhaps, as much effective matter in the English adaptation as in the original. A happier instance of the skilful transfer of a story from one period and country to another, and of adaptation from the French in the best sense of the phrase, than the *Sheep in Wolf's Clothing*, I have seldom seen. The Wife at the HAYMARKET is Miss Reynolds : at the OLYMPIC, Mrs. Stirling; and both ladies appear to great advantage in the part. At the HAYMARKET, the Finot of Mr. Compton strengthens the piece materially.

March 14.—*Richard II*, produced at the PRINCESS'S THEATRE for the first time on Thursday night, as to its mounting is, perhaps, the most elaborate and costly spectacle that Mr. Charles Kean has yet set upon the stage, and the splendours are all unimpeachable. Fine as are the opportunities afforded by the part of Richard II to a tragedian, no tragedian in recent times has made the play sufficiently attractive to the public. It is full of passages that have floated out of their place in the drama to live in the minds of the people ; the number of what are called "Beauties of Shakespeare" in the play is great ; it contains also what ought to be one of the best acting-characters, and it embodies a fine picture of the old, wild days of English civil

war. Only Shakespeare himself could have filled the stage
with a clash of arms, as we here find it, blended with so
many incidents of grief and terror.

It was a fair object of ambition so to perform *Richard II*
as to present this picture to the eye as well as to the mind.
Mr. Charles Kean has reproduced the people of the time,
has restored to our eyes Richard the Second in his court,
shown in their strength castles now known as ruins, reproduced with scrupulous fidelity the complete spectacle of
lists set out for a tournament on Gosford Green, and has
even interpolated between two acts of the play the triumph
of the entry of Bolingbroke with Richard into London,
which is a fine piece of stage-effect. The play gives reasonable opportunity for all these shows. They leave the mind
bewildered for a time, but ultimately settle on the memory
as a true picture of at least one phase of a past state of
society.

Of course it is necessary to make room for stage-appointments and processions by omissions from the poetry, and
Richard II was well chosen as a play from which certain
omissions may be made without serious damage to its effect
for acting purposes. Thus I hold Mr. Charles Kean to be
quite justified in omitting the scenes in the fifth act founded
on Aumerle's treason against Bolingbroke, though, if we
consider the position of each person concerned in the
episode, they contain truly the most vigorous sketch ever
conceived of the domestic misery that is among the incidents
of civil war. But it is to be regretted that to the necessities
of the scenery two passages have been sacrificed that are
most necessary to the play, and by the loss of which Mr.
Charles Kean impairs greatly the success of his own efforts
as an actor. At the end of the first act the curtain must
fall upon the spectacle of the tournament. The scene has,
therefore, to be sacrificed in which the audience is prepared
for Gaunt's death by tidings of his illness, and for Richard's

seizure of his plate by a distinct knowledge of the King's sore poverty, his need of means to fight the Irish rebels, and his consequent wish that Gaunt may die, and leave his wealth behind him. Thus prepared, we can see with less surprise and abhorrence Richard's act of seizure in the first scene of the act that follows. Still further to soften the impression against Richard, which, if too strongly excited in the first half of the drama, would check pity in the other half, the poet has taken care to remove Gaunt from the stage to die, so that when Richard, after receiving information of his death, turns promptly to the subject of the Irish wars and makes the seizure, he does not shock us by the rapacity and selfishness displayed while the very body of his uncle—dead but a minute since—lies before him. By the omission of the last scene in the first act, as the play is performed at the PRINCESS'S, we are brought suddenly from Gaunt in regal favour to Gaunt on his death-bed. He dies on the stage, and Richard, with the urgency of whose needs we have not been carefully impressed, becomes immediately a bird of prey beside the corpse, and loses irretrievably the goodwill of the audience. The other dangerous omission is that of the scene which should open the third act, and which immediately precedes the change of Richard's fortune, cunningly preparing us for pity by producing Bushy and Green for execution as the men who have "misled a prince, a royal king", etc. The effect of these two omissions is to impede seriously the course of sympathy in the audience for King Richard's misfortunes, and to throw great difficulty in the way of the actor by whom it is the whole purpose of the play that sympathy shall be excited. Mr. Charles Kean could not wholly overcome this difficulty by the most careful acting, though the skill with which he marked, as the turning point in Richard's story, the revoking of Bolingbroke's sentence of banishment, went far to win some pity for his hero. Mrs. Kean, too, conquered a few kind thoughts for Richard by the pathos which she threw into his Queen's parting from him at the Tower.

By other members of the company the parts less important were efficiently sustained, and there was much to praise in Mr. Ryder's Bolingbroke.   The revival earned a most complete and well-deserved success.

March 21.—Mr. Bayle Bernard's new play, *A Life's Trial,* may be described as an Adelphi drama suited to the actors and the audience at the HAYMARKÉT.   It is in four acts, of which the first three are so good and effective as to promise more than usual success, but the last ends with a scene to which expectation has been strongly directed only to be balked.   The scene itself—a West-end gambling club—is richly mounted; in it all the elements from which should arise the last conflict of love and passion are collected, and yet no dramatic use is made of them.   The hero is ruined at cards by conspirators at a quiet table, where no word is said; the heroine arrives too late to denounce the villain; the villain himself has run off.   Nobody has anything to say that is worth saying, somebody looks in to report that the villain of the piece has taken poison, and the curtain falls. Every preceding act had ended with a situation not only well conceived, but also powerfully wrought, and Mr. Bernard has only to re-write his concluding scene in such a way as to bring into play all the contending passions he has stirred, to make the close of the fourth act as triumphant as that of the second or the third, and to secure for the whole drama unusual success.   That for the fault of one scene, hurried in the writing, a play everywhere else written so skilfully, mounted so liberally, and acted throughout so well as the *Life's Trial*, should miss the success it deserves, is not to be tolerated.   Precedent may be against such a proceeding, but so easy does it appear to remove the sole bar to the durable success of this drama, by re-writing its close, that I hope precedent will not be in this case too strictly respected. Miss Reynolds, as the heroine, acted well, and received at the close of the third act a hearty call, while Mr. W. Farren, as the hero, in an expression of repressed hatred for a false friend, at the close of the second act, added one more to the number of his bits of acting in which he now and then mounts high above the ordinary level. Mr. Buckstone, as a tea-dealer who affects fine company, wears white waistcoats, and hums *Di tanti palpiti*, to the confusion of his business and to the beggary of himself, and Mr. Compton, as an adventurer in many forms, appear throughout to excellent advantage. The story extends over ten years, during which these two worthies are much buffeted by fortune.

March 28.—One of Mr. Robson's very best successes is his personation of the old rustic miser, Daddy Hardacre, in an English version of *La Fille de l'Avare*. The old man loves his daughter and his gold, handles and hugs them with so equal an affection, that to subdue either of the two loves, when it seems to have become inevitable that he must bring one into subjection to the other, is impossible. To save an uncle's life the miser's daughter robs him of five thousand pounds that he had stubbornly refused to lend. When he is frantic with his loss, the daughter owns herself to be the thief. He will fell her to the earth ; he will fondle her ; he will starve her into more confession. He has sent her to her room, and sits before the stairs that lead down to his money and the stairs that lead up to his daughter. He sees her weeping and praying. "Shut the door," he cries to the old servant, "I'll never forgive—— I didn't tell you to shut it close, you stupid fool !" The knot is untied at last without violence to either of the miser's ruling passions. It will be seen that there is full scope here given for Mr. Robson's power as an actor. He has put his entire strength into the part, filled it with minute touches of character, fantastic shifts of mood. The half-maniacal exultation over success in driving a hard bargain, an exultation that almost takes away speech and that brings tears to the eyes, he contrasts sharply with the pain it costs to pay even the small expenses upon executing deeds from which there is to accrue large profit. I say no more, for *Daddy Hardacre* ought to be seen, and will be seen, by every faithful playgoer. Miss Hughes, who made her first appearance at the OLYMPIC, as the miser's daughter, acted with a charming simplicity and truth. The other characters were so well sustained by Mr. George Vining, Mr. Cooke, and Miss Stevens, that there was no drawback whatever on the satisfaction of the audience.

April 18.—At HER' MAJESTY'S THEATRE the success of the season was decided on the first night by the substantial triumph of the new tenor, Signor Giuglini. The opera was *La Favorita*, and with one exception the singers were all new ; with no exception they were good, but Signor Giuglini won the honours of the night, and left upon all minds the certainty that he will win no mean share of the honours of the season. He has taste, feeling, sufficient power as an actor, and a perfect voice. No success could have been less spurious than his. The crowded audience was critical, the opera is weak and dull ; at the end of the first act (into which the first two had been wisely compressed) the applause expressed simply a mild content. As the opera proceeded the range of the new singer's powers was developed ; and when in the last act *Spirto gentil* was sung with a purity of voice and a delicacy of expression never to be surpassed, the audience surrendered at discretion. One of the best singers in Europe was before them, and no room was left for any doubt about the fact.

April 25.—*Maria di Rohan* has been reproduced at the LYCEUM Opera, and after an interval of four years the public is again surprised by the intensity of passion expressed in the last act by Signor Ronconi, whose Chevreuse is the one thing that keeps the opera upon our stage. In the first two acts he is the chivalrous and devoted friend and lover. Some people have sharp eyes. A daily critic, in a detailed analysis of Signor Ronconi's performance of this part, calls attention to the "seeds of suspicion" sown by the discovery of the lady's mask in his friend's room, and to the metamorphosis produced by a supposed knowledge that it is his wife's, which is fearful in its painfully suppressed emotion. The scene is, in fact, the only one in which Signor Ronconi has an opportunity of showing comic power. Ladies' masks all very much resemble one another, and the "fearful expression" seen by the critic was that of banter against a friend who has a lady in a closet, and has been affecting only a solicitude about his mother. Chevreuse after quitting the stage comes back to look in at the door, and leave a parting joke behind him. The suppressed emotion is in fact that of laughter. If any evidence were needed beyond that of one's eyes, the libretto clearly enough shows that the same man from the moment of his discovering that friend and wife have deceived him pants with an insane passion to bring back the betrayer to his grasp, yet after the discovery of the mask not only retires laughing, but fights the false friend's duel for him; and yet more, when peril from Richelieu threatens, although wounded already on his behalf, exerts himself to mount him on a horse and speed him into safety. But Chalais on the verge of the duel had written a parting letter to Maria, in which he returned her portrait. This Richelieu finding among his papers, sends to the deluded husband. "The manner in which Ronconi perused the letter, and his convulsive exclamation at the end," are then commented upon by the too observant critic. The manner was that of complete indifference. He was reading a farewell to some lady—it mattered little whom ; there was no doubt yet in the brave mind. The portrait was then opened carelessly ; and with a loud cry, passing rapidly, as the words of it denote,

from amazement into agony, and thence to wrath, the passion
that begets the whole catastrophe begins :

> " Che ?   Maria . . . dessa ! e Riccardo . .
> La scorse notte ! . .   Oh rabbia !"

The rest is all the work of passion.   The whole catastrophe
is brought about during the first terrible half-hour of fury.   I
am not sure whether the last glance at the actor as the
curtain falls does not show him with his wrath already half
repented.

May 23.—Mdlle. Parepa sang, for the first time in London,
at the LYCEUM Opera last Thusday evening, as the Elvira of
I Puritani.   She is very young, comely in person, graceful
in movement, and endowed with a sweet and flexible soprano
voice, which has all the fresh music of youth in it, and in the
use of which skill is not more apparent than quick feeling.
Mdlle. Parepa seems to have in her the material of a good
actress, and performs already with much tact and animation.
She deserved the honour of addition to the excellent Lyceum
company.

May 9.—No opera has been performed at HER MAJESTY'S
THEATRE this season so perfectly as the *Lucia di Lammermoor*
in which Mddle. Piccolomini and Signor Giuglini appeared
for the first time on Thursday night.

The Lucia of Mdlle. Piccolomini was a double success.
It was her fourth success as an actress, her first as a singer.
As actress she has a very wide range of emotion to express
—maidenly love, fear of the spirit-world, fear of man, hope,
doubt, despair, and a sort of madness in which all moods
mingle.   We need say only that she justified the highest
praisethat has been heretofore bestowed upon her skill.
The first expression of her madness is in a recitative,
beginning *Il dolce suono*, which, as Mdlle. Piccolomini
delivered it, was one of the most curious displays of a rare
power of dramatic expression that we can remember.   The

mood shifts with every line or every half-line, and the dramatic illustration was throughout exquisite. There occurs in it Lucia's fancy that she hears the nuptial hymn, and upon the words expressing this, Mdlle. Piccolomini seized, that she might put into them a rapture of tenderness which brought the lost life, and the happiness with which it might have overflowed, into a startling contrast with the girl's death and despair. With a like skill, by her delivery of the lines

"Nell' ira sua terribile, calpesta, oh Dio! l' anello . . .
Mi maledice!"

she not only flashes into every heart the reason of her madness, but makes it clear that sudden madness was to her the inevitable consequence of Edward's curse.

May 16.—At Her Majesty's Theatre, Madame Alboni has, during the past week, made her first appearance for the season in the *Barbiere di Seviglia,* and on that occasion the public had, for the first time this season, an opportunity of hearing one of Rossini's operas performed at either house. With that single exception, from the opening of the season to the present time, there has been no music heard either at Her Majesty's Theatre or at the Lyceum, except two operas of Bellini—who is, at any rate, not the most vigorous of composers—and the works of the two weakest writers who have compassed fame, Donizetti and Verdi. Of Donizetti, moreover, with a single exception, we have had only those works—his serious ones—in which he most distinctly made his weakness manifest. Is it the fault of the public, or of public singers, that with two opera-houses open we so seldom hear any first-class music? It is time to begin singing a better class of music than has been heard hitherto at either opera-house, for we cannot believe that the polite world wishes to place itself in unenviable contrast with the throngs that crammed the Surrey Music Hall last Monday evening to hear Mendelssohn's *Elijah*, or with the great shilling audience that will be regaled next Wednesday evening at St. Martin's Hall with Mozart's *Requiem* and Mendelssohn's *Hymn of Praise*.

ADELPHI.—Mr. Webster appeared last Monday evening, for the first time this season, acting with Madame Celeste in a new drama, entitled *Joseph Chavigny ; or, Under the Thumb*. *Joseph Chavigny* is an ADELPHI drama, unrelieved by comic passages, and burdened with a mass of verbiage under which a very fair plot sinks utterly exhausted in the second act. The first act is the best, and would tell capitally with only about one-fourth of the words omitted. Of the second act, three-fourths of the words ought to have been scored out before the piece was acted, and the third act would have borne reducing by about one-half. Unluckily the author, in his laudable desire to write his best for his best actors, had overloaded most especially with his *copia verborum* the parts of Mr. Webster and Madame Celeste, and a dialogue between those excellent performers, who are first favourites with the house and were putting forth all their best powers, was, on the first night, the most dangerous part of the whole drama, which but narrowly escaped damnation. No doubt it has already been compressed ; and as the story is good, and the Chavigny of Mr. Webster really a good piece of acting, the compressed play will have a reasonable power of attraction.

May 30.—The Bouffes-Parisiens are acting a variety of gay little pieces which now tempt the town with mirth, and raillery, and pleasant song. One of these is *Les Pantins de Violette*. Violette, under the care of an old enchanter, is bred to the belief that all the living things she sees are mechanical machines, and the person whom she is to love is then presented to her as the most beautiful of all the puppets. This puppet performs until it wins her heart, and then—but why tell every turn of the story? The pleasant little conceit is worked out gracefully, merrily, and cleverly.

June 13.—Mdlle. Piccolomini can do nothing without showing the originality of her genius as an actress, and as Zerlina in *Don Giovanni* she especially gave with a new force certain dramatic points in the *La ci darem ;* her rustic elbowings and wheedlings in *Batti batti* were devised as a true artist would devise them ; and in the ball scene she accounts cleverly for Zerlina's withdrawal by showing her as a country girl absorbed in the business of watching the steps of the other dancers that she may see what she herself ought to be doing. Nevertheless, Zerlina is her least successful part. She does not owe her triumph as an actress to her piquant ways. If there be no depths to be stirred, no hidden springs of emotion to be loosened, no spiritual meaning to express, her strength is only as the strength of actresses and actors who can please without possessing any genius at all. Her comparative failure as Norina in *Don Pasquale* indicated this, and her almost positive failure as Zerlina proves it. Some of the best melodies in the opera are here entrusted to her voice, and as a vocalist she is, by a great deal, less perfect than as an actress.

The Don Giovanni of Signor Ronconi is not perfectly sung ; but I differ altogether from those who do not appreciate it as a piece of acting, and who sigh for the gentlemanly grace of Tamburini. It is admitted that Signor Ronconi, as Chevreuse, assumes perfectly the dignity and bearing of the noble chevalier of the Court of Louis Quatorze; if, therefore, his Don Giovanni be not an agreeable and pleasant gentleman, the reason must needs be that Signor Ronconi does not choose to represent him so. A hero who in the last scene of a play or opera, goes down alive into hell before the presence of the audience ought, one humbly suggests, to be shown as something else than a most gentle-

manly person in the early scenes. The character which
Signor Ronconi imprints on his Don Giovanni is one of
defiant wickedness. That is the true character of one who
delights in insulting the weak women whom he has betrayed.
He charms women with the serpent's power of fascination,
not with the noble bearing and the courtesy that are the
attributes of better men. He is wicked and defiant to the
last. Because he remains defiant, the last hope of rescue
from perdition leaves him. It is odd that the same censors
of the stage who object against Mdlle. Piccolomini that she
wins too much sympathy for the struggle of a dissolute girl
to wipe away her stains and falter back upon the road to
heaven, should think it a fault in Signor Ronconi that he
has not made sufficiently *débonnaire* and agreeable the
character of a licentious man who travels with his best
speed in the contrary direction.

June 27.—Madame Ristori has been acting the part of
Bianca in an Italian version of the *Fazio* of Dr. Milman.
It is an Italian rendering of an Italian tale, and when we
see it acted by Italians we are less sensible than usual of
that inadequacy of motive for their actions which in the
English play takes force out of the three leading characters,
Bianca, Fazio, and Aldabella. The Italian element in the
tale being more vividly presented to the mind, it proves
a better story than we take it to be when told in English
fashion to our English eyes and ears. In her own part of
Bianca, which is the one part of the piece, and for the sake
of which it keeps a place upon our stage, Madame Ristori
sees the weak point, and exerts her skill successfully to
strengthen it. By touching upon one or two characteristic
passages in her performance, we may indicate her reading
of the play.

She is a fond wife, but an Italian wife. In the first
scene she marks strongly the repose of wedded happiness
with Fazio. The repose is broken only by a natural impa-

tience at the mention of her husband's early love for the proud Aldabella, who had scorned him in his poverty, and by a weariness at his search for the secret of alchemy. She is not the last speaker when she leaves the stage, but it is a rule with Madame Ristori never to quit the stage without making a point as she does so, and Fazio's last words were a jesting reference to Aldabella. Bianca, therefore, turns towards him at her chamber door, and with two little parting gestures of the hand only—one representing playful but half-earnest warning, and the other trusting love— impossible to any English actress, natural to an Italian, sums up in two instants the meaning of the scene.

Then the stabbed miser from next door enters and dies, whereupon Fazio, yielding to temptation, buries him secretly and steals his wealth. When Fazio, madly elated, shows the treasure to his wife, Madame Ristori does not—as Dr. Milman directs—burst into tears, but shrinks from it with a panting dread. Fazio is a weak fool, and, love him as she may, instinctively she knows it. What will he do, with his head turned by riches?

When she appears next upon the stage, Fazio's head has been turned not only by riches, but by the flatteries of Aldabella, who has sought to win him again to her lure. As he was before delirious with wealth, so is he now delirious with flattery of woman; and as he talks to her of the noble lady whom she may see drinking light out of his eyes, Madame Ristori's action is again full of significance. Listening to her husband with mute astonishment, she stirs twice only during the rhapsody: once to look narrowly into his face for the meaning of it, once to look round towards the street for any outward cause of his disturbance. That leads to her presently divining that he must have seen her rival. A reasonable jealousy is now, of course, set boiling in her blood; but when she warns Fazio of the extremities to which a woman may be driven in her passion, of the possible change from love to hate, she lets the word *odio* suddenly fall broken on a sigh of woman's inextinguishable love, and into a few tones breathes the entire spirit of the character she plays.   Fazio promises well, but when for the second time Bianca parts with him, it is with an expression of more hopeless dread than the sight of the gold had caused in her.

We see Bianca next as a home-keeping wife, troubled by Fazio's night-long absence, and soon learning that he had supped at the house of Aldabella.   She hears at the same time that the Duke sits in council over the mysterious disappearance of the old miser, she as a trusted wife being, of course, mistress of the mystery.   Then comes the dangerous part of the story.   It occurs to her to accuse her husband, simply that he may be dragged from Aldabella's arms.   The least hint of reflection here would be the ruin of the part, and we again appreciate Madame Ristori's perception of the difficulty when with a peculiar action, as the thought rises, she flashes to its execution.   Perfectly original is the way in which she contrives to pass from the stage, leaving behind her an impression of eager swiftness and at the same time of an intense preoccupation of the mind which bars all reasoning.

When she appears before the Duke as the accuser of her husband, Madame Ristori represents Bianca as a woman transferred into a world of new sensations, who continues almost mechanically to move in the direction taken after the first impulse to go somewhere and do something was received.   Her mind is as a ball rolling in a straight line, of which the pace begins to slacken.   She enters slowly as one in a dream, self-occupied; she does not appear to see the counsellors, answers their questions according to her first purpose, slowly and with the manner of one speaking to herself.   It moves her a little when, by the course of inquiry, she is reminded that she is Fazio's wife; but she is little stirred until her husband enters as a prisoner, then suddenly she flies across the stage and hides her face, because she does not meet him, as of old, with the true features of a wife.   Compelled to show herself as his accuser, when he doubts her reality, and asks to see her marriage-ring, she nervously attempts to cover the ring-finger with her other hand.   But with what frenzy she becomes Fazio's defender when he receives sentence of death, how she pleads for him, humbles herself in the dust before him, it is needless to go on to tell.   The last half of the play gives scope for nearly all Madame Ristori's powers. Having shown how she understands the part, how skilfully also she surmounts the difficulty of the play itself, I need not describe in detail how she triumphs when she has simply to display the usual resources of her art as a *tragédienne*.

July 18.—Mdlle. Piccolomini's Adina in *Elisir d'Amore* is, or rather should be, one of her most genuine successes. Certainly, though her reading of the part is all plainly enough set down in the libretto, Mdlle Piccolomini is the first person who has taught us to see in Adina more than a mere coquette.

Mdlle. Piccolomini's Adina has from first to last her heart set upon the over-modest Nemorino.   She knows herself to be the prettiest girl in the village, is well-to-do in the world, and happy in her sense of power as well as in possession of the lover whom out of pure gaiety she teases.   When the over-bold Sergeant Belcore addresses her in the come-see-and-conquer vein, she is tickled by his conceit, humours him in the mock-ing way of a girl who knows how far he is from ever making an impression on her heart, amuses herself with him as an agreeable absurdity.   In the succeeding scene with Nemorino, while Adina plays with his affection, Mdlle. Piccolomini makes it most evident that her playfulness is of another character.   She worries out of him incessant pro-testations of his love, at every fond word her face brightens

with an innocent happiness, there are touches of respect also
in her behaviour.   She is as much in love with Nemorino
as he is in love with her, but that swain has not courage to
believe it.

We see Adina next when she finds Nemorino foolishly
singing after he has taken the elixir which is to compel her
love on the day following.   When she is coming to him,
and first notices his reckless, joyous manner, she stops
suddenly with a serious look of doubt and concern, her
love is for a moment openly betrayed; but before Nemorino
sees her she has leapt to the conclusion that he is endavour-
ing to take her at her word and break from her.   Gay with
the expectation of to-morrow's victory, he encourages the
notion; she affects unconcern on her part, yet reminds him
of his vows, and contradicts her former counsel by suggesting that he may attempt to break them, but will not know
how.   He abides by his gay mood.   Adina, piqued a little,
must needs bring him back to his allegiance, and at that
moment Belcore's drum is heard.   The drum suggests him
to her as a puppet of which she can make use for the
reconquest of her lover.   Mdlle. Piccolomini shows here in
by-play how suddenly the thought of turning to her use the
empty sergeant is suggested.   By the time he enters, her
mind is made up, and in a preoccupied, determined way—
every third gesture a glance at Nemorino—she begins to
court him.   She watches her lover throughout.   She barely
does so much as think about the sergeant.   He is a vain
man, ready to believe that she can love him in an instant.
He has told her so; and if she takes him up, plays with
him, and puts him down at the last moment, he deserves
the lesson.   It is his vanity that will be wounded, not his
heart, and in the meantime he may be serviceable as a
puppet-figure.   Narrowly watching Nemorino, therefore,
Adina gives herself up to the soldier, promising more and
more as her pique rises, because her lover maintains his

gay humour. When the order for departure of the soldier arrives, and she has been bidding higher and higher in the hope to frighten back her truant to his old allegiance, and she at last promises marriage to the sergeant on that very day—before the happy morrow to which Nemorino has been looking forward—her end seems to be half gained, for the old lover shows signs of despair. She scolds him then, she parades Belcore up and down before his eyes, she turns the laugh against him; but she hovers near him instinctively, her love shows through her anger, and once, when the sergeant raises his hand to push Nemorino roughly, she bounds forward to his rescue.

In the next act Adina finds that she had no just cause of pique against her modest lover, and she not only throws aside, as she meant always to throw aside, the sergeant, for whom, as she frankly owns, "*pieno di donne è il mondo*", but she throws aside much of her own feminine pride ; and when she really fears that she may lose the husband of her choice, makes, in a scene charmingly diversified with lights and shades of feeling, first timidly and modestly by implication, then, when he has not courage to act upon that, with a frank energy, the plainest and most unequivocal confession of her love.

And this is the part of Adina, which opera-goers have for many years been accustomed to regard as the part of a mere hard-hearted village coquette, in which there is no play given to the skill of a good actress. We have been so long used to look for no more, that many, whose attention to the suggestions of the actress is divided by attention to familiar and pleasant music, may fail to observe what otherwise is manifest enough. The music, too, is in this opera quite within Mdlle. Piccolomini's reach.

July 25.—Of course it is hard for an Englishman to reconcile himself to a *Duncano, Re di Scozia ;* to believe in Macbetto as he believes in Macbeth. It is impossible for

Signor Giulio Carcano to translate *Macbeth*, though he
deserves credit for the result of the effort he has made ; and
it is amazing to see how Signor Vitaliani acts Macbeth.
His purpose is obvious enough. Macbeth is not the hero
of the play in the Italian version : it is his business to serve
as foil and contrast to his lady.

Madame Ristori conceives Lady Macbeth as a woman who
pens up her emotions, who is watchful, self-contained, who
fights against compunctious visitings of nature without
letting a stir be seen or any note of aches within to escape
her lips, until her heart too sorely charged gives way under
the weight it is forced secretly and silently to bear. She
contrasts the innate force of this wife's character with the
weakness of the man who cannot keep his troubles to himself, who gives all his emotions tongue, who when he
shrinks with his mind shrinks with his body also, who when
he is startled mentally starts bodily, and so, instead of
being self-contained, is always pouring himself out, even at
the very finger-tips. We suppose that she has asked Signor
Vitaliani to mark strongly this contrast between Macbeth
and his lady. In his excess of zeal accordingly that gentleman invents a performance equalled only in its more frantic
passages by the dancing of Mr. Robson in the choruses of
Vilikins and his Dinah. He wriggles, leaps, and pirouettes,
serving undoubtedly as a tremendous foil to the impassive
figure of the lady who when his fits are most distressing
commonly stands by his side.

Lady Macbeth is, of course, the entire play at the
Lyceum, and Madame Ristori can have studied no part
with more care than is manifest from her presentment of
this character. These are some of the main points in her
conception of it.

In Macbeth's letter, which she is reading when she enters
first, it is not to be overlooked that, by her intonation of
the passage, "They made themselves air into which they

vanished", she expresses the deep awe which supernatural occurrences awaken in her. She is not less sensitive than Macbeth to the terror they produce.

After her first interview with her husband, when she has been nerving him to murder Duncan, and her face has brightened with contentment at a half-accomplished purpose, on his saying to her "We will speak further", the manner of exit is peculiar; she has her hands upon him, and with a persuasive yet compelling force urges him on, smiling the while with firm-set lips and nodding satisfaction at her work. He is in her power; he moves at her urging.

When Lady Macbeth appears next she is inviting Duncan with false courtesies into the castle that shall be his tomb, and there is much subtlety in the art which makes the spirit of the fox apparent in the manner of these humble and graceful solicitations. It is not overacted. There is a false tone in her voice, a false expression playing faintly now and then across her face, always intensest when the spoken words are humblest; they are courtesies with which women may lead men to their death, exciting no suspicion in their victims. Then follows the scene in which she breaks her entire purpose to Macbeth. When at the close he, for the first time, speaks as an accomplice, her face brightens with exultation at a purpose all accomplished, and as the act closes she repeats the old manner of exit. He is in her hands, and she, with a gentle familiarity persuading yet compelling, urges him on.

So the act ends. Again in the next act, when the murder is to be done, she, nerved to the deed, outwardly impassive and disdainful of his starts and contortions, again pushes him before with her own hands, persuading and compelling him across the threshold of King Duncan's chamber. Afterwards there is a wild—but not a loud—defiance in her tone when she shows him her own hands red with the blood of the grooms. When the house has been alarmed, and she affects

dismay and anxiety, Madame Ristori, without making the
terror that is assumed too manifestly hypocritical, marks
clearly to the spectators the difference between that and the
terror that is real.   She does not know how her husband
has dealt with the grooms, and listens with intense and real
anxiety till he has told her as well as all the rest that he has
killed them.   Presently afterwards she is struck with a real
horror as Macbeth tells how he had found the murdered
king, "His silver skin laced with his golden blood".   She
had before passed rapidly over the admission to herself that
she with her own hand would have killed Duncan "had he
not resembled her father as he slept".   She had hurried
over the thought as one not to be dwelt upon, and showed
a fine taste in so doing.   Macbeth afterwards inadvertently
thrusts it home into her heart, and then the point is made
that ninety-nine actresses in a hundred would assuredly have
tried to make before.

In the next act, during the banquet scene, Lady Macbeth
is supposed to ascribe her husband's horror at the ghost to
the death not of Banquo but of Duncan.   Madame Ristori's
timing of the glances of anxiety towards her husband, and
of the solicitous courtesies towards the guests, is always
excellent.   Her recurrence to the aspect of face in which
she had nerved him for the murder, when she attempts now
to nerve Macbeth against the terror of the spectre, is suggestive.   When Macbeth says—

> "The times have been
> That, when the brains were out, the man would die,
> And there an end, but now they rise again,"

Lady Macbeth drinks from a large bowl of wine; the cup is
in her hand when she tries to recall her husband to the
guests; she does not lay it down until after the next appearance of the spectre.   On the night of Duncan's murder she
had made addition to her courage by the help of wine.   She
feels it sinking now.

When she next goes to Macbeth, after having anxiously provided occupation for each guest, and warns him in the old way, at Macbeth's retort upon her of his marvel,

> " When I now think you can behold such sights,
> And keep the natural ruby of your cheeks,"

the sight before her mind's eye is the murdered Duncan. Her spirit has been on the rack, but she has kept down every cry, no eye has seen the torture she has borne; from this last wrench she flinches bodily, and we see now that her strength begins to fail. Those words of Macbeth mark the turning point in Madame Ristori's personation of the lady's character. She meets them with the action of an eager, startled hush! She hurries away the guests in a voice of which the tone betrays intense nervous emotion. Then, when she is alone with her husband, and he in his wild pacing up and down comes suddenly upon her still face, over which a new expression is now creeping, he recoils as from another spectre. After that she replies to his questions in the tone of one wearily disregardful of their import. As Macbeth continues talking, and his talk is of domestic treachery, of the weird sisters, of wading in blood, she watches him with a face of which the expression becomes more and more spectral, and when she says,

> "You lack the season of all natures, sleep,"

there is a weariness of soul and body in her voice and manner, and with a weary step she quits the stage with him.

We see her next, for the last time, in the sleep-walking scene. Her look is haggard, utterly haggard, her whole aspect is spectral, her action slow and painfully nervous in its manner, her voice low, full of such weariness as follows acute and exhausting pain. Her exit, when her mind has recurred to the night of the murder, is with a ghostly repetition of the old gesture of urging Macbeth on before her.

This scene over, and Lady Macbeth's death announced, short work is made by the adapter of the following part of the play, which is condensed into a single page of the libretto.

August 1.—At the farewell benefit of Mr. Alfred Wigan the quality of the retiring actor was expressed significantly by the nature of the audience assembled in his honour. The best intellect of London was, on that occasion, fully represented on the benches of the small OLYMPIC THEATRE. Mr. Wigan had attained perfection in some branches of his art, was appreciated, and had, as all thought, many years before him to be used in widening the bounds of his success. What he has already done, however, would suffice to satisfy no mean ambition, even if public success were the one aim and comfort of existence. But every man's happiness has many sources, and when one spring dies another may increase its flow.

August 15.—The transfer of the management of this theatre into the hands of Mr. Robson and Mr. Emden was marked by the production before a crowded auditory of Mr. Wilkie Collins's dramatic story, *The Lighthouse*, which then for the first time passed to the public stage out of the drawing-room theatres at Tavistock or Campden House. It may be that one's judgment was obscured by an involuntary comparison, in each passage, of the acting of Mr. Robson with the intensity of life that Mr. Dickens gave to the same character. The public has had recent opportunity of seeing that the genius of Mr. Dickens can take hold of us as surely through the spoken as the written word. But I believe the truth to be that Mr. Robson is most perfectly at home, and can be seen to the best advantage, in those parts by which his reputation has been made ; and that his success in parts of serious interest will be greatest in those which, like Daddy Hardacre, permit him to add to his strokes of passion some fantastic touches that provoke us unexpectedly to mirth. In Aaron Gurnock the whole interest is serious ; he has an enfeebled body and a stricken soul, solemn awe of the spirit-world, emotions shifting with the changes of his bodily condition and of the events that pass around him. Full of interest, full of fine touches of the artist's power, is Mr. Robson's personation of the part ; but it is not one of his triumphs.

August 29.—Immediately upon the expiration of Mr. Charles Kean's dramatic season, the PRINCESS'S THEATRE was reopened by Mr. Willert Beale for twelve nights of opera.

Mr. Charles Kean's season is memorable for the liberality by which it was distinguished. Four plays were produced, all mounted not only in the most costly way, but so mounted as to create out of the theatre a brilliant museum for the student, in which Mexican antiquities, the days of English chivalry, Greek and Etruscan forms were presented, not as dusty, broken relics, but as living truths, and made attractive as well by their splendour as by the haze of poetry through which they were to be seen. True, there is not much poetry in *Pizarro*, and *Pizarro* was the least successful of the four revivals. Mr. Charles Kean is right in feeling that there is no Atlas except Shakespeare for the world he fashions. Energetic, conscientious in exact fulfilment of his purpose, working hard without a sordid motive, although followed always by success on the peculiar path he has adopted, Mr. Kean does the work he has appointed for himself, and he has never done it more efficiently than during the last twelve months.

The new opera season is of a kind to maintain the accustomed state of the benches in the theatre. The operas most in fashion—not the best—sung by a company which includes Madame Grisi, Madame Alboni, Madame Gassier, and Signor Mario, and helped by a band and chorus chosen honestly out of the staff of the great opera-houses, entertains the town at play-house prices, and defies the weather. The stalls and boxes fill ; the pit does not quite fill. Your true man of the pit prefers Mozart and Rossini.

September 19.—ADELPHI.—*The Pilot* has been reproduced, with most effective scenery, machinery, and costume, for the purpose of restoring to the stage Mr. T. P. Cooke's super-essential representation of the model stage-sailor, as Long Tom Coffin. His performance is a marvel. The singing voice is gone, and that is all; nevertheless the songs are given with effect. For about five minutes of hornpipe the veteran's breath is good, and his feet are as nimble as they were when they twinkled for the pleasure of our forefathers. The acting is as full of quiet touches that bespeak the actor's genius, and for all that belongs to the stage-sailor—love of salt water, grogs, quids of tobacco, devotion, patriotism, power of engaging in terrific combat any dozen of another nation, dying true to his ship, and recovering suddenly from death at the call of duty—Mr. Fitzball has determined that the gods shall accuse him of shortcoming in no one particular. The plot of *The Pilot* is clear enough to keep the audience well inter-ested, and just misty enough to amuse them with its puzzles. No doubt it is all right, but I for my own part never can make out whether the sentimental hero is not at last rewarded for his goodness by obtaining leave to contract marriage with his sister. If the renegade who turns out to be his father be also, as I take him to be, Cecilia's father, and this hero marry at last the Cecilia of his love—as the final tableau, in the midst of a sea-fight, leads us to suppose he will—what will they say at Doctors' Commons?

October 10.—As Harry Hallyard, Mr. T. P. Cooke is again faithful to My Poll and my Partner Joe, though sorely tried at last by doubts of the fidelity of both. In this drama he is both a fresh-water and a salt-water sailor, a Thames waterman in the first act, and afterwards (having been taken by the press-gang out of the midst of the frolic that was to precede his wedding) the most heroic sailor on board H.M.S. *Polyphemus*. He dances a double hornpipe; fights the man who "never forgives an injury"—the diabolical captain of a slaver; comes home, is heartbroken by what he finds, and then is made heart-whole again. The piece is mounted with new and effective scenery. Mimic watermen tug at their boats upon a mimic Thames. The slaveship in the second act seems to be speeding through the waters, and when it is boarded by the men of the *Polyphemus*, there is such brisk fighting, such firing of guns, hand-to-hand battle, with an unexpected shooting down of the wicked slave captain at a critical moment by the comic character who lies hidden inside a barrel, that the audience is worked up to an exceedingly high point of jubilation. To the comic character—Watchful Waxend, a psalm-singing cobbler—Mr. Wright's acting gives importance. In the first act, throughout which Mr. Waxend, who has many weaknesses of the flesh, is to a limited extent fuddled, Mr. Wright found substance in his part on which to found a very finished bit of acting. Afterwards little was asked of him except simple extravagance.

October 24.—A new comedy by Mr. Adolphus Troughton, entitled *Leading Strings*, was produced last Monday evening at the OLYMPIC. It is an early work by M. Scribe, planned afresh and rewritten, therefore a new comedy. The most noticeable fact in the performance was the complete transformation of Mr. Addison into a faithful, addleheaded, old family butler, Binnings, who has also a son to manage, and who, as a father, clothes himself in thunder. The other day, Mr. Addison had so perfectly transformed himself into the old boatman at the Lighthouse that he shared honours with Mr. Robson. Now, in a part altogether different, he divides honours with Mrs. Stirling, and has proved himself an artist in the true sense of the word. Dramas always have been well acted at the OLYMPIC, and Mr. Addison has borne his part well in a most efficient company; but if he can keep the ground he has won in *The Lighthouse* and in *Leading Strings*, as we believe he can, there is a new pleasure established for the playgoer.

Love's Labour's Lost—The Comedy of Leisure—ought to

be acceptable as a relief to busy men in anxious times. It has been observed that there is only one morsel of business in the whole play, and that is mentioned to be postponed till to-morrow. The play as now acted at SADLER'S WELLS runs daintily and pleasantly. They err who see in it only a caricature of euphuism. Euphuism, when the comedy appeared, was a language of compliment congenial to the temper of the times, and in many of its forms, while it was not less absurd than the tone of compliment conventional in our own day, it was a great deal wittier and wiser. There was room for wit in the invention of conceits, and an amusing ingenuity in their extravagance.

> "Thou shin'st in every tear that I do weep;
> No drop but as a coach doth carry thee."

Shakespeare undoubtedly took pleasure in this way of frolic with the wit; it is a form of fancy, and over the whole range of fancy he was lord. Pleasant euphuisms find their way even into his graver plays, and in this play, which he devoted to a chasing of conceit through all its forms, the most poetical and the most prosy, it is manifest that he not only heartily enjoyed the sport himself, but that it must have given special pleasure to the men of his own day.

He laughed no doubt at the hollowness of all conceits, and represented them as labour lost, his sharpest satire being expressed in the part of "Don Adriano de Armado, a fantastical Spaniard". This is the part assumed at SADLER'S WELLS by Mr. Phelps.

It has a certain general resemblance to his Malvolio, inasmuch as these are both fantastical and foolish men; but Mr. Phelps defines clearly the essential difference between the two. One was a substantial and not ignorant steward, covering with affectations a substantial ambition to become the husband of his rich and beautiful mistress, and to be a lord. The other is a man who carries all his bravery outside. He talks conceitedly of love, and in his soul carries enshrined the image of a country drab, its best

ideal. He affects finery of speech, and is so utterly destitute of ideas that to count three he must depend upon the
help of a child who is his servant, and his master in all
passages of wit. He carries a brave outside of clothes, but
cannot fight in his shirt, because, as he is driven to admit,
"the naked truth of it is, I have no shirt". This is the
view of his character to which Mr. Phelps gives prominence
by many a clever touch, such as the empty drawl on the
word love, whenever Armado uses it, or the lumbering
helplessness of wit displayed by the great Spaniard when
magnificently and heavily conversing with the tiny Moth,
in which part little Miss Rose Williams has been taught to
bring out very perfectly some telling points.

We must not part from the play without praising the
Biron of Mr. Henry Marston, the clever rendering of the
conceits of the Schoolmaster and Curate by Mr. Williams
and Mr. C. Fenton, and the Ferdinand of Mr. F. Robinson.
Mrs. Charles Young—who is new to London, and has,
during the last few weeks, taken honours at SADLER'S
WELLS in two or three characters—looked and spoke like a
lady as Princess of France, and Miss Fitzpatrick did fair
justice to her talent as the laughing Rosaline.

November 14.—HAYMARKET.—Mr. Tom Taylor's three-
act drama, *An Unequal Match*, was produced for the first
time at this house last Saturday night with unequivocal
success. As a literary work it is by no means the best of
Mr. Taylor's plays, but as a new play, exactly suited to the
company by which it is performed, it is very good indeed.
The hero, retired from disappointment in love with a
woman of the world, becomes enamoured of a child of
nature in a Yorkshire dale. She is a blacksmith's daughter,
and he is found by his fine friends carrying her milking-
cans and offering her marriage. Though he learns now
that by an uncle's death during the time of his withdrawal
from society he has become a baronet, he abides by his
troth. Sir Harry Arncliffe takes to wife the blacksmith's

daughter, Hester Grazebrook, in spite of the amusement of his fashionable friends and the profound consternation of his man Blenkinsop.

In the second act we find the world, represented by a crowd of polite visitors at Arncliffe Manor, shrugging its shoulders at the frank way in which Lady Arncliffe gives expression to her natural tastes and affections. The husband chafes, instructs his wife how she must do at Rome as Rome does, and then leaves her, on a plea of business, to go to Ems for recovery from a first outbreak of consumption that he has concealed from her. His old love, the woman of the world—Lady Montresor—is among the guests at the manor, and has been sowing sorrow between man and wife. She also starts for Ems, and Hester believes herself wronged. She resolves then to fight the world with its own weapons.

The scene of the third act is the German watering-place. Arncliffe is taking his ease there with restored health. Lady Montresor is there flirting. Hester, who has spent a twelve-month at home in learning everything, and has become an Admirable Crichton of her sex, is creating a sensation at German courts as *die schöne Engländerin*. She appears at last, plays the fine lady's part, shows herself perfect in all her husband's lessons, discomfits her rival utterly, and only at last shows that she has rubbed in the polish without rubbing out the better nature underneath. The marriage of the baronet and blacksmith's daughter made the first unequal match, but more unequal is the match when a right-hearted woman accepts battle with those who can bring to the combat only artificial weapons. That is the tenor of the closing sentiment.

The plot is of a hackneyed character, but Mr. Tom Taylor does not work it out by use of only hackneyed details. There is a complete change of circumstance in every act; this keeps alive the attention of the audience. There are three phases of character to be presented by the heroine, Miss Amy Sedgwick, who is in the first act naïve to the utmost degree as a country lass, and in the last act, to the utmost degree short of burlesque, the manufactured lady of high fashion.   This was Miss Sedgwick's first appearance here in a part for the acting of which she was without help from traditions of the stage.   Her success was great, and it was fairly earned.   Then, again, as a gentleman's gentleman, Mr. Compton had the best opportunity of bringing his peculiar humour to the support of the play. Mr. Buckstone, fitted with a less amusing part, first as a rustic Æsculapius, touched with sentiment, then as a fine lady's body doctor, then as the betitled and bestarred physician to a little German duke, also pervades the piece, and keeps the audience in perpetual good-humour.   All the other parts are well sustained, and Mr. W. Farren brings out quietly and well what few points of character the author has accorded to his hero.

November 28.—OLYMPIC.— *What will they say at Brompton ?* is an elegant little piece, properly called a comedietta.   The laughter it excites is moderate, the pleasure it gives great.   The author, Mr. Stirling Coyne, has planned it ingeniously for the purpose of placing Mr. Robson in a very ludicrously serious position, and then working him up by successive disclosures to a climax of grotesque terror. The actor's terror is so real that, while there is much laughter at its odd manifestations, there is enough of serious impression made to check any great outbreak of mirth.

December 12.—The place of *Boots at the Swan,* heretofore occupied by Mr. Keeley, has been taken, and will for a long time be kept, by Mr. Robson.   Mr. Keeley was a true Boots; Mr. Robson also is a true Boots.   To the same order of Boots each actor refers his part most clearly, but not to the same genus of that order.   Mr. Keeley was not only deaf but humorously stolid; Mr. Robson, although deaf, is humorously wide-awake.   He is the Boots who is brisk,

and alive to all the humour of the street, who would be pre-
ternaturally knowing if he could but hear what people say.
In word and look and action he is more the *gamin* than the
simpleton.   The extravagance of a most laughable farce is
heightened by him to the utmost, and there is not a long
face to be seen in the house while he is busy on the stage.

1858, *January* 23.—There has not been produced for
some years so dainty a little play as Mr. Leigh Hunt's
Lovers' Amazements, first acted on Wednesday last at the
LYCEUM.   For a time one might be in doubt whether it
did not make its appeal to a more refined audience than
that which is usually addressed in this country by the
dramatic author, but the doubt was unjust to the poet.
The genial spirit of his work was not to be resisted.   A
cleverly devised web of small perplexities leading to neat
and original dramatic situations, a dialogue passing frequently from delicate raillery or brisk battle of wit into
some strain of unaffected poetry that puts the heart's best
thoughts into a simple music, welcome even to the most
untrained ear, had their effect.   Moreover, there is an air
of chivalry about the play.   Homage to woman is the
essence of its plot.   The charm of the story lies in the fact
that it sets two pairs of lovers wandering in a maze to meet
each other at most unexpected turns, and become hopelessly entangled, until one of them, dashing against a barrier,
breaks a way through for them all.   This he does in a
most reprehensible and unfair manner, and yet to the
satisfaction of them all.   " I have done it, though," he
says, and there's the comfort.   The story is not one to
be told otherwise than as the author tells it.   I can only
say that it is the story of two ladies and two gentlemen ;
that each lady in the party of four has fancied love for one
gentleman, and felt it for the other ; that each gentleman
has done as much by the two ladies ; and that exaggerated
records of the likings help to mystify the loves.   All the
four people are lovable people and good friends, however

they may cross swords or wits ; the character of each is defined with pleasant touches, and the gentlemen, who take high ground—one as a brave lord of creation, and the other as a brave, good-natured fop—are effectually humbled before the ladies, who in many a pleasant line put to the blush the pomp and pride of man, and the unequal bargain that he generally offers to his mate.

February 27.—HAYMARKET.—Beatrice, in *Much Ado about Nothing*, is not one of Miss Amy Sedgwick's best characters. In the earlier scenes the stage-laugh is too forced and too frequent, but in the later scenes she succeeds better. As Mr. Howe, who excels in this play, without abating any of the mirth of Benedick, presents him as a soldier and a gentleman, so does Miss Sedgwick show, in Beatrice, behind the mask of a gay mockery, the gentle spirit of a woman. In the garden scene, after listening to Hero and Ursula, she shows that her heart had not been filled with a new thought, but only opened—

> " For others say thou dost deserve ; and I
> Believe it *better* than reportingly."

Miss Sedgwick's Beatrice is in fact hearty in her love as in her mirth, and that is right. The distinct representing of this is the best feature in her performance. As for Mr. Compton, Shakespeare himself would have liked to shake hands with an actor who could play his Dogberry so well.

Louis XI is a melodrama in five acts. The first act is unnecessary, for it tells nothing that could not have been expressed by four minutes' conversation following the old stage-direction, " Enter two gentlemen, meeting." The last two acts only work out, at twice the necessary length, an idea that has been already expressed. Louis XI is the chief person of the play, and is the play. Parricide, fratricide, cunningly wicked, he is an old man on the borders of the grave, painfully hovering between earth and hell. To fix his hold on earth he clings to his body physician, to secure rescue from hell he grasps the skirt of the priest, but he still loads his conscience with offence and has the executioner for his companion.   To present such a man's character with all its deep contrasts brought into direct apposition for the production of those bold effects which please the melodramatist has been the business of M. Casimir Delavigne.   The English version of the play, reproduced this week at the PRINCESS's, supplies Mr. Charles Kean with his finest character.   His Louis XI is a striking picture, painted no doubt in the bold way which accepts none but the brightest colours of the prism, after the manner of the old illuminators, but none the less striking for that.   It is in such characters that Mr. Kean excels, and he mingles with the presentment of this one a quaint, half-humorous sense of the grotesque that greatly heightens its effect.   Whatever faults there may be in the piece—and they are neither few nor small—there is none in the actor, who depicts the mind of an old king as the illuminators would have shown his body to us, and completely hides under the work his own identity.

March 13.—At the OLYMPIC Mr. Morton's farce of *Ticklish Times* is full of practical fun, and supplies Mr. Robson with a part in which he may produce laughter without limit by the boldest plunge into the grotesque.   He is Mr. Griggs, a newly-married husband with a somewhat weak brain, and an intolerance of the tickle of a whisper in his ear, who in the days of the Pretender went to London upon patriotic business, came back and found his wife sheltering a man who claimed also to be Griggs.   This man is an attainted baronet, the husband of the dearest friend of Mrs Griggs, but the real Mr. Griggs will not be whispered to, and cannot understand.   His mind gives way under bewilderment. Mr. Robson has then the whole world of grotesque before him, and he knows his way through it to a substantial success.

April 17.—The HAYMARKET Opera has this week opened

with *The Huguenots*, and a new prima donna, Mdlle. Titiens, to give freshness to the part of Valentine. Mdlle. Titiens did not receive extravagant applause, but she was heartily appreciated. She has a clear, not very sweet soprano, steady, accurate, and of extensive range, a voice quite under her control, that gives the comfort of reliable sound to the ear. I did not observe any indication of original genius as an actress, but among conventional actresses she is one of the best upon the lyric stage. This impression is set down after a first hearing only. Better acquaintance may disclose in her yet higher faculties.

May 22.—Mdlle. Titiens has since the last report given new strength to the cast of *Don Giovanni* by an admirable performance of the part of Donna Anna. I admire her less in the *Trovatore*, though the Leonora of that opera gives her opportunity of further proving the range, power, and stability of voice, which we may hope ere long to see employed in doing justice to another Leonora. I suspect that Mdlle. Titiens can both sing and act as Beethoven's Leonora better than any lady who has yet enabled us to hear *Fidelio* on the Italian stage.

June 19.—It is announced that the engagement of this lady is now drawing to a close, but she has earned a permanent position in the London opera, and will not be lost to the public. We cannot spare from our double opera troupe a good actress and an accomplished singer, who is most at home in the best music.

At the PRINCESS'S *The Merchant of Venice* is the new Shakespearean spectacle. Beyond question this is the best of Mr. Kean's revivals. The literary alterations that have been made in the acted play consist only in judicious restorations of the text, which give not only more interest to the play, but also more importance to the character of Portia. Mrs. Charles Kean's Portia is known as one of the parts in which she best displays her power as an artist, while Mr. Charles Kean is seldom seen to more advantage than as

Shylock. The scenery is so contrived as to suggest the whole idea of Venice, and the play is only better understood when thus presented with the local colouring that was in Shakespeare's mind, marked strongly by the scene-painter. Even the interpolated dance, which in some former revivals has appeared to me inopportune, being introduced here, at the close of an act, as that music and dance of masqued revellers in the street under Jessica's window, against which Shylock had warned her to lock up his doors and shut his house's ears, is such a show as Shakespeare might have been content to see appended to his text.

June 26.—Madame Ristori having appeared this week in two characters translated from Rachel's French *répertoire,* one or two words of comparison become inevitable. The two actresses differ widely from each other. Rachel dazzled and startled us by flashing an electric life into words and lines. She was unrivalled in the power of giving an intensity of meaning to a single phrase. Madame Ristori has this kind of power, but she has it in a less degree ; her excellence appears to lie in a clear artistic conception of each part she represents, a resolute subordination of every detail to the just working out of the central thought, and this not seldom to the sacrifice of stage-effects easily produced, sure of applause, but false in taste.

Perhaps I cannot define Madame Ristori's genius better than by dwelling on her treatment of the part of Phèdre ; the result being that, where Rachel inspired terror, Madame Ristori awakens pity. The new Phèdre is a woman full of all honour and modesty, cursed by the supernatural wrath of Venus with an impure passion. Her natural modesty struggles in vain against relentless fate, but that it does struggle, that Phèdre is a hapless woman, victim to the passions of the gods, Madame Ristori sets forth as the fact that is the soul of the whole tragedy. Racine herein exactly followed the plan of the Greek tragedians, whose purpose was not to develop character, but to display in some great passion the fulfilment of a Fate.

In the first act Phèdre tells Œnone, with all womanly shame, the passion for Hippolytus that had been raised within her by the hatred of Venus. She is resisting it while it is killing her. She keeps him from her sight, forbids the mention of his name, battles against the curse with what weapons are in a woman's power, and still feels its edge. All this in the first act Madame Ristori paints by many touches of her art. Then follows presently her interview with Hippolytus, which she has sought, after the supposed death of her husband Theseus, for honest purposes of state. She approaches timidly and with averted eyes; and while her eyes are still averted, her speech begins to run as Fate wills that it must, she half looks towards Hippolytus, then wholly looks, and only by a strong effort restrains herself from running to embrace him. The passion of animal love masters her. In marvellous contrast to her natural manner, the modest Phèdre, possessed by her curse, yearns with a supernatural intensity of lust towards Hippolytus. When she has bared her secret to the youth a look of intense horror marks her sense of her position; she struggles to recover ground, and is again lost in a fury of desire. When, at last, seeing no friendship in the face of Hippolytus, she is suddenly attempting to slay herself with his sword, there is a strange hurry of madness in her passion, and she is drawn away with face convulsed as one exhausted by the paroxysms of a fit that is upon her still. Phèdre has won our sympathy and pity, even here.

In the next act Phèdre is with Œnone, and her first passages enable Madame Ristori to mark strongly again the natural instincts of the woman shrinking from the shame and terror of her curse. But the passion soon returns to overwhelm the shame. Then come the tidings that her husband is alive and has returned. She is all woman again, too honest to keep her secret, welcoming death, but dreading shame, and

dwelling with intensity of womanly pathos on the future day
when her children shall blush for their mother's memory.
Exquisite is Madame Ristori's by-play while the insidious
counsel of Œnone is being given. When she counsels
accusation of the innocent Hippolytus, Phèdre with the
whole energy of her soul repels the crime, and, as Œnone
stills counsels, covers her face, stops her ears. But Theseus
comes, she sees Hippolytus, and becomes powerless. Her
words to Theseus, when she retires from his presence, are
spoken from the heart of a sad woman, not with the guileful
purpose of an assassin. Œnone takes her away. The wrath
of Theseus against Hippolytus Phèdre at once hurries to
appease, even at the cost of her own disgrace, but the
current of her thoughts is violently checked by the discovery
that upon Aricie alone the affections of Hippolytus are
fixed. While her mind pauses under the shock of this new
thought, Theseus has left her, and her evil counsellor Œnone
comes. In the succeeding dialogue Madame Ristori em-
ploys all her skill for the complete definition of her reading
of the part. She dwells with the purest tenderness upon
those lines which change a cry of passion into womanly
perception of the beauty of innocent love in Hippolytus and
Aricie, and pass on to a sigh for her own misery. Presently,
in a transport of passion, she desires the ruin of Aricie, but
from that passion falls into the deepest horror at the thoughts
of her own heart. She cries for a hiding-place from gods
and men. But the gods are her kindred, and she finds them
everywhere ; her tone of supernatural awe thrills through the
audience at the words

> "Il padre e rè de' Numi
> Avo mi fu : degli avi miei son pieni
> La terra, il mar, l' Olimpo.   Ove celarmi ?"

In hell her father Minos is the judge ; she pictures herself
before him, and here Madame Ristori is at the very crisis of
her part.   She acts the judgment scene with the energy of a

wild terror, she pleads to her father and judge that it was
the wrath of a hostile god that fell upon her in that shape of
sin. Flying, shrinking, cowering, pressing her hands down
over the head upon which, while she speaks, the scathing
lightnings seem to be rained down, she cries with a wild
despair,

> "Ah! nò perdona !
> Un Dio crudele, un Dio la tua progenie
> Tutta dannò !"

and falls senseless beneath the stroke. Beyond those lines
the speech of Phèdre runs in Racine, and in the Italian translation, to a simple plaint. This Madame Ristori properly
omits. She has struck the key-note of the tragedy with a
power beyond anything Racine ever supposed to lie. in his
couplets when he wound the speech up with five lines of anti-
climax. From her swoon Phèdre is aroused by the voice of
Œnone giving impure counsel. She passionately spurns the
tempter who has made the downward way for her so smooth.
In the last act, when we have heard of the death of Hippolytus, we see Madame Ristori's Phèdre but once more, at
all cost to her own fame, serving truth and honour with her
latest breath. Fate is fulfilled, and she is now quietly dying
as a stainless woman in the arms of her maidens ; stainless,
yet in such deep debasement at the memory of her great
shame that her last thought is of closing in death eyes that
by their immodest glances have defiled the light of heaven.

I need not show wherein a conception of this kind, carefully and harmoniously elaborated in every detail, differs
from the Phèdre of Rachel. In as far as it is the development of a Fate, it is, of course, and so was Rachel's, the
Phèdre of Racine. As the development of a character it is
certainly the most poetical, and we think also the most
legitimate, deduction from the words that are to be said.
Dramatists of Racine's school never have painted character
with a firm hand in distinct and consistent touches ; they
leave always something for the actor to create.

In the modern play, *Adrienne Lecouvreur,* there is no
Fate, and there is development of character, but that we
have after the manner of the melodramatist, who, as he now
plies his art, differs as much from the true dramatist as
any second-class scene-painter may differ from a Turner.
In a play like *Adrienne Lecouvreur* there is nothing to interpret ; the writer stimulates and satisfies dull wits with a
series of broad and obvious stage-effects, and provides his
leading personage with the greatest possible number of
showy points and situations.   An English fashionable
audience can lift itself by an effort to the comprehension of
an *Adrienne Lecouvreur* in the drama, as in music it can
grasp such ideas as those of Donizetti or the Earl of Westmoreland.   But *Adrienne* is a clever work after its kind,
and Madame Ristori has a rare courage in refusing points,
however sure to fetch applause, when it is bad taste in
the dramatist that has obtruded them for her acceptance.
Take for example the famous declamation scene.   Throughout the play Adrienne moves like a breath of fresh air and
sunshine through the stifling atmosphere of a licentious
court.   She comes as the actress of the day to recite before
a brilliant company in the salons of the Princess, who is her
unknown rival.   The two women become known to each
other.   It is only when the smooth hypocrisy and un-
womanly cruelty of the Princess have stirred her blood
to the utmost that, upon being forced to recite under torture, she chooses that passage from *Phèdre* which closes
with a stroke into the heart of the smooth sinner.   Very
characteristic of Madame Ristori is the way in which this
recitation is delivered.   She does not, as the dramatist intended, and as Rachel acted the passage, work up to a
grand stage-effect by visible and bodily denunciation of her
enemy.   She is an actress, and a simple-minded one, re-
citing before a grand assemblage ; after the recitation she
is handed to her carriage, and departs with all formal
exchange of courtesies, and therefore in the recitation she

is guilty of no breach of etiquette. When she begins, the Princess, to torture her the more, is toying and trifling with her lover. As she proceeds there is a strangeness about her manner that attracts even the Princess's attention ; the intensity of the direction of her mind causes in Adrienne a slight and instinctive approach of the body towards her tormentor, but she hardly looks at her, she does not point at her by any discourteous outward sign, when suddenly she brands her in the poet's lines with all the forces of her soul. Rachel's was for most people the more effective, but unquestionably this is the finer reading of the situation. Then follows the business with the poisoned bouquet, which gives room for an unlimited display of dramatic power. Madame Ristori, as in duty bound, elaborately paints the pains of death, but she dwells on the spiritual part of the suffering, and reduces to as little as will satisfy her sense of what is natural the presentation of mere physical distress. The low, quick, unearthly cry with which she draws her face back from the box which she has just opened, when the scent of the poisoned bouquet rises from it and strikes death into her, is a marvellous dramatic sound, wholly distinct from the voice of misery that follows when she looks on the returned bouquet as an insult from the man she loved. When Maurice the Count comes to her with his love in her last hour, and she in her delirium is fancying herself upon the stage again, with Maurice in a box, to whom the Princess enters, he may hear how large a part he was in the poor girl's life by the agony of expostulation in the cry " Maurizio ! Maurizio !" by which she seeks to draw him from the rival's side. Indeed, there are several words and passages in the last act of *Adrienne Lecouvreur* which Madame Ristori delivers with an intensity of dramatic expression that reminds us of the peculiar powers of Rachel. But the whole spirit in which she acts is different. The quiet fondness with which the dying girl places her lover's head in her lap, the last look of affection towards him, and of friendship towards the old prompter as she joins their palms within hers, in one gesture of prayer, when in the act of death, are in the true manner of an actress all whose characters are women, and as natural women as, in each case, the dramatist will suffer her to make them.

July 3.—Alfieri has made of Ottavia, the wronged wife of Nero, an impossible woman. The play he founded on her is remarkably well developed, and especially to be noticed for its skilful opening, but his depiction of the heroine is a distinct example of the bad character-painting that often occurs in the "pure drama" of the Continent. Nero sends for her from banishment, and she comes home to stand as a lamb before her butcher, impatient of the presence of her base rival Poppæa, but to Nero obedient and loving; she has been silent while he slaughtered her mother, her brother, and her friend—now she waits, brimful of love, to be slaughtered in her turn; her love does not disappear, though some of her patience does, when she is threatened with infamy as well as death, and at last, when shrinking from shame and torture she gets poison from Seneca, she, not altogether in bitterness, asks pardon of her husband for depriving him of the pleasure of killing her himself at his own leisure. And yet this mild lady says hard things at odd times, because the poet often thought more of the point in his lines than of the substance in his characters. Probably the defect of the play would have been lessened if some touch of human nature had been given to the character of Nero, if it were only some glimpse of a past life to account for Ottavia's love. But there is nothing. He is such a tyrant as a boy might paint. Having this impression of Ottavia, we were unable to foresee how Madame Ristori would read the part.

She so reads it as to reconcile not all its contradictions, but more than we had been used to consider reconcilable. Ottavia, she remembers, is a Roman matron, and, moreover, a Roman queen, last of a royal line. She represents her, therefore, stately in every gesture, her attitudes are royal attitudes, and magnificent in every look and tone and movement is the expression of the height from which she looks down as the daughter of a line of kings, and as a wife without reproach, upon the base-born and immodest Poppæa. In her fidelity to Nero, again, Madame Ristori represents Ottavia as animated, not by sentimental love, but by the virtue of a Roman matron. She is true to her duty, but submissive in a Roman and a queenly way; she does not flinch before her husband, and can tell him a stern truth sometimes. The charge of incontinence bewilders and astonishes before it angers her, but that such a charge should be laid upon her by Poppæa is the deepest wrong. Immeasurable is the quiet scorn that Madame Ristori puts into the words

"Poppea
Bassi amori mi appone."

In scenes with Poppæa she usually will not deign to look at her, to notice that she speaks; when she obtrudes herself Ottavia turns to Nero; but whenever the Queen, proud of her lineage and of her virtue, does speak of her or to her, exquisitely cruel and quiet is the expression of a disdain to which her deep wrath against the woman who so shamelessly usurps Ottavia's place gives only a more settled intensity.

"Ben m' è vergogna in ver, rival nomarmi
Di Poppea——"

She twists the very name of the unfortunate woman who writhes under its sting into a word of scorn that has a dozen cruel modulations, and she dies with that word on her lips, or its equivalent,—

"Conoscerai frattanto un dì—*costei*."

We have dwelt only on the main feature in Madame Ristori's Ottavia. The patient gentleness of spirit is not left out of the study, but the portraiture is taken from the land of dreams, and made a thing of life by that addition of

a strong emphasis upon Ottavia's position as a Roman
empress strong in her own dignity, and proud that she is,
even against all discouragement, in every sense faithful to
her duty as a wife.

June 10.—The Italian version of Schiller's *Mary Stuart,*
following the lights and shades of the original, differs so
essentially from the adaptation into French by M. Pierre
Lebrun, that all comparison between the Mary Stuart of
Madame Ristori and that of Rachel is at once put out of court.
The superficial resemblance between the two versions is very
close, but Schiller's Mary Stuart had a character too full of
light and shade for the French taste, and from M. Lebrun's
version there accordingly disappear altogether those points
in which the dramatic force of the character especially
resides. Schiller's Mary Stuart is not, like M. Lebrun's, an
angel of light, who once in a great scene, that stands apart
from the rest of the play, triumphs as a scold over Queen
Elizabeth; she is not only a sad captive, but a sad woman,
much hated and much loved, with passions that have
brought a stain of murder on her soul. At the very outset
of the play she is presented, shrinking from the thought
that Darnley's ghost is abroad and will not rest until her
crime is expiated. Her death is that expiation. This,
being the core of the play, M. Lebrun cut out; to make his
picture prettier, he wiped away the shades. Madame
Ristori, happy in a character conceived with real dramatic
energy, carefully adjusts throughout the emphasis on each
detail, and, thanks to the good material on which she works,
establishes Maria Stuarda as one of the best and most interesting of her representations. We lose no sympathy for
Mary, since the evil she bears we see her bearing, and the
evil she has done we see only in her repentance over it.
Under her stillness are yet smouldering the passions that
she now repents, and in the scene with Elizabeth there is
sufficient provocation to set them again for a short time
fiercely raging. The true place of that proud, wild outbreak,

in Schiller's whole conception, is lost, if we are to regard
Mary as one who has been an angel of light from her youth
upward. And where was M. Lebrun's soul when he accepted the necessity his change of character enforced, and
in his last act changed to the mere reception of a blessing
the scene in which Mary, finding an ordained priest in
Melvil, lays at his feet her load of sin and sorrow? Madame
Ristori shows us the sad queen not only with all the pathos
of her leave-takings, but abased, content to die as expiation
for a crime that has deserved death, though innocent of
that for which she was condemned to suffer; anxiously,
painfully striving to subdue all earthly passion and to fix her
thoughts on heaven. Her eyes are nervously fixed on the
cross, as if she dared not loosen herself from it for an instant,
lest again some of the old worldly turbulence arise within
her. Then on her way to the scaffold she encounters
Leicester, the lover who has betrayed her hopes; she
struggles in vain to keep woman's thoughts out of her speech,
a faint spark of woman's passion shines through her last
words, and admirably conceived is then the eager rush of
the terror-stricken woman back to the cross, her fall upon
her knees, her anxious fastening back of her thoughts upon
it, and the still, nervous, preoccupied way in which she
walks to her death as one afraid lest any chance word or
sight should, by seizing her attention, draw her back among
the passions of the world.

By many and exquisite touches, Madame Ristori gives
prominence to the softer elements in Mary's ideal nature,
by which the poet represents her winning love, but I have
chosen rather to dwell upon those details in which lies the
distinctive character of her performance.

July 17.—With this week, Madame Ristori's performances
end for the season, and she will take her farewell benefit on
Monday in the COVENT GARDEN Opera House. For that
occasion she has chosen to appear in her last and newest
part of Queen Elizabeth in Signor Giacometti's play of

Elisabetta, Regina d'Inghilterra. The choice was wise, for there is no part in which it is so advisable that the Italian actress should be seen by those who would learn all they can of the range of her powers in a single evening. Moreover, the play is by no means bad. Signor Giacometti takes the common notions about Queen Elizabeth, and brings into bold apposition many odd contrasts of character ; she is tender and cruel, vain and heroic, playful and grim, punishing a slight with death and pardoning a deadly treason; we even see her young in one act and old in another. Simply by accepting a tradition, Signor Giacometti shelters himself against all reproach in furnishing an actress with a character that gives her opportunity of showing skill alike in comedy and tragedy, and of running up and down the whole scale of her art. He has done his work also in a pleasant spirit ; there are no inflated speeches in his play, his dialogue is rather lively than severe, and where there is passion he contents himself with indicating by a series of words what the actress must express. He works into his play all the most popular bits of the history of Queen Elizabeth, and allows all his *dramatis personæ* to grow grey before he parts with them. With Queen Elizabeth he does not part till she has died upon the stage. Unity of thought is secured by centering everything upon the love of Elizabeth for Essex. Madame Ristori, who always gives prominence to the essentials and runs lightly over the accessories in her reading of a part, works out this feature of the character with every elaboration. In illustration of her manner of dealing with accessories, take the scene in which she pardons Maria Lambourn an attempt upon her life. A dozen strong points might be made, and would be striven for by an inferior artist, but the scene is only a bit of colour meant to embody the notion that Elizabeth joined magnanimity to littleness ; it is not one of the essential portions of the story, and with a light touch, therefore, Madame Ristori runs over it, because she will not mar the just proportions of her picture. During a long play of five acts, the heroine is almost incessantly upon the stage. She sets out with comedy and ends with tragedy. She is Elizabeth with her red hair, her great frill, and her furbelow ; capricious, handsome, dangerous, hiding a love in her heart. She signs her lover's death-warrant with haggard face, ages at once when he is dead, and appears years afterwards a decrepit woman eaten with remorse and spectre-haunted ; but still vain, denying her own feebleness, still proud, asserting her own dignity ; bowed down, heart-broken, when in any snatch of solitude she dares permit her thoughts to dwell upon the lover whom she cut off in the blossom of his youth.

The play is well acted by the other members of the company, who, though they second Madame Ristori feebly enough in classical plays, know how to give life to a romantic drama.

July 31.—Signor Mario's Don Giovanni as an acted character seems to me weak. As I have said before, a hero who is presented revelling in crime with such defiant recklessness that the librettist must needs end by giving him over visibly to the torment of devils, ought to be acted as if there were meant by him something more than a graceful gentleman, with manners seductive in the daintiest and best sense of the term. I abide by the belief that Signor Ronconi's Don Giovanni was, as a dramatic conception, better than any other that has been seen on the English stage for the last twenty years.

> " Da quel ceffo si dovria
> La ner' alma giudicar"—

Elvira does not speak to the purpose when she says that, and points to the affable lover of all womankind expressed by Signor Mario. Signor Ronconi showed the cold and cruel heart of the seducer, gave prominence to his impiety, a tragic rage to his last act of defiance, and terror to the depiction of his doom. By the tradition of Tamburini, who had sung the part much better, but conceived it with less power, Signor Ronconi was judged, and his Don Giovanni was pronounced to be his one failure. He acquiesces in the decision and retires from the part. Signor Mario attempts it, and, as he makes of the part what Signor Tamburini made of it—the perfection of a stage-gentleman—he doubtless will be said to act it well.

Signor Ronconi now tries Leporello, and therein follows, as a main rule, the line laid down by Lablache, in whose buffoonery—when he conceived that he had a farce character to support—there was an unction that made it welcome even when most out of place. Signor Ronconi, being a man of original genius, and indeed by a great deal the best actor now upon the lyric stage, was of course not merely a copyist. He succeeded perfectly in the great buffo song of his part, filling it up with whimsical details and a full dramatic expression following the course of every word. He took pains to give life and natural colour to his part by showing Leporello as a serving-man with not enough of independent character to carry him out of the circle of his master's influence—a coward, volatile, unstable of purpose, ignorant, and superstitious. During the short duel in which the commandant is killed he leaps on a bench and crouches in the shadow of a wall. When one combatant has fallen he quietly takes off his hat in reverence or prayer for the dead, but he comes forward only to speak foolishness or fall into a witless levity. In the last scene also Signor Ronconi takes care to subdue his part by look and attitude into some keeping with the gravity of the situation ; but, after all, Signor Ronconi's Leporello disappoints me. Checked in his independence of conception by the scant appreciation that was the reward of his originality as Don Giovanni, probably he did not care to risk a second failure by revision of the part of Leporello as an acted character. Whatever the librettist meant, Mozart

meant more. It is possible to refer every incident in the
part of Leporello to the one central idea of cowardice,
physical and moral, and through all incidents to work out
a representation of this—and not essentially a comic one—
in a way that should be in harmony with all the music in
its gayest and its gravest strains, and should account perfectly for Leporello's otherwise most awkward retention
upon the stage during the whole of the last scene.

August 7.—As a good specimen of the music of the
French school the management of the COVENT GARDEN
OPERA has been just to the frequenters of that house, in
adding *Zampa* to the *répertoire.*

Zampa is the Don Giovanni of a Frenchman, bearing to
that of Mozart the proportion of a penny whistle to a
trumpet. He is a seductive corsair, who turns out to be
a count. Having destroyed the virtue and the life of a
saintly girl, Albina, he comes, in the presence of her statue,
to rob his brother of his bride. In defiance of the statue
he marries it with a ring. On the way to the wedding to
which he forces an unhappy bride, Albina's tomb opens,
and the statue ghost displays from it her ring. Finally, on
the wedding-night, the statue comes and carries down the
impious man through a trap-door, out of which shoot flames.
There are situations of all kinds proper to operas : lovers
wail, peasants sing wedding-songs ; hymns sound from a
church ; there is a gondolier's song under a window ; corsairs
sing a barcarole ; men dispute fiercely ; a sword is to be
proudly broken across a knee ; comic scenes of love or
terror are freely interspersed ; and it is all set to good light
music, which should please a Frenchman, but which,
because there is not a spark in it of fun or feeling—
because it is simply so much vocalisation and so much in-
strumentation—is received with dulness by an English
audience. As music, Hérold's *Zampa* is a better opera than
Flotow's *Martha.* But there is a glow of mirth and pleasure
infused into *Martha* that will retain it as a favourite upon
the stage.

September 25.—At SADLER'S WELLS the play of *The Provoked Husband* has been produced this week, and here again we have had an example of the finish with which a company well trained to work together may present a play demanding no little variety of talent. SADLER'S WELLS has a reputation for its acting of old comedy, as well earned as its credit for fidelity to Shakespeare. *The Provoked Husband* is an excellent example of the merit upon which this reputation has been based. Mr. Phelps here presents a play not because it presents a notable part for himself, but because it brings out all the force of his company. Two renderings of the part of Lord Townley are possible: one, which is not the one selected, contains a display of restless uneasiness, breaking out here and there into passion, an effective and therefore a tempting version. In the other rendering, which Mr. Phelps has chosen, Lord Townley appears with all the dignity and self-command proper to a nobleman of the old school who had a warm, strong heart, but had learnt how to contain his passions. The repose and dignity thus given to the figure of the husband serve as an admirable foil to the wife's restless levity; just as the worldly sense of Manly in the play is a foil to the folly of the Wronghead family. We are disposed to think too that this reading of the part of Lord Townley gives a solidity of light and shade to the whole play, which would not be derived from the old-fashioned proprieties of courtship between Manly and Lady Grace. And while Mr. Phelps denies himself all but the subtler indications of the feelings by which he, as a stately lord, is not to be compelled into loud bodily passion, he adds brilliancy to the part of Lady Townley. If the play has been produced for the special increase of any one artist's reputation, it has been produced for the credit of Mrs. Charles Young. This lady won her first laurels at SADLER'S WELLS, and is provided there with the best opportunities of triumph. In *The Provoked Husband* she is as truly the high-bred lady as her husband is the high-bred lord, but she is the lady who floats lightly on the surface of society, while her sedate lord is one of its foundations. She is fascinating in her folly, innocent even in the seeming heartlessness of her frivolity, so light that none can hope to fix her attention long enough to find a passage through it to her heart; and when her attention is at last rivetted by the strong measure that her husband is compelled to take, she is a woman, with a woman's nature, beautiful after all in its distress. Lady Townley is, perhaps, the part in which Mrs. Charles Young has found herself most free to exercise her skill. The other parts in the play are all well filled. Mr. Marston, always a judicious actor, did his duty by the part of Manly, and everyone concerned in working out the almost farcial underplot of the adventures of the Wronghead family in London—the "Wrongheads", as its chief observes, "were a considerable family ever since England were England"—carried on the jest with an unflagging spirit.

At the OLYMPIC there is constant mirth over comediettas bordering on farce. In *Hush Money* notice is due to the excellence of Mrs. Emden's acting as the practical clearstarcher who inflicts so terrible a shock upon the nerves of Mr. Jasper Touchwood. Mrs. Emden in this little piece really divides applause with Mr. Robson.

October 16.—At the OLYMPIC we have had, during the week, the opening of Mr. Wilkie Collins's *Red Vial*. Intent upon the the course of his narrative, the author has in this instance forgotten that in a drama characters are not less essential than a plot. There is not a character in *The Red Vial*. One person is, indeed, benevolent; another rigid in the sense of probity; another, represented by Mrs. Stirling, weak in the same, and wicked; and another, represented by Mr. Robson, a maniac, with wits of dimensions varying according to the convenience of the story; but they are all shadows for a tale that should be read in ten minutes, not characters to be offered bodily to our senses, for a two hours' study. Still with the same exclusive care about the story, it happens also that the author of *The Red Vial* has taken no pains to secure pithiness of expression; there is no effort to say good things pointedly, and sometimes even a tendency to say commonplace things tediously, as if they were worth elaborating into speeches.

But the defect fatal to the success of this melodrama, probably, is something in itself apparently more trivial than any of these faults. The morality of the play is, indeed, to a certain extent, bad; we are asked for some sort of sympathy with mother's love that begets robbery and murder; but plays seldom are condemned for bad morality. Crowded houses at the Haymarket have this week taken harmless delight in *London Assurance*, of which the whole story shines only through a bright halo of swindling and lying; a play without the faintest recognition in it of such a principle as honour, except by a weak tag at the end about two gentlemen. That play succeeds because it has a fairly managed story, a pleasant variety of well-marked stage-characters, enough of sparkle in the dialogue, although it is by no means good, and an easy sense of the ridiculous everywhere paramount. Want of power in the writing does not much offend an audience that is otherwise contented. When will *Boots at the Swan* fail to attract playgoers to the Olympic, and to awaken peals of laughter there? Yet as a piece of writing it is utterly unreadable. The fatal defect in *The Red Vial* is that it makes no allowance for the good or bad habit that an English audience has of looking out for something upon which to feed its appetite for the absurd. The orthodox writer of melodramas satisfies that hunger with a comic underplot, and by so doing saves his terrors whole. But Mr. Wilkie Collins has experimented in a drama without one break in the chain of crime and terror, and the audience therefore makes breaks for itself at very inconvenient places. That a play so contrived should contain frequent solemn references to a doctor's shop, blue, green, and red bottles, drops and tablespoonfuls, small matter as that may be, is in the presence of a laughter-loving public very perilous. It needs the highest and the truest exaltation of the language of the drama to keep an audience in an English playhouse in a state of unbroken solemnity for two hours at a stretch. Mr. Robson and Mrs. Stirling raise the story to the utmost possible height by their acting ; every help of effective scenery has been supplied on the most liberal scale. The piece is the work of a popular writer, admirably mounted, perfectly acted, with the favourite actor of the day labouring his utmost in what should have been a striking part. Nevertheless it was condemned, and condemned, as we believe, not for any serious demerit, but for a defect arising from misapprehension of the temper of an English audience. It is no new temper among us. Even Shakespeare felt that to King Lear the Fool was necessary. Such plays as *Jane Shore*, or Otway's *Orphan*, never had healthy life upon our stage; and as a nation we have for the style of the serious French drama an ingrained antipathy. There must be a deeper earnestness than plays can demand, in whatever serious thing Englishmen are to look at without exercise of that sense of the humorous which is part of their life ; so natural a part that every man is in every grade of society regarded as a bore who wants it ; and the very phrase with thousands even among our educated men for not finding a thing acceptable is "seeing no fun" in it.

October 23.—Our English *Tartuffe*, Bickerstaff's *Hypocrite*, has been revived at SADLER'S WELLS with more than the usual success. It is a bright old comedy, with a brisk dialogue, well-defined and amusing characters, and a hard hit at the mean traders in piety, whom honest men detest more heartily than any other sort of sinner. Mr. Phelps's Dr. Cantwell must rank with his Sir Pertinax as a particular success ; one of the personations which give strength to the

argument of those who believe that his genius for his art
is most conspicuous as a comedian. The "make-up" of
the character is wonderfully good, the actor has transformed
his face, and a German critic might spend a chapter on dis-
cussion of the artist's fine æsthetical treatment of his own
nose.   A couple of touches of black paint have given the
effect of a true Cantwell pinch to the nostrils.   The hypocrite's mouth that he makes in speaking; the large hand
with its outspread grasping fingers, that he lays upon his
heart in protest; the houndish snuffing of the air with
which he scents a frailty in his patron's wife; the change,
when he is unmasked, to a vulgar brutality of tone that
without one touch of caricature expresses the lowness of
his position among men and beasts; his coarse, excited
triumph, and his miserable collapse when all his schemes
have crumbled about his head, and he has not the spirit of
a mole to set against the fall of all his mole-heaps and
the crushing in of the underground passages he has been
mining so industriously—are a few only of the points that
attest the pains bestowed upon the study of this part by an
accomplished actor.   Mrs. Charles Young adds also a great
charm to the acted play by the sparkle and refinement of
her version of the lively, wilful, and kind-hearted Charlotte.
There is no actress now in London who in comedy of this
sort can so completely look her part, and at the same time
maintain with equal vivacity the stage-illusion, without
making the spectator conscious of the artifices of the stage.
Mr. Charles Young is the Mawworm, and the part in his
hands is sufficiently amusing, but he makes too obvious
the low-comedy intention.   The canting sermon suddenly
preached from a chair behind the screen, at the close of
the play, is well given by Mr. Young, in the true Bethel
manner; and exquisitely quiet in its humour is the way in
which Mrs. H. Marston, who has been making the most
throughout of the part of the sanctified grandmother, here
displays the force of habit.   The moment Mawworm's head

rises above the screen, and he begins to sound the first note of his discourse, she turns her chair so that she may directly face him, settles herself as naturally as if she were at chapel, and "sits under him" in proper form, while he informs them all that he is to go up, up, up, but they are to go down, down down; they'll all want to cling to his skirts, but they'll be disappointed, for he'll wear a spencer. Miss Atkinson's Young Lady Lambert was a quiet, un-obtrusive bit of acting, and Mr. Henry Marston and Mr. Belford as Charlotte's brother and her lover, kept up the good-humour of the play with an unflagging spirit. Not only were the individual actors equal to their parts, but numerous little concerted effects of grouping and stage-management gave life and spirit to the business of the scene.

December 4.—The theatrical event of the last day or two is the production at the OLYMPIC of a "new serio-comic drama" which adds one more to the number of remarkable successes by which the small house in Wych Street is distinguished. It is called *The Porter's Knot*, and is an adaptation from the French by Mr. Oxenford, but an adaptation made so skilfully that the adapter is entitled to full honours for the applause it wins.

Its hero, Sampson Burr, was an honest porter in a Kentish seaport town, who toiled early and late; he and his wife denying themselves all but the barest necessaries, that they might make a doctor of their only child, a darling son. They saved enough not only to send their son to London, but also to retire with comfort to a little cottage, where they were maintaining and cherishing an orphan niece, who was to be, one day, their daughter, when the son came home with his diploma; and the diploma was hung up in a grand frame, and the father's heart danced with delight at the boy's glory, and the mother's heart was satisfied at having her child by her side again. Any friend of their son's was welcome, and into the ears of a fast student from town, the companion of his son's follies, the proud father told the story of his life's ambition and its crown.   But there followed a mysterious visit from a smooth, hard money-lender, and it appeared that in secret extravagance the son had incurred a debt equal to nearly all the old man's savings.   Then Sampson Burr did battle with his heart, and resolved nobly to bear not only his own sorrow but as much of his old wife's burden as he could take upon himself.   They had a friend in a stout-hearted captain, with whom Sampson sent his son across the seas for the retrieval of his honour.   He paid then his son's debts, and, taking to himself in "a speculation in which he had foolishly staked all" the blame of ruin, went back to his truck and porter's knot, labouring day by day and month by month, with his niece for accomplice, to keep out of the tender mother's heart a knowledge that would bring the bitterest of sorrows.   What innocent frauds, what heroic endurance, what generosities of love spring out of this situation, are shown in the second act of the little drama of *The Porter's Knot*.   I have told only half its story. Seldom has there been a story told upon the stage more perfectly than this is told at the OLYMPIC.

Mr. Robson's Sampson Burr is a piece of acting not less perfect in its truth and its quaint mingling of comedy with pathos than his Daddy Hardacre.   There is the same rustic dialect and manner, but there ends all likeness between the two characters, except the perfect way in which each is expressed.   Sampson Burr's trouble in his chimney-corner, or his talk with his wife when she has brought him his dinner to the pier and they sit together on the truck while he is eating it, cannot be seen without an emotion, expressed either by laughter or by tears.   And it is not by Mr. Robson only that this piece is well acted.   Mrs. Leigh Murray as the mother, and Miss Herbert as the niece, leave nothing wanting to the picture of the Porter's home, or of the hearts that make it when its other wealth is lost.   Mr. G. Vining displays all that can be looked for in the fast man from the hospitals, whose better nature shows itself at last. Mr. W. Gordon is the prodigal son, and Mr. H. Wigan is the money-lender, of whose one appearance he makes such good use that he has never before been seen as an actor to such good advantage.

December 18.—HAYMARKET.—It is not easy to be out of humour with a comedy like Mr. Bayle Bernard's *Tide of Time*, the original work of a playwright who does not look to France for his material, and, though he wants the Frenchman's art in the construction of a plot, is well furnished with English wit and English earnestness of feeling. The story places a new factory next door to an old park, and sets Manchester to work upon the good heart of a fashionable daughter of the landed interest. Familiar conflicts of opinion through which the country has advanced during the last twenty years reappear upon the stage deprived of all their bitterness ; justice is done to honest principle on either side, extravagance is subjected to a genial ridicule, and familiar truths, brightened with apt touches of fancy, delight the audience throughout, partly by reason of the wit upon their backs, partly by reason of their own homely and honest faces.

1859, *January* 22.—ADELPHI.—The metrical translation of Molière's *Tartuffe*, which in the old house brought an accession of fame to Mr. Webster, is the first work of note produced in the new theatre opened upon the old site on the 27th of last December. The play is worthy of the house, and the players certainly are not unworthy of the play. Mr. Webster's Tartuffe is well known and appreciated ; he has made the part his own. But not less truly Molière's creation than her own is the Dorine of Mrs. Mellon. A new member of the company, Miss Henrietta Simms, has won credit at once by her performance of Elmire. Miss Mary Keeley gives abundant life to Mariane ; and Mr. Selby is an irritable Orgon, worthy of his position in the centre of the plot. It is a pleasant thing to see a thoroughly good play so well acted, and to sit at ease in seeing it, for the new theatre proves to be at all points one of the most comfortable as well as one of the prettiest yet built.

March 5.—The theatrical event of the past week has been the return to the London stage of Mr. Alfred Wigan, who appeared with Mrs. Wigan for the first time on Monday evening at this theatre, in one of his best characters, that of John Mildmay in *Still Waters Run Deep.* Mrs. Wigan, who supported him most admirably in the part of Mrs. Hector Sternhold, was visibly affected by the cordiality of the welcome showered down upon her husband when the curtain rose. There was more in the plaudits of the public than expression of a selfish pleasure at the recovery of one of its best entertainers. It meant a true sympathy well founded upon personal respect, and genuine congratulation.

March 19.—Mr. and Mrs. Wigan have also been playing together in *The Bengal Tiger.* It is hard to say whether the playgoer will find most reason to be pleased with Mr. Wigan as the irritable old Indian, or with Mrs. Wigan as Mrs. Yellowleaf, the ambling old maid by whom he is courted. A bit of cleverer farce-acting is seldom to be seen.

April 9.—HAYMARKET.—Mr. Stirling Coyne has written for Mr. and Mrs. Charles Mathews, Mr. Buckstone, Mr. Compton, Mrs. Wilkins, and Miss Reynolds, a new comedy-farce, which consists mainly of original variations upon Murphy's *Way to Keep Him.* It is called *Everybody's Friend,* and the design of the author seems to have been the production of a three-act play that will, during the engagement of Mr. and Mrs. Charles Mathews, employ the whole resources of the company for the amusement of the audience. One advantage of the new play is, that, although it provides Mrs. Charles Mathews with the heroine's part, it does not overtask her limited skill, as it was overtasked in *The Royal Salute.* The contrast, however, between Mrs. Charles Mathews's performance and the skilful acting of

Miss Reynolds, when the two ladies are on the stage together, is not to be overlooked by the most inexperienced playgoer. ·

April 16.—At the COVENT GARDEN Opera, Mdlle. Lotti has, in *Maria di Rohan*, given reason for believing that she will know how to win her way to higher ground from year to year, following the brave example set by Madame Bosio, whose energy enabled her to conquer for herself the first place as a singer on our lyric stage.

This was written before Thursday, when the telegraph brought news to London of the loss of Madame Bosio, who died at St. Petersburg on Tuesday last, after a short illness. By a wide circle of private friends she will be missed, and her memory will be long honoured for her more substantial worth. Although to the public Madame Bosio was nothing but a singer, yet in the never-failing courtesy with which she filled her place upon the stage, and the complete dissociation of her name from every rumour of professional dispute or jealousy, her private character undoubtedly went far to add something of the cordiality of friendship to a public admiration of her talent. That which she presented on the stage was not the sole talent cultivated by her, but that one all London could see how she cultivated to the utmost. The natural gift of a rare voice was joined by her to an energy of character that secured her steady advance as an artist. From the first season in which she sang to us, open to exception upon this account and that, constant advance was made until last year, when she was unequalled—perhaps perfect—as a singer of the true Italian school. Then there were also certain parts which she had conquered to herself, even as an actress, and she was bent evidently upon further increase of a dramatic power in which she had once seemed to be utterly deficient. Of such an artist we can hardly say that she died in the perfection of her fame. There was always more to be achieved. Enough was done, however, to secure for her a lasting reputation; and by the memory

of her example many a young artist will hereafter be nerved
for the steady, patient work through which alone in every
profession the true honours can be reached.

At the OLYMPIC Mr. Tom Taylor has produced a very
successful comedietta, founded upon Mr. Savage's story
of Clover Cottage, and entitled *Nine Points of the Law.*
Mrs. Stirling is the widow in possession, Mr. Addison is the
rightful owner, transformed by the dramatist into a kind-
hearted Manchester man; the honest lawyer of the story is
a knavish lawyer in the comedy, and there are other changes
made in adaptation of the plot. The little piece is acted to
perfection, Mr. Addison's Manchester Man being another
of those curiously happy personations with which during the
last year or two it has occasionally pleased him to surprise
the town.

October 1.—Even in farce there was a sense of truth about
Mr. David Fisher's acting, and a finish that is too rare to
pass unobserved. Mr. Fisher is now added to the strength
of the ADELPHI staff, and in the drama of *The Willow
Copse* creates a character out of the part of Hulks. He
attempts no caricature, and now and then so delivers himself as to make of a melodramatic effect in the way of
speech, something much less galvanic, but at the same time
more living and more interesting, than the authors meant.
Hard, cunning, self-possessed; a loser by his cunning, as a
lawyer struck off the rolls; a fast man, with a shabby dress
and hang-dog air; one self-possessed, who does not look men
in the face, and who watches tracings of his stick upon the
ground when he is rigidly speaking in accordance with his
plots—that is the Hulks of Mr. Fisher. When in the last
part of the story Hulks assumes the disguise of a subscrip-
tion-begging preacher, he does not at all caricature the
affected twang of the pulpit orator, but fairly reproduces it,
as it is daily to be heard in public meetings.

At the PRINCESS'S THEATRE, under the new management
of Mr. Augustus Harris, everything is fresh. There is new

and elegant decoration, there is a new drama and a new
burlesque; there are also several performers new to London
boards. Oxford Street audiences have been trained to
appreciate good scenery much better than good acting, and
their first want is still satisfied abundantly. Messrs. Grieve,
Telbin, and Beverley provide throughout both the new
pieces, one long feast to the eyes. In the new drama, *Ivy
Hall*, traditional scenery of the days of the old English
gentleman, in hall and park, is displayed to perfection.
Genuine old English airs furnish the music to the piece,
and all serves for illustration of a story taken from the
French. *Ivy Hall* is adapted (with much alteration to procure the local colouring) from a drama, *The Romance of a
Poor Youth*, which has been very popular in Paris. The
chief law of such a drama is, that there shall be a good
story and plenty of it, that the action shall go forward
swiftly, and that, except in comic passages, there shall be
little talk that does not actively advance the plot. It must
be written with the tact of a man who knows what can be
said effectively upon the stage, and pays no heed to the
opinion of any reader in a closet. It must allow the scene-
painter as well as the actor to give all the pleasure that he can,
and may tickle the ear now and then with a popular air, or
a lively dance-tune with a dance-accompaniment. But it
may do all that, and, like *Ivy Hall*, be tedious.

With the other novelty at the PRINCESS'S, Mr. Planché's
burlesque of *Love and Fortune*, not a fault is to be found.
It is exquisite trifling, very fanciful to hear, and very beautiful to see. The dainty garden-scenes in which Watteau
revelled are peopled with bright Arcadians of the eighteenth
century, and are a playground for the fantastic persons with
which southern fancy furnished the burlesques belonging to
the ancestry of pantomime. Louis Quatorze, even when
real sheep bleated before him in the mimic paradise of
shepherds, never was treated with a better show, or better
pleasantry, than Mr. Beverley and Mr. Planché have pro-

vided for the public at this theatre. Bright animated pictures, song and dance, and jest that never is impertinent, amuse the audience till the curtain drops.

October 15.—The tediousness of *Ivy Hall* having been found incurable, that drama has been withdrawn; but every night adds to the attraction of Mr. Planché's elegant burlesque, with the arch speaking and remarkably good singing of Miss Louisa Keeley in her part of Cupid.

October 22.—Mr. Tom Taylor this week has especially shown his dexterity in fitting any company of actors with a play that will develop their particular resources and those of their theatre. For ASTLEY'S he has produced a hippodrame upon the life of *Garibaldi* full of horses and gunpowder explosions. For SADLER'S WELLS he has written a play in blank verse, *The Fool's Revenge*, suggested by *Le Roi s'amuse* and *Rigoletto*. It is, however, really new as to its plot, and in fact an original play, well designed and written with all care.

November 19.—In *The Fool's Revenge*, Mr. Tom Taylor has transformed the nightmare story, best known to Londoners in association with the opera of *Rigoletto*, into a wholesome English-natured plot. The character of the jester is entirely altered. The old Count Monterone, whose wrath at the Duke's seduction of his child is mocked by Rigoletto, here becomes a nobleman, respectable in age, who, in his youth, brought the wife of Bertuccio to shame and death. Her little daughter was sent to a convent, while her husband, who had been an honest notary, went to a madhouse. He recovered his wits, subject only to one sharp twist, the determination on revenge. He became the court fool, bent upon retaliation for the wrong done to him. His enemy was then become the husband of a young, innocent wife. Oppressed by his loneliness and yearning for his child, Bertuccio brought his daughter from her convent, cherished her in seclusion, almost relented when, his revenge being in his heart, her doctrine of love

entered his ear.   The lady, to whose ruin he was guiding
the Duke, had earned, as he knew, his daughter's prayers
by protecting her against an insult.   It is not the
licentious Duke himself who in Mr. Taylor's play has won,
under disguise, the affections of the jester's daughter.   For
this there is substituted a pure maidenly affection for a
brave and modest poet.   He intervenes to save her from
abduction, but his intervention is ingeniously made to produce, with increase of dramatic force, the scene in which
the father helps, unwittingly, the Duke's design upon his
child.

For the Nemesis of the scene, the Duke's offended wife—
a character left undeveloped in the opera—is used.   The
jester had prepared her to appear at the right moment,
resolved to consummate such vengeance as befits the
character of an Italian duchess of the fifteenth century.
The moral of the play is expressed in the Fool's cry towards
its close—

> "I would have grasped Heaven's vengeance, and have drawn
>   The bolt on my own head."

The title of the piece carries, in fact, the suggestion with it,
that Revenge is a Fool's business.   The situations being
altogether changed, the poison of the angry Duchess, who
has brought also an army to the gates, stands for the dagger
and sack of Sparafucile; but the Duke suffers all punish-
ment, and Bertuccio, after enduring the last agony of his
despair, receives his daughter back.   Furthermore for the
daughter there is a good husband waiting.

All this accords with the sense of right and justice in an
English audience, while by the change some of the most
effective points in the old story are increased in power.   A
solidity of character is given to the Fool which accords
perfectly with the genius of Mr. Phelps.   While the lips
gibe lightly, the hands clutch at the Fool's bauble as if it
were a sword.   It is the instrument of his revenge, and the

actor tacitly suggests this by the manner of its handling.
The dignity and tenderness of Bertuccio's relation as a
father with his child, the struggle of his revengeful spirit
with the counsels of her simple piety and purity of heart,
presently to be followed by the ferocity of exultation at
what he believes to be the success of his relentless plotting,
yield occasion for fine contrasts of dramatic colour.   In
the last act the Fool's glorying, the baseness of his triumph
passing by swift stages, the terror of his doubt, the agony of
his despair, employ incessantly the actor's energies.   Miss
Heath, a refined and graceful actress, aids the play very
much by her unstrained performance of the daughter's part.
The other characters are well sustained; the scenery is
excellent.   The scene of the first act, indeed, is a charming
picture, although it ventures to present at one view both
the outside and the inside of a palace wall.

November 5.—The new drama produced at the PRINCESS'S
THEATRE, *The Master Passion*, is capital up to the end of
the second act.   The third and last act requires the excision
of about three-fourths of the author's words, and some revision of the incidents.   If nothing whatever is to come of
the plan for carrying off the hero in the last scene, why
mention it?   The smelling-bottle, said to contain poison, is
an old matter of scorn with English audiences, and, as in
this case nobody drinks the poison, I should recommend
the heroine to keep her bottle in her pocket.   It may be
observed also that the adapter has throughout punished
excessively the English language, under the belief that by
so doing he can make blank verse of it.   What he may
have taken for blank verse is prose in convulsions.   Liberty
might, perhaps, wisely be given to each actor to make simple
English of his or her part, and omit every syllable that can
be spared.   The supernumerary who has to refer to the
heroine as Snoria, might be permitted to say "Miss".   Only
we would not deprive Mr. Ryder of a syllable supplied for
him.   It was a grand thought to provide that actor so com-

pletely with a part to tear a cat in, and, after setting him to rave through three acts, make him burst in the last scene. If the scissors are not spared, and the English be a little cured of its convulsions, there may be a long run for *The Master Passion.* The public will be sure always to laugh in the wrong places, but it will be pleased. Rant and fustian are good things in their way, and there is sense of its own in a brilliant medley of robed doges, red spies with crimped legs, romance-heroes in picturesque armour who thrust fists into the lion's mouth, picturesque Venetian groups, romantic bandits, robbers' strongholds, wild heaps of glittering plunder, dances, the perfection of stage-grouping, dagger-fighting, heroine in white satin, ditto in fancy costumes, both with their hair now and then let down, both in love with the same hero-robber and invincible defier of hereditary foes. There is plenty also of the kind of story men and women have all loved as boys and girls. The brilliant bustling melodrama has in fact very much the effect of a pantomime. It will delight any child, and make the old feel young again. Only let three-fourths of the rubbish of its words be shot into the waste-basket, and the piece will be the gay beginning of a pleasant entertainment.

A French jest has been adapted at this house for Miss Louisa Keeley. That young lady, for reasons which a farce-writer is entitled to regard as sufficient, makes it her business to persuade a dreary German student that she is his cat transformed into a woman. This she does in a way that more than confirms the impression made by her bright acting and good singing in the charming burlesque that still closes the entertainment at this house. Miss Louisa Keeley has in her the spirit of an actress.

November 12.—A NEW ADELPHI drama on the most elaborate scale, *The Dead Heart*, occupied on the first night four hours in performance, and was nevertheless perfectly successful. When compressed, as it must be, to three-fourths of its present bulk, it will become a stock-piece at the NEW ADELPHI.   Its faults are that the hero's character is consistent to no ordinary standard, its inharmonious elements are only to be taken for granted on the ground that, after seventeen years' neglect in the Bastille, nobody knows what a man will say or do.   The smooth, dissolute, and cruel Abbé Latour is the only character in the piece fairly and consistently worked out, and it is thoroughly expressed by Mr. David Fisher's acting. Mr. Webster, as the hero, presents an elaborate and most effective study of a character that is not fairly comprehensible, and wins unflagging attention to a part that is much overlaid with words.   The writing of the drama is unstrained and unaffected, but as it never rises above the common level of thought and expression, no advantage is obtained from the liberality with which words have been supplied to the actor upon whom alone reliance is placed for the production of any desired effect upon the audience.   Mr. Toole has a comic part sketched out for him, which as a written part would amuse nobody, but which he knows how to make amusing.   Upon Mrs. Mellon (Miss Woolgar) no hint of a possible pathos has been thrown away ; and other members of the company have filled up very cleverly the author's outlines, which were not the more distinct for being large.   But in spite of these faults, the author is entitled to a principal share of the credit earned by the success of his new play.   He has skilfully produced an unbroken series of strong dramatic situations and effective groupings on the stage, he has never sunk below the common level in his dialogue, either into absolute dulness or by the more wearisome pretension of fine writing.   If there had been a weak situation anywhere, the audience, on the first night, being a little wearied by the quantity of matter, might have become discontented ; but success was absolute, as it deserved to be.   It will be also permanent. The scenes of the French Revolution produced in it, the taking of the Bastille, the Conciergerie, the Guillotine itself, are so represented as to seize on the imagination of spectators. Cured of its wordiness, the drama may become a treasure to the house.

December 3.—The dramatic event of the past week has been the opening by Madame Celeste of the LYCEUM, with a lively piece, *Paris and Pleasure*, presented with great brilliancy, full of smart dresses, tasteful decoration, and effective grouping. As it affords Madame Celeste herself an opportunity of personating half-a-dozen characters, its light bustle and agreeable surprises do not fail of their effect.

December 31.—At the PRINCESS'S THEATRE this Christmas *Jack the Giant Killer* has a famous representative in Miss Louisa Keeley, who is small enough, brisk enough, clever enough, to be Jack himself in every child's eyes. Such a giant, also, as is built up here was surely never before seen on any stage. Mr. Shore animates, it is in vain to guess how, a real giant form which opens its mouth where the mouth should be, bends its knees where the knees should be, walks about not more clumsily than giants ought to walk, handles his great club dexterously, and turns up an enormous pair of boot-soles when he dies. The introduction to this pantomime by Mr. H. J. Byron is, of course, liberally supplied with puns, but it deals playfully and ingeniously with the old child's-tale, and represents the matter of it very effectively in comic fashion.

At the OLYMPIC Mr. Robert Brough has written for Mr. Robson, on the subject of *King Alfred the Great*, a medley of puns, parodies, burlesque anachronisms, and defiance of invasion. There seems to be a story in the piece, but I could comprehend nothing of it, except that Alfred the Great was Mr. Robson, who burnt oat-cakes and defied the Danes. King Alfred imitates Blondin's performance on the tight-rope, and ends a song about the "Four Liverpool Merchants" with the chorus of "Riflemen, form!" The ballet presents evolutions of fair archers instead of rifle-women, but a rifleman is conjured from a caldron, and is an important figure in the last tableau. Of all the Christmas pieces this is the most exuberant in its defiance of invaders.

1860, *January* 14.—At the ADELPHI Mr. Dickens's *Christmas Carol* has introduced Mr. Toole for the first time as an actor capable of more than amusing extravagance. His Bob Cratchit contains homely natural touches that enable it to stand its ground beside the Mrs. Cratchit of Miss Woolgar (Mrs. Mellon), one of the neatest possible stage-pictures of a bustling, bothered, scolding, and kind-hearted mother of a poor man's family, at home with many cares.

February 25.—At the HAYMARKET Mr. Tom Taylor's *Overland Mail* shows during two acts the outside humours and airs of the passengers on board the *Simoon* homeward bound, and in the third act presents them as wrecked people upon a rock, with their true natures that underlie the humours forced into full view. The scheme of the drama is a pleasant one. It is a drama of life and manners rather than of incident, cleverly adapted to its actors, and at the same time written with unusual care. Mr. Buckstone, Mr. Compton, and Mr. Charles Mathews add their strength to that of the whole Haymarket company for its effective performance; and the result is another of those thorough successes with which the HAYMARKET has of late been favoured.

March 10.—At the LYCEUM, by winning Mrs. Keeley to the stage again, Madame Celeste has conferred no small favour on playgoers. That lady reappeared this week in one of her earliest parts as Margot in the drama of *The Sergeant's Wife*, Madame Celeste herself playing Lisette. *The Sergeant's Wife*, as now acted at the LYCEUM, is a piece to be seen; and as it has not been performed for the last thirty years, it will be new to most playgoers. It is not a good sort of play, but it is a wonderfully good play of its sort. Its topic is the night-adventure of a wayworn and belated sergeant's wife, on the way to her husband, with a lame old soldier who sups himself helpless in a ruined château with two murderers, one cruel smooth, the other cruel rough. Margot (Mrs. Keeley) is their maid, who with her husband (Mr. Rouse) had discovered the trade of their employers just before the arrival of the strangers. The drama means to inspire terror, and so passes without rest from one critical situation to another yet more frightful, allows no underplot or change of place to distract attention, and contrives even out of terror, in its comic aspect, all its incidental fun. The unity and energy of its intention, and the absence of all waste writing, as well as of waste incident, gives to the piece all the value that belongs to a production perfect of its kind. The consoling certainty that everything is to come right at last relieves the play of any painful effect it might have, and the admirable melodramatic acting, not by the two ladies only, but by all who take part in the piece, secures the fixed attention of the house. Madame Celeste identifies herself with the part of Lisette, and Mrs. Keeley as Margot, blending her grotesque terror with fine womanly sympathies for the victim upon whose behalf she becomes active, and with a visible sense of profound awe, plays like an artist. Mr. Rouse is a shade too farcical as Margot's husband, and appears to disadvantage in association with an actress who is in every gesture true to the picture she is representing.

March 24.—For the benefit of Miss Louise Keeley, at the Princess's last Thursday, Mr. Keeley himself reappeared upon the stage ; while Mrs. Keeley, who is strengthening the hands of Madame Celeste at the Lyceum, acted on that night at both theatres. Mr. Keeley remains for a night or two at the Princess's, acting in *London Assurance* and *Twice Killed*.

At the Olympic, Mr. Robson, in the farce of *B. B.*, first produced on Thursday night, represents a mild and somewhat timid gentleman, having those initials on his luggage, who arrives at an inn in Northumberland by the train from which the American prize-fighter calling himself the Benicia Boy is expected, and who undergoes much torture and bewilderment. His suffering proceeds from the enthusiastic interest taken in him by a sporting waiter and chambermaid, a sympathising landlady, and the retired Chicken by whom she is courted, as well as by the squire of the parish, who is "a patron". The farce, which is received with hearty laughter, is designed to exhibit Mr. Robson's skill in representing ludicrous mystification and alarm. It also shows to great advantage Mr. Horace Wigan, who has made a small character-sketch of his part as the retired pugilist.

April 14.—In the interval between two of his dramatic sessions at Islington, Mr. Phelps, engaged at the PRINCESS'S THEATRE, has been representing one of his favourite comedy parts, Sir Pertinax Macsycophant, in *The Man of the World.* Sir Pertinax Macsycophant, pliant in flattery and hard in purpose, determined to grasp worldly success, and utterly insensible to degradation that is not accompanied with loss of worldly influence, is represented by the actor even in what must pass for the repose of his face when on the stage. The features are cunningly hardened ; the keen eyes, and a certain slight but frequent turn of the head, with its ready ear and fixed averted face, shrewdly suggests an intent, secret watchfulness. Even when his schemes of family aggrandisement are being foiled by love and honour in his son, when the depths of his miserable passion have been stirred into an almost tragic agony of meanness, he commonly abides by the same habit of listening with open ear, keen, watchful eye, and face impenetrable. Mean, selfish worldliness, utterly dead to the perception of a man's honour and dishonour, is all that has to be represented, but of this the actor seizes the whole range. If the house roars with laughter at the littleness of the passion, it has also to note with a more silent and more powerful emotion its intensity.

April 21.—A sense of the intolerable in literature has, perhaps, been attained already by some of our burlesque writers. There is, indeed, still somebody who can select *Lucrezia Borgia* or *Jane Shore* for a subject, and there is an appearance in advertisements of a burlesque by somebody of fashion, who has written *Arthur, or the Hi-diddle diddles of the King.* But this Easter at any rate we are not condemned to hear laborious vulgarities connected with the names of King Alfred or of William Tell. Mr. William Brough's burlesque on the story of the Mountain Sylph, produced as *The Sylphide* at the PRINCESS'S, takes fair game in a fanciful tale, works out the story pointedly, and is to be praised also for many evidences of a true spirit of fun that underlies and overlies the punning. The scene of the witch Hela at her toilet is merrily designed; the dances, that are now essential to burlesque, are cleverly joined to the story; and although a good deal of the word-splitting could be spared, many of the puns are also honest jokes. *The Sylphide*, in fact, is a good thing of a bad sort. *The Forty Thieves*, also, are game well hunted, and it is rather good than bad taste to make merry with *The Miller and his Men.* Mr. Byron, who is dull in *The Pilgrim of Love*, has shown that he knows how to be naturally merry, much as punning checks natural mirth. He produced at Christmas one of the heartiest and best pantomime openings that I have seen for many years. Mr. F. Talfourd, Mr. William Brough, and Mr. Byron, the chiefs of the modern school of burlesque, are all capable of dispensing with the affectations of wit that are now practised for delusion of the ignorant. A true power of fun, that is in all these gentlemen, makes itself felt by high and low. Is it not, then, worse than superfluous that they should spoil their sport with a mere strain after false wit, and aim also, by the use of slang words that take the place of humour with the idle and stupid, to amuse the worse at the cost of annoyance to the better half of any but a tap-room audience?

April 21.—So supreme is *Fidelio* among operas and the
name of Beethoven among musicians, that it might be
natural to refer to some vaguely remote classical period a
Shakespeare of sound, by whom this opera was written for
us and for all time within the present century, when his age
was only thirty-five or thirty-six. There may have been
some who had shaken hands with Beethoven himself among
those who witnessed on Thursday night the admirable representation of his opera at COVENT GARDEN. Most opera-
goers have heard the story of the first suggestion of the
subject of *Fidelio* to its composer. Paer had written an
opera upon the story, Beethoven went to hear it, and, when
the composer came into his box, expecting compliments,
met him with the exclamation, " Paer, I am delighted with
your opera ; I shall set it to music."

And to what wonderful music is it set ! After all first
misadventures, the performances in two forms for three
nights only, the remodellings, and the four overtures produced for it (the third or Leonora being the best, and the
fourth written because the third was thought too long, and
could not be shortened without hurt), Beethoven's *Fidelio*
as it now stands is, in music, of all secular works, the one
that appeals most worthily to what is *in* the listeners. The
music itself thinks and feels, blending its harmonies with
all the variety and mystery of human emotion. As the
words are sung the music lives along the line. The most
exquisite of Mozart's melodies have no such life in them as
this, but are as the fancy of Spenser, pure fancy unsurpassed,
beside Shakespeare's sounding of all notes that are to be
drawn out of man's heart.

Fidelio is now performed at COVENT GARDEN better than
it has been performed in London for more than a score of
years. Since the time of Madame Schroeder Devrient,
there was a performance by a German company with
Madame Stoeckel Heinefetter in the part of Leonora, and
the opera runs so much better with German than Italian

words that until this week that may have been reckoned as
the last best of the London representations. The Fidelio
of Mdlle. Cruvelli was a display of the young lady's power,
of the energy she could throw here and there into dramatic
points, but I greatly preferred the subsequent performance
of Mdlle. Jenny Ney. The young German singer who has
now adventured to represent her true German Fidelio
on the Italian stage has every requisite of voice, and perhaps is an accomplished actress. I suspect, however, that
her art would fail her in an uncongenial part. Her Fidelio
is good because she evidently puts her heart into the part,
and means its music. She was not to be distracted even by
the strange Italian words, but occupied the stage with a
beautiful earnestness; never betraying her self-consciousness,
never displaying a concern for stage-effect, straining at
points, or striking attitudes. There is one aspect of her
part that now becomes prominent in it for the first time at
one of our Italian operas. The Leonora of Beethoven's
opera is a heroic wife, with all the tenderness and purity of
Shakespeare's Imogen. Very refined is the delicacy with
which Mdlle. Csillag shadows the relation between herself,
as a supposed boy, and the gaoler's daughter. She is true
woman in every situation; most of all when clinging within
her husband's arms she braves his assassin, and following
him, pistol in hand, with excited firmness to the door, half
swoons at the threshold, to be revived directly by her husband's voice and the new stir of a love suddenly released
from its constraints. Her piercing cry is not the musical
shriek to which we are accustomed, no note that her voice
reaches is uncoloured by the feeling that it should express.
In the famous cry, *Io son sua sposa!* her intonation of
the word on which the whole force of the story and the
music rests is wonderfully true in meaning. It is the
natural result, I believe, of her full earnest realisation of her
part, but it has all the force of a dramatic effect peculiarly
her own. Of the strains of religious feeling woven by

Beethoven into the music of the brave wife's part, not one
was lost upon the voice of the young singer.   When Leonora
in the first words of the prisoner hears the voice of her
husband, it is upon her knees that she falls as the cry of
recognition escapes from her; kneeling not consciously or
in set form of worship, but instinctively, as one suddenly in
presence of an issue that had been so long inseparable from
her prayers.   The line in which she gives bread with benediction to her husband is felt with a new force from Mdlle.
Csillag, who, without any display of intensity, fills the whole
prison scene with an air of truth and pathos that accords
most exquisitely with the music.   A Leonora guiltless of
stage-trick, who achieves one of the most difficult of operatic
triumphs without once appearing to ask homage to herself,
but who is evidently paying her own homage to the genius
she interprets, is a Leonora to be valued to the utmost.

April 28.—At the OLYMPIC Mr. Tom Taylor's adaptation
of a French sentimental comic sketch into *The Christmas
Dinner* gives opportunity to Mrs. Stirling for some capital
acting, to Mr. Horace Wigan for a clever make-up of
Hogarth, and to Mrs. Emden for one of her sturdiest and
pleasantest sketches of maid-servants.   But although the
appeal seems to be throughout to the English home-feeling,
the expression of it is still somewhat foreign in its sentiment,
and it does not altogether come home to the audience.
What little applause the piece receives is earned, and is,
indeed, less than is earned, by Mrs. Stirling.

July 28.—Five London companies, that have been indebted to the pen of Mr. Robert Brough as a burlesque
writer, contributed to the entertainment at DRURY LANE
last Wednesday for the benefit of the wife and children of
that excellent amuser of the public.   Touching allusion was
made to the occasion of the benefit in the closing lines of
the address written by Mr. Shirley Brooks.   It was an
address, spoken by Mrs. Stirling, as prologue to *The
Enchanted Isle*, the earliest of Mr. Brough's burlesques,

which formed the last part of the entertainments in aid of
a fund for the benefit of his widow and his almost infant
children.   It was performed by an amateur company of the
deceased writer's literary friends and comrades.   Mr. Robert
Brough was but a young man, for his career as a producer
of light literature began at an unusually early age.   Deficient
health made it impossible for him to undertake the sustained
work by which alone large incomes that depend on labour
can be earned, and it raised also beyond reasonable means
the premium for life insurance.   He lived laborious days,
and he was chargeable with no improvidence.   Had he
survived even to middle age he might have left provision
for the household that depended on him safely while he
lived.   He died without a blot upon his social character,
and it is an honour to his memory, not a reproach, that he
has left at his death friends zealous enough and prompt to
give substantial aid to those of whom he had in life been
the protector.

September 15.—Mr. Boucicault's transformation of Gerald
Griffin's excellent novel of *The Collegians* into an ADELPHI
play again furnishes conspicuous evidence of his stage-tact.
The new drama of *The Colleen Bawn* would on its own merits
excel *The Green Bushes* in lasting popularity.   It will not,
however, like *The Green Bushes*, be connected with the
picturesque melodramatic power of one favourite actress, or
especially supported by the broad fun of two favourite
comedians.   The work of the piece is fairly distributed
among many persons, who all work together to ensure its
success.   Mr. Boucicault himself in a genial Irish part, and
Mrs. Boucicault, playing with much quiet grace as the
heroine ; Mrs. Mellon as a comedy heroine, winning,
perhaps, the foremost honours of the night ; Mrs. Billington
as a tragic heroine seizing an opportunity to show (as she
has once or twice enabled us to see) that she sometimes
can rise as an artist far above her ordinary level ; Mr.
Edmund Falconer as an Irishman, with terror of a crime

upon his mind, acting with an effective carefulness deserving of the highest praise that he has yet earned on the
London stage; Mr. Billington as the hero; Mr. David
Fisher, acting always well, but here able only to pass quietly
through a part of which there is not much to be made
beyond a contribution to the general effect—I have not
yet named all the performers, but should have to do so
were I to name all to whom the piece is indebted for its
very great success. It owes much, however, to the genius
of Gerald Griffin, who contrived the story, and most to the
constructive tact of the dramatist, in whose hands every
situation is effective, and from whom every phrase tells upon
the audience. Upon the scenery, of course, pains have
been spent, and the second act closes with some "ADELPHI
effects" of sea in a cavern, with incidents of plunging,
swimming, drowning, and fishing up, of which the illusion
provokes rounds of applause. The production of *The
Colleen Bawn* is the most thorough old-fashioned success
achieved by Mr. Webster since his new theatre was built.

September 22.—Mr. Phelps, who is now sole lessee of the
theatre with which his name will be hereafter associated,
fulfils at SADLER'S WELLS all those conditions which the
Freiherr von Wolzogen considers necessary to the honest
progress of the drama. He acts national plays in a house
small enough to allow all to see, though few may appreciate,
the subtlest and most delicate shades of expression proper
to the art of the actor; he has a company of performers
trained and accustomed to support each other steadily, and
peculiarly able to present each play as an effective whole.
The unhallowed union of music with the drama, so deeply
abhorred by Herr von Wolzogen, is not sanctioned at
SADLER'S WELLS; and while the stage is always well
appointed, scenic display is made, even to a remarkable
degree, expressive of poetical intention.

Mr. Phelps has opened the campaign with two plays of
Shakespeare—*As You Like It* and *Coriolanus*. *Coriolanus*

I have been to see, and here as ever the first mention is
due to the whole truth and harmony of the representation.
The actors are all in accord together; and although the
company includes few bright particular stars, yet each does
justice to the dignity of his profession.   Mr. Barrett is a
genial and genuine Menenius Agrippa ; Mr. Herman Vezin,
a new member of the company, who, I believe, has earned
honours as first tragedian in a transpontine house, is a
discreet and serious Aufidius, who mars nothing by errors
of commission, and errs only on the hopeful side by under-
acting his part.   The Roman mob, admirably grouped and
disciplined, cannot easily be represented by a better first
citizen than Mr. Lewis Ball.

The little part of the domestic friend and gossip of the
women in the hero's household is spoken delightfully by
Mrs. Marston.   Miss Kate Saxon, an intelligent actress,
who supplies one of the losses of the company, delivers
with all due simplicity the few sentences that fall to her lot
as the wife of Coriolanus, and expresses quietly by her
stage-bearing the modest, faithful gentleness that follows,
strong in love, the warrior's career.   As the proud mother
of the prouder son, Miss Atkinson also labours her best,
but she does not achieve her best.   When she desires with
face and gesture to express scorn, it not seldom happens
that she fails to suggest more than intensity of spite.   For
this reason her Volumnia is wanting in some of the dignity
with which the character has been invested by the poet.   It
is a hard trial, no doubt, to measure the expression of a
Roman mother's pride with the show of pride that a man can
put into the part of Coriolanus.   Pride, after all, is not a
woman's passion, for what passes by the name is often
vanity.

The pride of Coriolanus is heroic, and is a man's pride,
from which vanity is altogether absent.   His own praises
are irksome in his ears.   That which he is, he is ; and it is
little in his simple estimation of himself, for he esteems

himself by what he feels the power of becoming. Upon comparisons between himself and the base multitude he never wastes a thought. It matters not at what level other men are content to dwell; his mind abides on its own heights. Thus when Caius Marcius in the camp, beset with irksome praises that he is compelled to hear, is named Coriolanus, and there is added to this honour the exhortation " Bear the addition nobly ever", Mr. Phelps represents him stirred by the warning into a large sense of what is in his soul, and lifted upon tiptoe by his soaring thought. The same action gives grandeur to the words,

> " I'd rather be their servant in my way
>   Than sway with them in theirs,"

and is afterwards more than once used, not ostentatiously, and never without giving the emphasis intended.

As in the action of the piece, that pomp of processions with the constant noise of drum and trumpet, which in the good old days of the drama formed a prominent part of the play, is subdued, and made to follow instead of leading the march of the poem, so in the action of Coriolanus himself it is remembered that heroic pride is self-contained. The passion least to be concealed by it is impatience of subjection to the shifting voices of the mob. The pride of Coriolanus is a virtue overgrown, and is associated with the utmost purity and tenderness of home affections; next to his love of honour is his love of home. The two qualities belong naturally to the same mind, and in the end of this play we are left unable to determine which feeling has prevailed. It is meant, doubtless, to be questionable whether love would have conquered had not the mother made her son—as Mr. Phelps does not forget to mark very distinctly —flinch at such a pleading as,

> " Say my request's unjust
> And spurn me back ; but, if it be not so,
> *Thou art not honest.*"

The expulsion of Coriolanus from Rome is presented in a capital stage-picture by the grouping of the mob, and here the actor's reading of his part is marked very distinctly. He had been wrung by the urgency of his friends and the commands of his mother to attempt to flatter into quiet the excited mob. The attempt to do this is presented with all signs of suppressed passion, and impatient, yet in itself almost heroic, endurance of what is really intense torture. When the tribune calls Coriolanus traitor, he recoils as from a blow, and lets his wrath have way. But when the mob raising their staves expel him from the city, he mounts proudly the steps from which as from his mental height he looks down on them, and he is lord of himself, lord as he feels of Rome. With a sublimity of disdain he retorts on them that "I banish you", which Edmund Kean erred in delivering with an ungovernable passion.

The scenic effect of the view of Antium by the light of the rising moon, when the banished Coriolanus haunts the door of Aufidius, his deadly enemy, is contrived to give colour to the poetry. But there is no scene in the play more impressive to the eye than the succeeding picture of the muffled figure of Coriolanus, seated by the glowing embers of the brazier that represents his enemy's hearth. It is one of the omissions of Mr. Vezin that he makes no sign whatever when the stranger-guest discloses his name, though he had vowed that

> "Where I find him, were it
> At home, upon my brother's guard, even there,
> Against the hospitable canon, would I
> Wash my fierce hand in his heart."

If nothing more were to be done, hands tightly clenched at the hearing of the name, slowly relaxing till they are held out in friendship with the words

> " O Marcius, Marcius,
> Each word thou hast spoke hath weeded from my heart
> A root of ancient envy,"

would be better than absolute inaction.

I must not dwell much longer upon this performance. Let me add only that the meaning of the heroic close furnished by Shakespeare to the play is well brought out at SADLER'S WELLS. The lofty pride that when defied by Rome had defied Rome herself, and was to set a foot upon the neck of the world's ruler, had, after painful struggle, knelt at the voice of a mother, yielding nobly when to yield was dangerous, if not mortal. When Coriolanus has attained his greatest height, Aufidius, fallen to his lowest, has sunk into a dastardly chief of assassins. All hearts are thus secured for sympathy with the pride with which, as Mr. Phelps shows us, the hero resents the taunt of an enemy basely triumphant. His whole frame enlarges, and his hands press on the expanding breast, as he cries,

> " Measureless liar, thou hast made my heart
> Too great for what contains it ! "

And so at last the loftiness of his disdain carries all sympathies with it when he whets the swords of the conspirators by telling them

> " How, like an eagle in a dovecote, I
> Fluttered your Volsces in Corioli :
> Alone I did it.—Boy ! "

October 6.—The LYCEUM opened on Monday for Madame Celeste's winter season with a new play by Mr. Tom Taylor, *The Brigand and his Banker*, founded on Edmond About's novel, "Le Roi des Montagnes". The LYCEUM play, however, was so ill-contrived and feebly written that not even the personal efforts of Mrs. Keeley and Madame Celeste, the beautiful scenery and dresses, and indulgence for an opening night, could save it from the fate it merited.

October 13.—Mr. Boucicault's comedy of *The Irish Heiress*, in which the American actress, Miss Gougenheim, has appeared this week at the LYCEUM before a London audience, is a poor work, and it may be well to defer judgment on the lady's talent until she has been seen in another part, a part also in which she has English to speak. It is very difficult to use the voice as an instrument of expression when it is condemned to an incessant artifice of intonation.

Miss Gougenheim's notion of an Irish brogue, picked up too manifestly on the other side of the Atlantic, is so nasal that there is only the difference of a stage-Irish trill between it and the talk of the ladies who have presented Yankee "gals" at the ADELPHI. There are two parts of Yankee to one part of Irish; and when a character has to be expressed throughout in such a dialect, it is not easy to tell whether the actress can make any or no good use of her voice. Miss Gougenheim may be an attractive performer because she is lively and good-looking, but whether as an actress she has more than average ability I am disposed to doubt. Mr. Henry Neville, from Liverpool, who also made a first appearance in this play, is a new actor of real mark, who, without much of a part, made good his title to a place in Madame Celeste's excellent company.

October 27.—The PRINCESS'S THEATRE opens to-night with the Parisian Mr. Fechter as an English actor in an English version of *Ruy Blas*. On Monday evening the ST. JAMES'S THEATRE will open under Mr. Alfred Wigan's management with a new play upon Anglo-Indian life, by Mr. Tom Taylor, and a revived extravaganza by Mr. Planché. Next week, therefore, the accusation against the public that it does not support the stage will be met by the fact, unprecedented I believe for many years, that in the winter season all the theatres in London from HER MAJESTY'S to the SOHO are open together. The neglect of English musical talent is met by the fact that, to say

nothing of the GREAT NATIONAL OPERA at the East-end of
town, the two opera-houses of the West are engaged in the
production of English music.

At the LYCEUM Madame Celeste, strong in herself and in
the help of Mrs. Keeley, has brought together some good
actors, and is labouring hard for the attainment of a strong
and effective working company.   Miss Gougenheim will
hardly be a valuable member of it; she has animal spirit,
but her performance in *The Love Chase* shows that she is
no artist, while her English proves to be, if possible, more
Yankee than her Irish.   Miss Amy Sedgwick has been
acting Constance in the same play at the HAYMARKET, and
between the art of these two ladies there can be no comparison.   But, on the other hand, the Widow Green of
Mrs. Wilkins, pleasant and genial as it is, only serves as a
foil to the humour with which Mrs. Keeley has enriched the
part.   Miss Florence Hayden at the HAYMARKET is pleasant,
but her Lydia does not approach that at the LYCEUM of
Miss Kate Saville, an intellectual and refined actress, of
whom much is to be hoped.

November 10.—At the ST. JAMES'S THEATRE a new play by
Mr. Tom Taylor, entitled *Up at the Hills*, has been received
with moderate favour.   It had been written for Mr. and
Mrs. Wigan, and has a half-serious domestic plot of the
French school of intrigue and encounter of wits, because it
is in such dramas that these excellent artists have achieved
their best successes.   The actors are displayed and the
audience is interested.   No more is desired.

At the PRINCESS'S THEATRE Miss Heath, Mr. Walter Lacy,
and Mr. Fechter sustain the chief characters in *Ruy Blas*,
and the French actor, Mr. Fechter, as the hero in and
out of livery, draws crowded houses.   In melodrama Mr.
Fechter acts effectively without extravagance.   He suits
action to word with a nicety not usual upon the English
stage, and without obtrusion of his art where he is most artificial.   Thus, when he says to Mr. Walter Lacy in the last

scene, "I was your lacquey, now I am your executioner", by the help of a chair and a drawn sword he places himself —standing in the middle of the stage—in a natural position, instantly suggestive of the conventional attitude of the headsman, and draws loud applause. Few melodramatic actors could venture upon such an effect, for the least hardness or clumsiness of manner would make it ridiculous. Mr. Fechter speaks good English with no more of his own accent than clings usually to an educated Frenchman resident among us.

November 17.—At the HAYMARKET Mr. Tom Taylor, clever and ready as he is, miscalculated the proportion between plot and dialogue in his *Babes in the Wood.* The plot is so thin and transparent that no interest attaches to it, and as first performed the play was a good deal longer than *Hamlet.* Shortened now by an hour and a quarter, the *Babes* ought to have a tolerable run; for there is a capital part supplied to Mr. Buckstone, and Mr. Compton is strong as a Bore of the Backstairs, though the author has made him so exact a counterpart of the bore that, in spite (or perhaps partly by help) of the marvellously true "make-up", and the ingenious acting, the audience itself is at last bored. It is noticeable that there is more clever writing in this half-successful play than in some of its luckier predecessors, and that there is a good artistic intention in some of those very passages which proved the weakest in stage-representation.

December 1.—To the success of a melodrama Madame Celeste has now added a yet greater success in a new Irish comedian, Mr. John Drew, who is by far the best Irish comedian seen in London since the days of Power, and who in the drama of *Handy Andy*, judiciously compressed and adapted into a mere vehicle for Irish fun, keeps the house in as genuine a roar of mirth as is to be heard in any of the playhouses. [Mr. Drew is dead and almost forgotten. 1866.]

At the HAYMARKET there is a new farce too closely resembling in its construction the *B. B.* in which Mr. Robson has this week been playing before Her Majesty at Windsor. Mr. Compton is the hero, taken for a Lion Slayer. The house is amused, but the curtain falls to slight applause. The play of *The Babes in the Wood*, as now acted, runs smoothly and merrily.

December 29.—At the OLYMPIC Mr. Robson is fierce Timour the Tartar in a burlesque written by Mr. Oxenford and Mr. Shirley Brooks, who have been as successful in the manufacture of puns as if they really had what they have not, the punster's emptiness of wit. *Timour* is a good entertainment of its kind. Its four scenes are admirably appointed, and, though not the costliest, perhaps the best of the burlesque scenes of the year. Mr. Robson is but moderately well fitted with his part. The attempt to give him in one scene a fit of jealousy double that of Othello, because it is jealousy of two ladies instead of one, falls dead. It is a gratuitous excrescence from the plot, and Mr. Robson seems to have given up any attempt to turn it to account.

At the ADELPHI the Christmas burlesque is by Mr. Byron, and its subject *Bluebeard.* Mr. Toole is the Bluebeard, really furnished with Othello's temper and that of a Timour into the bargain. After seeing both, I must come to the conclusion that Mr. Toole's Bluebeard is to be preferred to Mr. Robson's Timour, the advantage being, perhaps, in the part, not in the actor.

1861, *January* 19.—At the PRINCESS'S THEATRE Mr. Garden, behind *Robinson Crusoe's* pantomime mask, surprises the old playgoer by the comic force that he displays. It is to be remembered, too, that he shone for the first time as Dr. Caius.

January 26.—At the PRINCESS'S there is the French-English actor, Mr. Fechter, acting in *The Corsican Brothers*, and distinguishing the town-bred from the country-bred brother, with a subtlety that makes us for the first time fairly aware of what a good actor may get out of his part in such a melodrama.

At the St. James's Mr. Wigan is still acting in the very French *Isle of St. Tropez*, and is a fair match for Mr. Fechter in any part that he may play. Mr. Wigan, as an English actor, meets the French on their own strongest ground, and reproduces life and suffering, disease and death, in French dramatic form with a delicacy and fidelity that no living actor could surpass. Such art surely is worth better material.

April 6.—At the Olympic *The Chimney Corner* has its run—a piece not equal to *The Porter's Knot* or *Daddy Hardacre*, upon recollection of both of which it appears to be founded, and too hurriedly worked out in the catastrophe. The abruptness of the old man's miraculously opportune appearance, with the immediately following tableau at the finding of the money, is weak in conception, and there is wearisome adoption of the old-fashioned use of a catch-phrase in the grandfather's incessantly-recurring question, "Where's my snuff-box?" Mr. Craven has nevertheless shown ability as a playwright that makes his productions worth friendly attention.

April 27.—Two new plays have been noticeably well produced this week, both with complete success—an "original comedy", *Black Sheep*, by Mr. J. Stirling Coyne, at the Haymarket, and a new version, the second on the London stage, of the French *Pattes des Mouches* at the St. James's. The plottings of Mr. Coyne's *Black Sheep*, the dishonest lawyer and the hypocritical philanthropist, are the centre of action in his piece; there is a story of the author's own finding that interests the audience sufficiently, and there is plenty of fun. The writing, too, is equal to the best that we have had of late years. It is not a comedy, because it does not mirror life; its plot is impossible, and it contains no characters. It is simply impossible that a poor artist very much in love, whose sweetheart was, with his mother, perfectly at home in his studio, should paint seven successive portraits of a city widow, and either care or be able to conceal the fact. At least she must have seen the portraits often enough to recognise the presence of the original. But that she knows nothing whatever about her is the supposition with which we are to set out. There is no approach to a clear sketch of character. Even of the hero and heroine we can assert only that they are parted by impossible misunderstanding and some indistinct traces of the traditional stage-pride. Mr. Compton's Shorter is rich in absurdity and fun, but it is a farce character; and Mr. Buckstone's Bunny, although whimsical enough, is but a feeble descendant of Tartuffe through a long line of more or less ridiculous stage-hypocrites with sleek hair and smooth tongues. The number of things that are written, said, and done in the last act of the play at a lawyer's annual evening party, with the grand finale of revelations and heart-utterances in one of the reception-rooms, would greatly edify a foreigner who should look to the English stage for a fair, humorous sketch of English manners.

Still less are to be found English manners, or even French life, represented in the clever French play which, after having served Mr. Charles Mathews for some time, is now translated afresh for Mr. and Mrs. Wigan, under the title of *A Scrap of Paper*. It is a mere piece of stage-ingenuity, as pleasant in its way of artifice and intrigue as Mr. Stirling Coyne's piece in its way—and let me own, as to that, its honest English way—of fun. The temptation to adapt the piece was irresistible. Mr. and Mrs. Wigan are perhaps never seen to so much advantage on the stage as when they represent a man and woman of the world dealing politely while measuring wits against each other. Therefore it was that Mr. Tom Taylor, in the half-successful piece with which their house was opened, endeavoured to fit them with such characters. *Les Pattes des Mouches* does for them all that the English writer sought to do.

June 1.—The *King Lear* of Mr. Phelps draws full houses to the PRINCESS'S. In the opening of the play the actor represents the Lear of the old legend. Infirm with age, he is led to his seat. His hands tremble, and everything indicates the weakness of body in which a weak mind is working. The curse upon Goneril is spoken, as the whole character is conceived, with a sense rather of the pathetic than the terrible. But I miss the majesty of absolute dominion in the royal Lear whom Shakespeare brought into grand contrast with the Lear in the storm, slave of the elements, "a poor, infirm, weak, and despised old man", who goes shivering to the straw of the hovel. Mr. Phelps does not make full use of all the hints given by Shakespeare to the actor for expressing the imperious habit of King Lear, who had grown old in despotic rule. Even in his entry from the hunt, when at Albany's castle, with the "Let me not wait a jot for dinner", which Mr. Charles Kean interpreted as the words of a jovially hungry man (generally treating Lear at this stage of his tragedy as a comic character), Mr. Phelps misses the true dramatic meaning of the words. In all the first scene the impatient majesty upon which Shakespeare dwelt is sacrificed to representation of the age and infirmity of which alone the legend teaches us. But the infirmity has in a great measure to be laid aside. The shaking head and trembling hands cannot be carried through the play. Thus there is double loss rather than gain in laying at the outset too much stress upon infirmity. There is another shortcoming in the early part of Mr. Phelps's Lear. With unusual literalness, Shakespeare indicates to the actor of Lear the exact course of the change to madness. It is preceded by a pang of terror in the close of the first act :—

> " O let me not be mad, not mad, sweet heaven !
> Keep me in temper ; I would not be mad !"

There are well-marked struggles with the rising pang at

his heart indicated throughout the scenes in the second
act; where the character formed by long habit of rule overlies even the natural agony of the father. Of Kent set in
the stocks by his son and daughter, the first exclamation is
"They *durst* not do 't"; and in the scene which opens with
their denial to speak with him, it is the wounded majesty
that rages first, and the wrung heart that appears through
it. The first act ended for Lear with terror lest he should
go mad. In the second his last words are, "O fool,
I shall go mad". In the third act the first scene on the
heath is a sane frenzy; and towards the close of it, as
majesty creeps to the hovel, Lear simply defines his state:
"My wits begin to turn." He is not mad when, in the
next scene, he reads one of the grand lessons of the play,
praying in the storm outside the hovel, mindful of the
world's "looped and windowed raggedness".

> " Take physic, pomp ;
> Expose thyself to feel what wretches feel."

Just before, when thinking of his daughters, he had
shuddered and recoiled at the thought, "that way madness
lies; let me shun that". But the night of exposure
to the storm completes the ruin. "This cold night," says
the Fool, "will turn us all to fools and madmen"; and
the wild talk of Edgar, in his assumed madness, precipi-
tates the real madness of Lear. When he is talking with
this philosopher, Kent urges Gloster to importune him to
go, because "his wits begin to unsettle"; and when he is
brought by Gloster into the farmhouse, we are, at last,
warned by Kent's first words that "all the power of his
wits have given way to his impatience". Now, although
Mr. Phelps gives a fine reading of the part, I do not think that
he contrasts sufficiently the royal state with the abject misery;
the imperious way, strong in weak characters, with the
lowest humility of the infirm, weak, and despised old man.
Neither in the accession of Lear's madness do we get from

Mr. Phelps, what, indeed, no actor in our time has altogether given, a satisfactory embodiment of Shakespeare's conception. But from the time that Lear enters with his robes washed almost colourless by the rain, a feeble old man, weary and witless after his night's wandering under the storm, everything is exquisitely done, the story being read wholly with regard to its pathos, not to its terror. The king is utterly lost in the father. The wound to the heart has struck, as no hurt to the dignity of royal robes can strike a man. Majesty has been contemned in its rags. Humanity lives to assert itself. The quiet broken spirit, the strayed wits, the tender nursing and rocking of the body of Cordelia in the closing scene ; the faint interest in all but her by whose love Lear's broken heart was held together ; the tenderness with which he lays her down, as for an instant, while he lifts his hands to the throat in which the last convulsive throe of death is rising ; his quiet death, with his eyes, his pointing hands, and his last words directed to her lips, are exquisitely touching.

October 26.—The dignity of the heroic Moor, who fetches "life and being from men of noble siege", Mr. Fechter appears in the first two acts of *Othello* willing rather than able to represent. At once, therefore, we have attention called especially to his quick impressionable character.

In the very first passage of special note—Othello's speech before the senators in answer to the charge of having taken Desdemona from her father—the quickness of emotion in Mr. Fechter's Othello is strongly marked. While Brabantio complains to the Duke, he looks like a man conscious of a good reply in store, which he is impatient to utter. He is eager to speak. He begins so instantly upon the Duke's question, "What, in your own part, can you say to this?" that Brabantio's interpolation, "Nothing, but this is so", comes as an interruption to be swept aside. And when he does utter the well-known speech, standing near to the table under the Doge's chair which has Brabantio and two

or three senators about it, having confessed that he has
" ta'en away this old man's daughter"—

> " It is most true ; true, I have married her ;
> The very head and front of my offending
> Hath this extent, no more,"—

he utters the "no more" as one violently repelling a foul
imputation on his honour, with fierce gesture of advance
towards the table.   Upon this senators rise as if they almost
expected an attack, and Othello gives the next eight or nine
lines, "Rude am I in speech", etc., as a special apology called
for by that show of violence—an apology given, with Mr.
Fechter's French accent, in a tone that might seem, to a
critic, out of tune with the actor, oddly suggestive of a
French politeness by no means in accord with the speaker's
own estimate of his character.   But we have no right to
speak of it so lightly.   The device is new and ingenious, it
gives a lively break to the speech, and carries it to the end
in true colloquial fashion.   Shakespeare, however, meant
dignity of expression here ; and whatever force his true
interpreter would give to the "no more" was not such as
to make the court rise at Othello, or convert his simple
soldierly words in the following lines into a French apology
for his excitement, considered as a rudeness.   The subsequent description of the wooing is given with a colloquial
ease that is most clever and agreeable, though not at all
"unvarnished".

In the second act, Mr. Fechter's Othello first appears in
Cyprus less as the soldier than as the newly-married husband who rejoins the bride from whom he was parted on
the wedding-day.   When, roused from his bridal bed, he
enters to quell the riot following Cassio's drunkenness, there
is more dignity of manner ; but the quick temper breaks
into a tone of passion almost petulant as he turns round
upon the tolling of the alarm-bell to cry, "Silence that
dreadful bell !"—rather as if its noise had worried him,

than as if there were any special significance in the word
"dreadful", related to the reason he adds—as passionate
men are not apt to do in the same breath with a command—

> "It frights the isle
> From her propriety."

But the scene is well sustained, and Mr. Fechter, in the
first two acts of *Othello*, though he wins no laurels, loses
none.

I do not understand why, when Iago brings Othello to
the room where Cassio is taking leave of Desdemona,
Othello sees their parting with a spasm of emotion preceding Iago's "Ha! I like not that". There was no suspicion planted in his mind, and the disturbance expressed
is beyond what should be excited by the sight of the dis-
graced Cassio, whom yet he loves. Mr. Fechter, too,
himself, goes on to prolong the period of complete trust
through much of the succeeding colloquy, and is not disturbed by Iago's hints until he says,

> "She did deceive her father, marrying you ;
> And when she seem'd to shake, and fear your looks,
> She loved them most.
> > And so she did."

Here our new actor represents Othello tortured with a
deep, nervous thoughtfulness. He stands aside with his
eye fixed on vacancy, as one reasoning out in contemplation the path shown him to the hell whither it leads. Few
passages in Mr. Fechter's rendering of the part are more
finely conceived than the manner of the sudden stop with
a sense of bitter shame and humiliation followed by
"Leave me, Iago", when Othello finds himself, having so
far accepted the poison offered to his mind, impelled to say
to his ancient, "Set on thy wife to observe".

The soliloquy of Othello after Iago has left him Mr.
Fechter delivers with admirable emphasis, and the manner

of his address to Desdemona in the little scene next follow ing, when he throws down her handkerchief, is in its distressful hardness perfectly expressed. As the passion grows the action becomes more wholly emotional, and Mr. Fechter shows the physical effect of mental suffering in con- vulsive twitchings and involuntary drawings of the corners of the mouth till all the teeth are bare. The epilepsy into which Shakespeare represents Othello as falling in the first scene of the fourth act, and which is now wisely restored, Mr. Fechter foreshadows by these signs of physical yielding to the mental torture. When Othello demands the hand- kerchief of Desdemona, the scene is enriched with some new touches of tenderness. His face is averted when she says, "It is not lost", and he turns suddenly with all his love and trust flowing back on him, to take her to his arms, when she repels him with the addition, "but what an' if it were?" A like expression, only more prolonged, is given to the scene in Desdemona's chamber, where Emilia waits at the door. The "O Desdemona" is given as a cry of irrepressible tenderness, at which the lovers wind insensibly into each other's arms, and the following passage is spoken by Othello seated with Desdemona at his feet, her face between his hands, in tones of the old gentleness, that are to give place to a renewal of the fury.

The scene between Cassio and Bianca having been re- stored at the beginning of the fourth act, which opens upon Othello insensible with epilepsy, and so passes to what seems the strongest proof of Desdemona's guilt, the sense of pity becomes strengthened. The appeal is, by Mr. Fechter's rendering, more simply to pity for Othello than we suppose Shakespeare to have intended, but it is most effective, is made powerfully and with much success. The gentler sympathies of the whole audience are secured, and the fifth act therefore becomes very painful.

Here, too, Mr. Fechter has made noticeable innovations.

The Bedchamber is elaborately set, and the bed, no longer in an alcove at the back, is a pompous structure at the side of the stage, with its back to the audience, so as to conceal the sleeping Desdemona, and raised on a dais with several steps; so that it looks as portentous as a catafalque prepared for a great funeral pomp. Othello is in the room already ; and although one door is closed, open doors lead to the outer world, where operatic boatmen perform Desdemona's willow song, whereto he listens. That is a small effect unworthy of Shakespeare; and the showy effects now got with a great bed are rather more melodramatic than Shakespearean. Othello bolts the door that leads from within the house, but the doors by which there may be entry from without are left wide open. The murder also is too ostentatiously a murder, morally and physically.

When in the last act Othello enters Desdemona's chamber to inflict upon his wife what he regards as the just penalty of her offence, because his soul shrinks from the contemplated act, he strengthens it by bidding it look not to the bloody deed, but to the reason justifying it.

> " It is the cause, it is the cause, my soul !
> Let me not name it to you, ye chaste stars," etc.

When Mr. Fechter spoke these lines holding a hand-glass like a hair-brush that he had deliberately gone to fetch from Desdemona's bed, and which he threw, after speaking a few lines in dudgeon, to the carpenter, I had not imagination strong enough to conceive what he meant. Probably, I thought, Desdemona's vanity is being symbolised as the cause of her fall—a very poor notion, but let it pass. Now Mr. Fechter's explanatory book shows me that here Othello looks at his face in the glass, and is telling his soul that his skin is the cause of his misfortunes ! It is his skin that he will not name to the chaste stars !

Othello is, as he should be, in his own eyes executing justice, and when stirred to passion cries—

> " O perjur'd woman ! thou dost stone my heart,
>   And make me call what I intend to do,
>   A murder—which I thought a sacrifice."

The act, in Mr. Fechter's reading of it, is full of passion
and emotion, and the audience is deeply stirred, but the
effects in some respects belong rather to French melodrama
than to English tragedy, and Mr. Fechter even closes his
Othello with a melodramatic but false reading, by half-
throttling Iago—whom he wounded before his sword was
taken from him, whom he would not be suffered again to lay
hold of with a dagger in his hand, and on whom in his last
speech he is very far from spending thought.   For it is then
that he accuses himself only for one, " whose hand,

> " Like the base Judean, threw a pearl away,
>   Richer than all his tribe."

Instead of telling his tale of the circumcised dog whom he
took by the throat and smote him—"thus", in contempt of
himself mixed with a reminder of his old soldierly prowess,
Mr. Fechter's Othello is pulling Iago about with uplifted
dagger, and at the "thus"—to flash surprise—stabs not
Iago but himself.

November 2.—Mr. Robson reappeared at the OLYMPIC on
Monday after a second absence enforced on him by illness,
and was received with the most cordial and prolonged applause, which evoked from him a quiet " God bless you !"
His reappearance was in a new farce by Mr. Oxenford, *A
Legal Impediment*, of which the whole value consists in the
abundant opportunity it gives the actor to be droll in his own
way.   Mr. Robson is the outdoor man of a firm of griping
lawyers, pinched himself, and bespattered with mud of the
streets, where he has caught, in spite of his little camlet
cloak, a permanent cold that allows him to get no farther
in the announcement of his own name Slush, than H ''ush.
Mistaken for a better man in eccentric disguise, Mr. H ''ush
is invited to make himself at home over the fruit and

wine of a City man's dessert in his suburban paradise ; and he does make himself at home. Mr. Robson's toasts and sentiments after the manner of the Pork Pie Club, his sentimental song, his disgust and astonishment on getting an olive in his mouth—"they looks", he says, "like gooseberries, they tastes like periwinkles"—are all occasion for uproarious mirth. A farcical entertainment, in its way more thoroughly Robsonian, none could desire.

November 16.—*Our American Cousin* is a piece of Transatlantic extravagance which will have a long run at the HAYMARKET, not only because it is well mounted and acted, and presents Mr. Buckstone in a Yankee character, but more especially for the sake of a sketch new to our stage, given by an actor hitherto unknown in London, Mr. Sothern, with an eccentric and whimsical elaboration that is irresistibly amusing. It is the republican American's contemptuous notion of an English lord. There is absolute vacuity in the head of Lord Dundreary, but his whiskers are, with help of dye, in good condition. He is polite and good-natured, although inane, and very indulgent to an outside world that puzzles him sorely, by consisting chiefly of people whom he takes to be lunatics. The stale jokes and the extravagant suggestions of emptiness—his Lordship does not know what butter is, and has trouble to fit the name to the thing in speaking of a cow—would be intolerably stupid in the hands of almost any actor. But Mr. Sothern has overlaid it all with innumerable ludicrous touches of manner and byplay, and is so imperturbably extravagant that shouts of laughter follow almost every look and gesture. He contrives, in the midst of all the extravagance, to maintain for his inane lord the air of a well-bred, good-natured gentleman, and shows an art in his absurdity that makes us curious to see what he can do in some other character. But it will be long before he has leave from the public to do anything but identify himself with Lord Dundreary. The piece is sure of a long run.

December 7.—At the minor houses, including, alas!
DRURY LANE, *The Colleen Bawn*, in licensed reproduction
or unlicensed burlesque, is to be seen in all directions.
DRURY LANE and the SURREY give it in burlesque; the
DRURY LANE version, enriched with a version of the water-
cave scene by Mr. Beverley and the acting of Miss Louisa
Keeley, has attractions.   The burlesque acting by the company is also more welcome now that Mr. H. J. Byron,
instead of Shakespeare, furnishes the text.   The SURREY
burlesque parodies the title of the popular play by calling
itself *The Cooleen Drawn*, and doubtless has a dialogue
about as clever as its title.

Meanwhile *The Octoroon* at the ADELPHI, though the
public does not greatly care for it, is clever enough to earn
an ordinary run.   And the opposition to *The Colleen Bawn*
at the LYCEUM, Mr. Falconer's *Peep o' Day*, now pruned of
much of its verbiage, commands and deserves full houses
with unbounded applause for what is called, according to
the new term in theatrical slang, which Mr. Boucicault
imported for us from the other side of the Atlantic, its
"sensation" scene.   At the HAYMARKET Mr. Sothern's Lord
Dundreary is a piece of fun with which the playgoer is apt
to recreate himself more than once.   Mr. Sothern has this
week appeared in a farce—an old friend, *Livre III, Chap.* 1,
with a new face—translated from the French for the fourth
or fifth time as *My Aunt's Advice*.   He acts with ease and
spirit, pleasant and manly in his serious tones, and lively in
his mirth.   At the OLYMPIC a new comedietta, also from the
French, has been produced under the name of *Court Cards*,
with good scenes, delightfully brilliant and picturesque last-
century court dresses, and finished acting of a gaily compli-
cated little drama of intrigue.   Mr. and Mrs. Wigan continue
to represent at the ST. JAMES'S another play from the French,
The Poor Nobleman, which displays the highest finish of
English acting in the French manner.

1862, *March* 8.—There are, as to the main idea, two ways

of representing on the stage Shakespeare's Iago. Both have been in use probably since Shakespeare's time. One is that obtrusive presentment of a diabolical villainy which caused it to be objected against the Iago of Cibber that it made an idiot of the Othello who was blind to so much patent rascality; the other is that presentment of an accomplished hypocrite—a gay, light-hearted monster, a careless, cordial, comfortable villain—which Hazlitt found in the Iago of Edmund Kean. Mr. Fechter follows in his view of Iago the sense of Edmund Kean, and, what is far more to the purpose, that of Shakespeare. He is careful even to mark —what is so seldom marked in the acting—Iago's gradual though ready passage, led by circumstance, from crime to crime, until the climax of the tragedy he works. A thoroughly Italian quickness and vivacity of movement, which is said to have been a character of Kean's Iago, is also one of the strong points in the Iago of Mr. Fechter. Nobody can be more instant to obey a bidding, more animated in attention, quick in perception. When he leaves Othello in torment of mind his fingers cast at him behind his back a swift Italian gesture of contempt, instantly followed by servile obeisance at the threshold as Othello turns his face. Sometimes the vivacity of gesture leads to a questionable interpretation of a passage; but so much of what is new in Mr. Fechter's manner bears consideration, and may justify itself, while the whole reading is so just, so free from tricks of interpretation, and so smoothly coherent —as a part well played must always be—that I think it is far better than his Othello, and prefer it to his Hamlet.

March 15.—At the HAYMARKET, Mr. Westland Marston's *Household Picture under two Lights*, called *The Wife's Portrait*, is the best dramatic sketch I have seen lately. It is *not* from the French, but a sketch from nature of true character cunningly expressed by varied light and shade. It is long since I have seen among the novelties of the theatre so delightful a little English piece, with a true and complete character in it delicately drawn alike by author and by actress.   Mrs. C. Young represents the heroine.

August 30.—Miss Avonia Jones has appeared this week as Adrienne Lecouvreur, and confirms the impression made by her Medea.   The piece suits better than *Medea* the ADELPHI company.   She is therefore sufficiently supported. Miss Jones is clever and in earnest, she takes pains, feels her words as she utters them, has the command of good and varied facial expression, is not ungraceful in her attitudes, and is altogether an actress entitled to public respect.   In the desire, probably, to feel that she may make others feel, she pauses on her words too long, and the result is that she seems to act on a theory that all persons who speak under strong emotion speak very slowly, or, to be plain, drawl. The language of emotion is far oftener rapid than slow, and an actress really quickened by the instincts of genius would almost be in danger of a bodily explosion if, with the intellectual steam up, she went at the pace taken by Miss Jones when passionate utterance is asked of her.   Variations in the rate of utterance, variations also of tone, have yet to be studied before Miss Jones can take the place that really is within her reach among those leading actresses without genius who, if they get their well and hardly-earned applause in their own day, are in no concern at all about the silence of posterity.

November 1.—A new lessee of the PRINCESS'S, Mr. Lindus, seems to be resolved on avoidance of all clap-trap and sensation drama.   He has brought together a very efficient company, including Miss Amy Sedgwick and Miss Oliver, Mr. George Vining, Mr. Marston, Mr. Herman Vezin, with other good performers, and his programme hitherto has been, after a pleasant, well-appointed comedietta, one of the plays of Mr. Sheridan Knowles, either *The Hunchback* or *The Love Chase*.   *The Hunchback*, as it is now acted, with Miss Sedgwick and Miss Oliver for the two heroines, Mr. Marston for the Hunchback, and Mr. Vezin for the chosen husband, draws a full house and gives satisfaction. There is a bad imitation of Elizabethan manner in the language and some clumsiness of invention in the plot of these plays, but they are immeasurably better entertainment than the extravagance of scenic melodrama by which alone many managers are now tempted to think that the public can be charmed. Mr. Lindus has begun his enterprise with a quiet good taste that deserves full recognition and support.

1863, *January* 17.—A clean and elegant house, efficient actors, a well-appointed stage, and a picturesque romantic play that interests the public, Mr. Fechter now has, in addition to the goodwill and high expectation of the town, to assure him success at the outset of his venture as an actor-manager at the LYCEUM. The house before the curtain looks its prettiest.

In the painted lace of the ceiling certain names from the roll of English dramatists are worked in those crabbed letters which only a heraldic ticket-writer is able to read without labour—and the names follow each other thus in unadmired confusion : Shakespeare, Massinger, Byron, Knowles, Wycherley, Dryden, Ben Jonson, Otway, Beaumont, Fletcher, Rowe, Sheridan. On the stage, to be sure, when the curtain rises, we don't see the English drama, but a translation from the French of *Le Bossu*, one of the three or four great Parisian dramatic hits of the year 1862, which may not prove a great London hit, but, at any rate, deserves to have a run. I give my confidence to Mr. Fechter, and believe that he does mean to dig in the great unworked mines of our dramatic literature. At present we have M. Paul Féval holding the stage, and the English dramatists stuck only as flies upon the ceiling.

Never mind. M. Paul Féval's play, under its new name of *The Duke's Motto*, is a sure success, as an English revival might not be. It gives Mr. Fechter time, therefore, to warm his house, start prosperously, and observe his public.

The play is all bright-picturesque romance. It even rivals *The Colleen Bawn* and *Peep o' Day* with a set "sensation" scene and acrobatic feat for the hero, Mr. Fechter, who hauls himself up a rope, hand over hand, with a baby in his arms. Why, if the baby instead of being only a doll were but a real live baby, with a decent chance of being dropped upon its head or squeezed to death, the piece might run till Christmas 1866. With that magnificent effect the prologue ends; and the curtain rises next on many twinkling feet, and a bright dance of Pyrenean Gipsies. Here we see the bold outlawed free-lance who had gone into the castle fosse of the Duke de Nevers, and, assuming to be Duke, by uttering at a window the motto, "I am here", had received the Ducal baby—why the Duke himself had intended to elope with his own baby is not at all clear;—and the bold free-lance who, when he looked at the baby, was on the spot converted from his ruder ways, so that, instead of fighting the Duke for vanity's sake, he fought with him for love of right against six cowardly assassins; and the bold free-lance who when he and the Duke had beaten off the six assassins saw Nevers shot from an ambush by his villainous enemy, the Prince George Vining—a Prince with a villainous hunchback for his familiar—and the bold free-lance, when he escaped for the Duke's baby's sake by running up the rope for want of stairs, denounced on Prince George Vining and his hirelings vengeance from a window-sill, "the valets first, the master afterwards". That same bold free-lance, whose deeds and merits outrun twenty breaths, we find among the gipsies, with the precious babe over whom he has ever since been watching—now a fair maid twenty years old, secretly loving him, and secretly beloved by him.

But, ah !—the Prince George Vining, having married the babe's mother, that is to say, the widow of the Duke he shot in the back, to get the estates, must find and kill also the missing child. He comes ; the Prince George Vining,

or Gonzagues, comes among these gipsies seeking a substitute for the real daughter of the Duke, and finds a charm
ing one in Miss Carlotta Leclerq, the Gipsy Queen. But,
as it happens, close at hand is the Chevalier Fechter, or
Lagardère, the free-lance become gipsy, with Miss Kate
Terry herself, who is the rightful child. And the wicked
hunchback, with averted face and a big wig, he recognises
them. Upon which hunchback's time is come, as the last
unslain of the valets, to be killed, and he walks off the
stage to be killed, followed by the gallant avenger, who
presently returns in the big wig and with the hunchback's
robe, and with an assumed crook in his body and with
averted face, to enter for his own ends into the service
of the villainous Prince. After the valets the master.
Besides, there is the rightful child to protect. Prince
George Vining never discovers that a stranger has assumed
the place of his familiar. But much romance comes of the
mystification, and much clever acting and much pleasure
and amusement to the audience. The master might,
indeed, have been sent very speedily after the valets; but
then that would have cut two clever acts out of the play.
As for improbability of incident, he is a dull fellow who
does not sometimes like it. Certainly there is plenty of it
in the mine of English drama that we hope soon to see
Mr. Fechter drawing wealth from in every sense, material
as well as intellectual. There were more startling dramatic
incidents set forth upon the stage of the old Globe Theatre
than we shall ever get out of the Porte St. Martin. That
is not my complaint. What I do miss in these French
dramas is the glow of impassioned poetry, the daring flight
now into and now and then beyond the sublime, but always
gloriously and nobly on the wings of energetic thought. I
miss this, and the strains of a truer pathos or the flashes of
more sterling wit that belong to one or two of the dramatists
whose names I see, and one or two whose names I do not
see, on Mr. Fechter's ceiling.

February 7.—Mr. Boucicault is at ASTLEY'S, transformed under his new management into the THEATRE ROYAL, WESTMINSTER. His version of *The Trial of Effie Deans* must have been originally written for an audience somewhat lower in taste than that which frequents the SURREY THEATRE. He has found it in him to construct out of *The Heart of Midlothian* a pure Old Bailey play in three acts.

All is done that can be done to make the audience as happy as if they had paid half-a-crown apiece for seats in the gallery of the Old Bailey to hear an interesting murder-case and enjoy the humours of a popular criminal barrister, who is to appear as counsel for the defence. It is all there, in the second act, in prosy detail, from the formal citation of the titles of our sovereign lord the King, including his supremacy over the Channel Islands, and the calling over the names of the jury, to the point of passing sentence of death, upon which the curtain falls. And there is, shining in brass, the popular criminal barrister, all his claptrap being caricatured with most undoubted cleverness by Mr. Boucicault. Mr. Boucicault appears as counsel for the defence. He had been described in the previous scene as a generous barrister touched by the situation of Effie Deans, who had volunteered to speak in her defence without a fee. He is presented by Mr. Boucicault as a bamboozler of juries, who affects an enthusiasm that he does not feel, and knows so little of the facts of his case that, in the midst of grand bursts of mock eloquence, he makes comic stoppages for dry asides to his junior, wherein he asks whether he may venture to say this or that, and, being told that he may, charges down on the jurymen again with his mock thunder. It is as good as a farce, no doubt, and is precisely that which makes a seat in the Old Bailey gallery delicious to the vulgar ; but it is absolutely at war with the dramatic situation. It is not at all the pleading of a barrister whose heart is in his cause, who has renounced his fee, and speaks for the pure love of right and mercy. Yet to this coarse Newgate entertainment Mr. Boucicault has reduced Scott's delicate romance.

February 14.—At the St. James's Theatre a new piece called *The Dark Cloud*, by the gentleman who is known to the public as Mr. Arthur Sketchley, is a drama of plot and counterplot, and so far of the French school that the plot turns on an attempt against the honour of a wife. But there is no lax French morality. A genial and wholesome English tone prevails throughout. The villain is no polished, smiling gentleman, but a rough fellow full of evil propensities and evil deeds, who, being in youth an unsuccessful rival to his friend in the love of the heroine, pushed jealousy to crime. He obtained the ruin and transportation of the innocent young husband, who died a convict; he was himself sent abroad, and after ten years of a wild criminal life in Australia, blended with successful gold-digging, came back with the rough and desperate impression of his early passion yet in his heart, to win the object of his perverted love by force or fraud. A new actor, Mr. Arthur Stirling, as the criminal, foully faithful to an old passion, when he in subdued voice pleads his cause, seeks to persuade with so clever and natural a suggestion of coarse tenderness that he appears to singular advantage. This advantage, however, he does not maintain in the other new piece lately produced at the St. James's Theatre, *The Merry Widow*. His part is not a promising one, but he makes it unnecessarily tedious.

The Merry Widow is a piece in two acts, adapted by Mr. Leicester Buckingham from a recent French piece, *Jeanne qui pleure, et Jeanne qui rit*. Jeanne qui pleure appears in the first act as a crocodile widow, who by false tears entraps into an engagement a young surgeon returned from India, where there died by his side, as he thought, a gallant friend whose wife's sister he has come home to marry. But he finds his friend's widow, who is the heroine of the second act, a Jeanne qui rit. She goes with her sister to balls, concerts, and all gay entertainments, though her husband's death is recent. She has forfeited all her good friends, and she is mocked behind her back in polite circles as the Merry Widow. But her mirth covers a breaking heart. She has not dared to tell the blind old mother of her husband, who lives with her and to whose life any great shock would be fatal, that her son is dead. The old lady forces her, therefore, to take her sister into society.

At home the sisters give lively accounts of their doings in the world, and once a month the wretched wife goes through the torture of reading an imaginary letter from her dead husband that professes to be written to his mother or to herself. Miss Herbert plays the wife, and the reading of such a letter to the old woman, at a moment when her own heart is wrung by the reappearance of her husband's friend, by the chilling words of taunt that have accompanied the delivery of her husband's last bequest of love, and by their friend's cold retractation of his suit for her sister, is the situation in which lies the whole interest and power of the piece. It is almost Ford's *Calantha* brought into a modern drawing-room. Miss Herbert's acting in this situation makes the fortune of the little drama. I care much less for her acting at its close, when she enters the room with haggard face while a real letter is being read from her husband, who has, after all, been in a prison and not in a grave. The transition from the belief that the old farce is being re-enacted, to wonder, doubt, eager curiosity, and a sudden assurance of joy, by which she is struck to the ground, is unnaturally slow, and the stroke of joy that felled a wife under such circumstances would not allow her to articulate " He lives", or whatever the tag may be, and place herself so as to form a tableau on which to bring the curtain down.

Of the two acts of the piece, the first is wholly superfluous. All that the first act shows for the interpretation of the second is implied clearly in the dialogue of the second, or, if not so implied to everybody, could be set forth by the addition of ten words.

March 14.—At the St. James's *Lady Audley's Secret* appears as a drama.   It is only in two acts ; and the putting of the superfluous husband into the well follows so closely on the bigamy, the glow of the arson, again, so closely on the stain of murder, and the interesting heroine goes mad so immediately, with the glow of the house she has burnt yet on her face, and the man she has burnt in it dying on a stretcher by her side, that the audience has a pudding all plums.

At the Princess's there was produced last Wednesday a version of *Aurora Floyd* in four acts, and in this play occurred the chief dramatic incident of the present week— the distinct advance of Mr. G. Belmore, who represents the half-witted murderer Stephen Hargreaves, from among the ranks of actors clever only in burlesque and farce, towards the higher ground occupied by Mr. Robson and Mr. Toole.

At the Olympic there is *The Lottery Ticket*, in which Mr. Robson as Wormwood, the misanthropic lawyer's clerk, enjoys "a heavenly day" of trouble to his neighbours.

March 21.—There was produced at the Adelphi on Wednesday evening another version of *Aurora Floyd*. The lowest form of literary taste in the uneducated having been forced into fashion among readers who have better fare at their command, the players, who seek only to please the palate of the town, will cook the garbage that is in demand. Omelets are accounted flavourless ; a strong taste in the mouth is the one thing desired. *Aurora Floyd*, as acted at the Adelphi, lasted on the first night four hours and twenty minutes in performance, being two hours longer than the Princess's version, and, upon the principle here applicable of the less the better, being in that proportion worse.

The life of the piece at the Adelphi, as at the Princess's, is in the impersonation of the murderer, the "softy" Stephen Hargreaves. Mr. Webster, in his representation of this part, does not take a leaf from the laurels won at the Princess's by Mr. Garstin Belmore. His conception is entirely different, a thing by itself. The weakness of intellect is shown only in the lowness of its degradation. The make-up of the actor, with deformed back, crooked limbs, a Caliban fore-head under a thief's crop of red hair, a penthouse of shaggy eyebrow over cunning eyes, and a great cruel, witless mouth that, we know not how, seems to be all fang, creates a being in whom not even an expert playgoer, without assurance of the playbill, would easily recognise Mr. Webster. Mr. Dickens's Quilp must have been suggested more than once to half the audience. In this spirit Mr. Webster acts the part through with a terrible energy. His greed, cunning, and malice become diabolical under unwonted excitement and temptation, and we part from him as he is dragged off screaming unmitigated hate—in strong contrast to the abject, entreating cries of animal fear with which the half-witted man, as Mr. Belmore represents him, is carried off, as he supposes, to be hanged like a dog straightway.

April 13.—The list of performances at London theatres this week would, with but one or two exceptions, be an insult to the taste of the town if it did not indicate a lament-able change in the class to which the drama looks for patronage. It is quite true that new conditions of society have somewhat altered the relations between stage and people. When there were few readers and few comfortable homes, the story told to the eye and ear attracted thousands whose imaginations needed active exercise. Now the story can be read at ease among home comforts. Out of the printed page graces of style and delicate suggestions of the fancy rise to the mind undisturbed by flare of gas and smell of orange-peel, and so it is that the men of genius who would have written plays for the Elizabethan public are the novelists of our own time.

How do the players meet this difficulty? Not often by resisting, too often by multiplying all the influences tending to decay. I am heartily with the players, seeing constantly how hard they work in their vocation, how well they honour

it by prudent charitable deeds, and how ready they sometimes are to honour it by acting good things that the public
will not come to see. When that excellent actor Mr. Frank
Matthews first became the lessee of the ST. JAMES'S THEATRE,
every old playgoer wishing well to his venture, he produced
the best new plays he could get of a creditable sort, and
though they were not bad, and were acted well, I saw one
evening his curtain rise to an audience of five in the stalls,
seven in the dress-circle, and thirty in the pit. He is
now acting to crowded houses *Lady Audley's Secret*, and
a burlesque of Mr. Boucicault's burlesque of *Effie Deans*.
Let us not underrate the difficulty and the temptation.
Theatrical prosperity is most precarious, as many people
know too well, in spite of Mr. Boucicault's advertisement of the glorious percentages to be made by speculation in a couple of theatres under such enlightened
management as his, producing, of course, an unlimited series
of Phantoms, Dots, and Octoroons. The temptation is
very great to meet debility by stimulants, but there can be
only one end to that course. It leads, through the degradation, sooner or later to the ruin of the stage.

In his worldly affairs, the actor has of late given conspicuous evidence to the public, in the excellent Dramatic
College, that he has the full average of prudence, with more
than the average of generosity and sound professional good-
fellowship. But, however hard the task, it must now be
expected of him that he should provide for the future of his
profession as well as of himself and his brethren. The
charm of a good play well acted is something wholly different from the enjoyment within reach of a home reader,
and it is most powerful over the most cultivated minds,
while it can hold the roughest crowd in thrall. The public
in the innyards and playhouses of Elizabeth's day was
rougher in its ways, and lower in its tastes, than the public
to which are now offered the vile, unintellectual, shambling
melodramas, bad punning, and senseless grotesque toeing

and heeling, recommended by much costly scenery.   Yet on the old rude stages before those rough audiences, actors strained their skill to express the force of human life and passion in words that at their wildest aimed towards some height of a true poetry.   There lie their plays, untouched. Some of the names of the old dramatists Mr. Fechter has glued to his ceiling, while he acts the translation of a French melo-drama that is romantic, picturesque, but not enlivened with a single word of power.   Why are their works shelved?   They contain "sensation" plots by the score; for the Elizabethan public also liked strong meat and mustard.   It would not take more trouble to adapt for the "sensation"-loving public Marlowe's *Faustus*, or his *Jew of Malta*, than to translate and adapt vapid French melodrama.   There would be plenty of room for scenery in such old English plays made new; plenty of wild marvel and startling situations: but instead of the poor slipslop words there would come home to the very souls of the audience, with a fair share of the bombast that I would by no means have expunged, the wild stir again of a true manly English poetry.   How can a man be or seem a great actor who has to speak night after night such words as are now commonly set down for him?   Put honest poetry of passion in the actors' mouths, let them begin by ranting if they will, and, if there be such stuff in them as I honestly believe there is in many actors of our day, they will warm to their new work, and soon win the educated as well as the uneducated public to their stage.

May 23.—Let our new school of burlesque writers be taught by the success of the amusing comedy, *Finesse*, pro-duced last Saturday at the HAYMARKET.   In the veins of the writer runs the blood of Sheridan, and the abundant mirth it causes is genuine mirth provoked by wit in its fair sport and its extravagance.   There is not a pun in the piece, although one scene is full of mirthful and witty play upon the double sense of words.   The writer of *Finesse* is the authoress of those *Lispings from Low Latitudes* which form

one of the merriest and most genial of table-books with pen
and pencil burlesques upon life, and the wit of the comedy
runs often into burlesque as genuine. It has higher merits,
for it interweaves curiously a thread of fine comedy with the
broad merriment of farce. The audience is heartily amused
by a bright flashing of wit and witty fun, and becomes
joyous upon this new sort of provision. No punning can
suggest a more whimsically extravagant idea than that put
in the mouth of Mr. Buckstone, who, as a nautical cockney
after a hard day's trouble at Messina, complains that he is
hungry, for he has had nothing to eat but three watermelons
and a peppermint lozenge. Only the blockheads would be
enemies to broad burlesque; grotesque absurdity is fair
source of recreation, and we may concede as much licence
to the decoration of burlesque and the provision of gay
ballets as Ben Jonson might have taken for the decorations
and the dumb-shows of a masque. Burlesques of the present day are wretched only by reason of the want of all true
fun, the inconceivable parade of poverty of wit that comes
of stuffing them with puns. Writers of this intolerable stuff
consider themselves complimented by the deprecation to
which punning has been always liable. They will tell you
themselves that he who will make a pun will pick a pocket,
and tell you that with a smile, as who should say, You know
what clever fellows we are nevertheless.

But punning is *not* a mark of cleverness. Except when
it involves a witty thought, the play on words is but the
mark of the mind too feeble to lay hold habitually with its
entire attention on the thoughts of which words are the
signs, but accustomed to stop at the mere perception of
their sound within the ear. It indicates the weakness of an
intellect so little attentive to sense that it is able to spend
what trifle of thought it connects with the use of words
on the jumping aside after any jingle that can be dragged
into false association with them. The social contempt
for the mere punster is not expressed as in playful joke

against a spoilt child of good-humour; it is the well-grounded and demonstrably just censure of a manner of speech that signifies commonly a want of intellect. Where a man of sound judgment has been, like Sidney Smith, also a punster, his puns always sent home a witty thought, and were not a mere brainless playing upon words.

It is perfectly manifest that a story, told in language contrived incessantly to divert attention from the sense of language to its sound, is told with such deficient use of human speech that it can be but dimly presented to the mind. The tale is inevitably sacrificed; nearly every natural source of fun in the writing is also dammed up by this wretched obstruction; and if the actors, who have all the mirth to make for themselves, are not lavishly grotesque, the piece becomes insufferably dull. The first and easiest step, then, towards a restoration of the credit of the stage is that managers, without lessening the scenic attraction, the gay ballets, or the grotesque action of their burlesques, should require the burlesque writers to cease their punning and begin to make use of their brains. There is, I know, in more than one of them a hearty sense of fun that would be glad to escape from the vile bondage that now chains together in one gang the wits and the dolts, and that would know how to revel to good purpose in true merriment of mind. While there is abundant absurdity, it is the absurdity of wit or humorist, in the Duke of Buckingham's *Rehearsal*, Fielding's *Tom Thumb*, Sheridan's *Critic*, or the German Tieck's fairy extravaganzas. But where fancy should be free to frolic, let us set up no models for imitation. I only pray for the abandonment of the delusion that there is proper entertainment for the public in a form of writing absolutely and incurably inane, and of which we might almost say that for facility in its production the possession of intelligence of any sort is the most serious disqualification.

July 4.—The first new part in which Madame Ristori has

appeared at HER MAJESTY'S THEATRE during her present visit to London has been that of Deborah in an Italian translation of a mildly benevolent and not unpoetical German play, called *Deborah*, by S. B. Mosenthal.   Herr Mosenthal, whose *Deborah*, a *Volks-Schauspiel* in prose and verse, was first produced about a dozen years ago, is also the author of a version into modern German verse of the works of old Austrian poets, and more recently of a clever fanciful play, *Das gefangene Bild*.   He belongs fairly to the more refined class of modern German *littérateurs*.   Doubtless his *Deborah* play was meant to be a lesson of toleration between Christian and Jew, for there is much said on behalf of toleration in the abstract.   And yet the young Albert, son of the village Mayor, having given his heart to the poor trusting Jewish Deborah (instead of the Christian Anna, the Pastor's niece, whom it is considered that he ought to marry), is smuggled away from the Jewess, married to the Christian, and becomes so wonderfully good, that the heart of the woman he has wronged, which in the third act poured the bitterness of its curses upon him, claiming eye for eye and tooth for tooth, is at the close of the play melted to exquisite tenderness ; and I don't think that the author, with all his tolerance, could have brought himself within five thousand miles of the assumption that Albert ought to have married the Jewess, for whom his God was her God and his ways her ways.

But his play is good.   The great wrong to the Jewess arises out of, and has everywhere for its background, the tattle of the village.   Every act but the last begins with a little tumult of small-talk, in which the affairs of the Mayor and his son, and the Pastor and his niece, and the opinions of the schoolmaster, the mercer, the baker, the hostess, or the representative of the superstitious old woman, Old Martha, are put forth and discussed.   The highest poetry of life is thus, for the author's purpose, cleverly and effectively set, as the world sets it, in its petty prose.

In the wood outside a Styrian village are some poor Jews who have been hunted out of Hungary. They are an old blind man, a helpless woman with a new-born child, and the high-hearted Deborah, daughter of a Rabbi, who is outcast with them, and who faithfully but somewhat sternly guides and succours them. Deborah has her mind stored with the poetical traditions of her fathers, but she is a young enthusiast who has her first and last love to bestow, and she has given it all to the young Christian from the village, Albert the Mayor's son, who secretly pours out his own love at her feet. The sensitive girl's nature—that had been exalted by the teaching of her father, the Rabbi, and the sorrows of her people, into a vivid realisation of the wail of the Jews at Babylon, and of their curse on the oppressor; that had been hardened by the sense of wrong; that had yearned for the restoration of Sion—is all turned to woman's love by the strong bidding of nature. Thus only we see her in the first act.

The good Anna has found the Jews in the wood, desires to bring Deborah's helpless charges into the village, and excites the ignorant outcry of the villagers. Into the midst of their chatter Deborah comes, looking for Albert. The villagers, did not Anna and her uncle the Pastor intercede, would haul her off to the ducking-pond. She stands at bay; and the author evidently intends a showy situation for the actress here. But Madame Ristori notes that in her next scene with Albert, when he refers to her danger in the village, she replies that she heard nothing, she thought only of him; and in this spirit alone, resisting every strong temptation to produce a false effect, she acts at her first entry. Even the apparent sanction of the author's stage-directions does not betray her to a false emphasis that would secure worthless applause. Not yet knowing her tale, one rather wonders, as if it were fault in her, why, baited thus, Deborah is so quiet. She seeks some one, when hunted is a little haughty and distraught, but not excited, showing no signs of deep

trouble. True actress as she is, Madame Ristori has read,
here as always, only for the true and deep sense of her part,
and she relies wholly for stage-effect upon the most exact
expression of its poetry. . But Deborah meets Albert as, protected by the Pastor, she is returning to the forest, and, in
exchange of a few rapid words, appoints a meeting with him
at the cross in the wood. Albert is left, guilty of mysterious
absences, to be the grief of his father and the perplexity of
Anna ; then for the rest of the act we have Deborah and
Albert in the wood. The poor Jews over whom Deborah
watches are asleep ; she awaits in the moonlight Albert, as
her Messiah, blending the girl's dream of love with solemn
memories of the mystical prayers learnt from the old Rabbi.
Albert comes, and she pours out on him her love and trust.
For him she has put to sleep the old wail of despair awaiting
vengeance, Cursed be thou, Babylon, and blessed he who
shall repay to thee the evil thou hast done ! As a weird
dream of the past this memory surges up in her talk with
him, as the moan of the sea under moonlight, that when the
clouds gather will rise into the fury of the tempest. Albert,
whom we find detestably weak, whatever Herr Mosenthal
meant us to think of him, has crude dreams of the perfec-
tibility of man in an American millennium. Deborah shall
be his wife and fly with him from all the petty discords of
small minds. He will be a priest of the rights of men. And
Deborah will do all as he shall order it, whither he goes she
will go, for he has taught her to know that his God is a God
of love. The old blind man, the helpless woman, the little
one—who will sustain them if she who is their eyes, their
feet, forsake them? But Albert urges, and she yields—
" *Dannabile non son colpe a te grate*"—and upon the solemn
tenderness of the poor Jewess's love the act closes, as she
blesses her departing lover.

With the opening of the second act we are again plunged
into the tattle of the village. Albert has spoken out at last,
and his father has had an apoplectic fit in consequence.

And then Albert is to be tenderly managed and reasoned
with after the manner of old people who wish to manage the
young, and is to be discussed after the manner of inquisitive
neighbours. Of course the young Jewess is a designing
person—neighbours do say that she fascinates by enchant-
ment—her sole object of course is to get money. Let her
have money and go. The schoolmaster has a secret of his
own, that he is a Jew turned Christian, and dreads any contact of villagers with other Jews who might make it known
that he also had been one of the hated race. He gladly
undertakes the errand to the forest, with a village guard or
two, to turn the nest of Jews out by main force if they will
not be bribed. He finds, not Deborah but the old man, who,
though blind, knows his voice, and betrays him to the
gossips of the guard (he will be turned out of his school for
this), and then he meets the woman who is not Deborah,
but who eagerly takes the money and at once promises that
they shall all depart. Upon which the schoolmaster de-
spatches instantly a message to Albert and his father saying
that the money has been taken.

Meanwhile Deborah has been seen solemnly commend-
ing to the God of Israel the care over the helpless ones
that she lays down with anxious heart, and her last words
to herself had been the cry, " *Forza, o mio cuor . . Alberto !
Abbimi tutta !*" But he does not come to her. The night
is stormy. She is drawn to the door of her beloved. In
the thunder she hears now Jehovah upon Sinai, and now
a voice that may cry to Albert of the sorrow of her heart
and bid him come to comfort her with kisses. She knocks
fainting at the gate, and Albert's father opens to her. He
tells her that she had fascinated his son only for gold, had
taken gold, and now—she yet returns. Deborah understands nothing ; she is faint, bewildered ; she follows him
only with a cry for Albert as he leaves her, and on her
knees before the old man yearns only for the sight of
Albert. The kindly Anna comes to her, still with the same

tale of her barter of her love for gold. There is no wild outbreak of passion here in Madame Ristori's Deborah; she is benumbed, confounded, questions herself vaguely, "*oro . . . . qual oro?*" and when these are shutting the gate upon her, her thought is, that, for forsaking in the darkness of the night the helpless who put trust in her, she also is now in the darkness helpless and alone. But Albert, the desire of her soul, is next to enter: with sudden happiness she lightens up at his coming step, and at his presence. He also disdains and formally discards her; insults her by throwing money at her feet. They leave her so, and with a piteous cry Deborah sinks at the threshold of the closed door.

The next act opens with the tattle and bustle over the marriage of Albert and Anna. Old Martha has an appetite for placing over the joined hands of each new married couple, as they go to church, her gift of a rosary with a cross fastened to it, a rosary that has been prayed over and made into a charm to preserve union and happiness in wedlock, and guard the souls of the children and the children's children. Albert and Anna receive such a rosary as the wedding procession forms upon its way to church. Ignorant of all that is passing, in the old churchyard behind the church *Deborah* has kept vigil for seven days and seven nights—for so long do her people mourn their dead—over her dead love. We see her there in sad lament, the spirit of vengeance stirs, but it is calmed by the solemn strains of the organ as the marriage-service is proceeding in the church. She hears voices as of a marriage-ceremony; and, passionately sensitive to the blessings of a happy consecrated love, she kneels to add her benediction. The dramatic situation is good, and nothing could be more exquisite in its pathetic tenderness than Madame Ristori's expression of the utterance of the bruised heart—

" anch 'io m' unisco, anch 'io
A benedirvi o sposi ! . . . oh ! Amen, Amen !"

She rises from her knees, curious to see those whom she
has blessed, and recoils with a wild horror when she recognises Albert. Her blessing withers in her heart, she revokes
it; and when Albert presently comes alone into the churchyard—for he had thought he heard the cry of Deborah—
Deborah herself is there in solemn majesty of Jewish wrath.
There is a tumult in her first of love and scorn. When
Albert seeks to explain, and tells his version of the story, of
her having taken money to go from him, the bitterest pang
strikes to the heart of Deborah, and marvellous is the
actress's delivery of the words, *Credermi capace!* which indicates the uprooting of that idolatry which had possessed her
soul. If this was his religion, she returned penitent to the
God of her fathers. Love is transitory, vengeance is eternal;
and with fixed gaze, in low rapt voice, as though she were a
prophetess, she pours rapidly into his ears a curse upon the
earth he tills, the wife he loves, the children she may bear.
The curse seems to cleave to him as he cowers under it.
Again she hears the wail of Babylon, but now it is wild and
pitiless. May his child bear the mark of Cain, and languish
in its mother's arms like the babe of the Jewish woman she
forsook for him; may his father like the poor old Abraham
thenceforth wander in darkness. And all is sealed with a
solemn intensity: *Maledetto, tre volte maledetto; E come all'*
Ebal Israel gridava Tre volte io grido; Amen! Amen! Amen!
The whole grandeur and terror of the malediction is expressed by the actress. Even his charmed rosary Deborah
snatches from the new-made husband, winds it about her
clenched hand, and as she leaves him points to the cross on
it with bitter and defiant scorn.

In the next act we see, after lapse of half-a-dozen years,
Deborah sternly waiting the fulfilment of her curse. She is
among her people, who are departing from the land that
casts them out. She will not go till she has looked on

Albert's ruin. The scene changes to Albert's house, happy and rich in wife and child, and smiling harvests, and the blessing of all men. Deborah enters upon this, and is met, as one poor and weary, by Anna's Christian tenderness. Albert is away, has been away some days on a good errand; but the miserable woman snatches at the hope that he may have forsaken wife and child, and presses eagerly vindictive fancies, until Anna shrinks from her, and bids her go, yet calls her back. The Angelus sounds, and Anna prays for Albert. Deborah will not hear that prayer, and withdraws. Albert returns, and from his talk with his wife Deborah learns that she is spoken of with love and tenderness between them. When they retire into the house, her heart is softened. Their child comes out, sees her and speaks to her; she fastens with a trace of her old passionate delight upon the features of its father born again in the child; discovers that Albert's child has been taught to remember Deborah in daily prayers, and kneels weeping; learns that the child's name is Deborah, and kisses its face, the hem of its dress; hangs the rosary upon its neck, and lays upon its head the tenderest blessing.

> "Te benedica Iddio .   .   .
> E gli Altri tutti."

Here the curtain should fall, for the pathos of the situation, perfectly rendered, cannot be surpassed, but the author has continued the scene into a weak final tableau.

July 11.—The difference between the representations of M. Gounod's *Faust* at HER MAJESTY's THEATRE and at COVENT GARDEN is so great and so distinctly marked that I believe it to have been designed by the author (who assisted at the production in each case), with no small advantage to his own work, and no prejudice at all to either house. There are two ways of reading Goethe's *Faust:* it may be read literally as the story of a village girl whose plain substantial love is stolen from her by unholy arts, who is betrayed and forsaken, yet in her hour of uttermost distress finds pity in heaven ; or it may be read mystically as a soul's tragedy of the devil's war against the innocent. At HER MAJESTY'S THEATRE we have the real, at COVENT GARDEN the ideal side of the conception. But the ideal to a great extent includes the real, and is clearly the point of view from which especially the music was composed. Goethe's own sketches of Margaret present distinctly in ideal outline the image of a real and artless village girl. That is the Margaret of Mdlle. Titiens, who plunges substantially into an abyss of love, and with the help of Signor Giuglini brings out in the garden scene the whole material and sensuous charm of the music.

Madame Miolan-Carvalho, who has been taught by M. Gounod himself how he intends her part of Margaret to be played, and for whom its music was written, represents not so much the girl as the girl's soul. Even in the dressing of the part this is remembered. Until her fall she walks in virgin white, the idealisation of the character marked strongly by contrast of her dress with the gay peasant costumes of the other girls. Betrayed and forsaken, the white has been changed for grey. After the death of her brother, his last words laying his death at her door, she enters the cathedral with dress black as ink ; no white, but in great sleeves like wings about the arms she lifts in prayer. In prison she wears grey again, with a white lining ; and she ascends at last in pure white to the skies.

In her acting, Madame Miolan-Carvalho represents first the still pure maiden spirit, on the way to church when Faust first meets her. Afterwards, re-entering her garden, prayer-book in hand, and through a strain of sacred melody wondering who was the stranger that accosted her, she does not fling away Siebel's flowers, but drops them unconsciously as she submits with an innocent grace to the fascination of the devil's jewels. When Faust and Mephistopheles arrive, at the first near approach of Mephistopheles to Margaret there is a sudden jar in the music, Margaret is fluttered and half faints, and there is an exclamation of defiant hatred from the disguised fiend ; but that first shock of the contending principles underlies natural dialogue that accounts otherwise for the fiend's cry and for Margaret's faintness. In the HAY-MARKET reading of the piece, the thought here intended is conveyed ; but it seems rather a small detached effect than, as at COVENT GARDEN, necessary to the harmony of the entire performance. In the more spiritual version, Margaret under fascination does not seek Faust, hardly dares to look at him, delivers her love up wonderingly ; and so throughout until the closing plaint of Margaret at her window, which she begins sitting, and during which she rises pressed with the magical longing to her full height in the window, Madame Miolan-Carvalho maintains to the last the sense that it is Mephistopheles, not Faust, who has achieved the cruel victory.

In Mephistopheles as represented by M. Faure, instead of M. Gassier's hunted Figaro, we have a malignant fiend stricken with deadly terror, quaking, shrinking, gnashing his teeth, when Mephistopheles is banned with the crosses on the sword-hilts of the students. His mocking serenade at the door of forsaken Margaret is no longer the almost incomprehensible excrescence it appeared, as given by M. Gassier, in connection with the other reading of the opera. Here we have seen in the drama, and felt in the music, a conflict between a pure soul and a mocking fiend ; and the serenade, as given by M. Faure, has mockery for its natural tone, but is the devil's cruel song of triumph in its motive.

A transposition of scenes in this act, as performed at the HAYMARKET Opera, seems to confirm the impression that M. Gounod meant to show separately at the London houses the two sides, spiritual and human, of his work. In the HAYMARKET version, the fiend's interference with the prayers of Margaret takes place with diminished emphasis outside the cathedral, and is followed by the killing of Valentine and his curse on his sister, which forms the climax of the act. This is transposed from the original arrangement, and the effect of the change is to bring out with more emphasis the material incidents of the story, and to throw its allegorical sense more into the background. At COVENT GARDEN the original order is restored. The curse has fallen upon Margaret before the struggle in the church of the despairing soul with the demon who lurks to betray it, and that conflict forms in a great cathedral scene the climax of the act. Mephistopheles speaks to his victim from within a side-chapel, where, by a skilful arrangement of the lights and shadows, he stands like a spectre. Again— to hurry at once to the end—the redemption of Margaret's soul is not represented slightly by a transparency, but dwelt upon in a substantial group that fitly crowns an opera remarkable even at this house for the luxurious complete-ness of its stage-appointments, and so brings the allegory to its right, emphatic end. But Faust is held to his bargain. At the HAYMARKET, where he is chiefly shown as one of a pair of human lovers, he is, I believe, with M. Gounod's consent, saved.

And let me not forget to mention how finely in the rendering of Madame Miolan-Carvalho the soul of Margaret, strong in prayer and victorious over the tempter, at last strides forward and stands fearless breast to breast with its great enemy.

August 15.—Mr. Tom Taylor's play, written by two Frenchmen, the *Léonard* of MM. Edouard Brisbarre and Eugène Nus, Englished as *The Ticket-of-Leave Man*, has a great run of success. When this drama was first produced here Mr. Tom Taylor received from most people entire credit for the play, while some profound observations were made here and there as to his logic in illustrating the ticket-of-leave question by a man who was not really a criminal. We know what would be said of a writer in any other department of literature, except only the stage, who, having translated into English, with a few small changes and touches and a transformation of title, the book of any foreign author, should present it to the public as his own. The players themselves, who are often good adapters from the French, have lately taken to the honest way of naming their French author in the play-bills. An OLYMPIC actor, Mr. Horace Wigan, has thus acknowledged all his obligations for some time past. Of the source of *The Duke's Motto* we had two-thirds of an acknowledgment in the announcement that it was by " Paul Féval and John Brougham". For " and" read " through", and the acknowledgment is perfect.

If the actors disdain this mystification, surely the authors should be far above it. The plea of custom is, no doubt, admissible in bar of any question of literary dishonesty. The *suppressio veri* in this matter has not for some years past been considered dishonest, and it would, indeed, establish only a conventional fiction were the rule of translation and adaptation universal. But there are, perhaps, some writers who would try to be original if they could get credit for their originality ; and there are some who do try and do not get credit ; because against every new piece claimed as original the too common practice of dramatic writers tends to raise the suspicion that it hoists false colours. Some critics read, see, and try to remember, a mass of French pieces that are not worth reading or seeing, to say nothing of remembering, in order that they may maintain credit as detectives ; and the sources of this sort of mystification are so wide and obscure that, one might almost say, every English dramatic writer is supposed in this matter to be a licensed cheat, and nobody ever can be proved honest. Nobody is now before the public who is more able than Mr. Tom Taylor to give us a play

" From his own hand, without a coadjutor,
  Novice, journeyman, or tutor,"

or to adapt with utmost neatness to the manner of its English players, and the humour of its English public, a French drama worth his transplantation. For that reason, it is especially upon occasion of some clever work of his that one prefers to direct attention to a mischievous custom that must not be overlooked in any fair consideration of the present condition of the London stage.

And one could wish, also, that the very few managers who still believe in it would abandon their faith in that form of puffing which consists in stating what is not the fact. Where is now the THEATRE ROYAL, Westminster, that was to show a trustful company how thirty thousand, million, billion, or whatever other sum it was a year, formed the natural profits of a right system of theatrical management?

We have then, at present, for the support of the London stage behind the curtain, a well-organised, respectable profession, a large body of hard-working and well-meaning actors and actresses, among whom are many capable of aiding strongly in the elevation of the public taste. Let the public give the full weight of its support and respect to plain-speaking. Let it estimate mere puffery at its right value. Let it expect to be told in the play-bills, when a new piece is adapted from the French, who was the original author, and what work of his is presented to them. Let every branch and offshoot of the delusive system be thrown to the quacks, with whom players, like all other professional men, are infested, and throughout the middle and upper ranks of the players' calling let us have, as between players and public, an abandonment of every sort of customary falsehood.

The only difficulty I see, says the player, to stand in the way of a full accomplishment of this lies with the public. And he fancies that he finds reason every week to endorse Colley Cibber's opinion that "it is not to the actor, but to the vitiated and low taste of the spectator, that the corruptions of the stage (of what kind soever) have been owing. If the public by whom they must live had spirit enough to discountenance and declare against all the trash and fop-

peries they have been so frequently fond of, both the actors
and the authors, to the best of their power, must naturally
have served their daily table with sound and wholesome
diet."

October 17.—There are a few hopeful features in the
recent bills of the play. Unmistakable the other evening
was the enthusiastic testimony of a crammed house to the
satisfaction of the public at seeing Mr. Phelps in his right
place upon the boards of DRURY LANE. *Manfred* has the
best of successes, it brings what it should be the aim of
every manager to bring, the educated classes back into the
theatre. Mr. Falconer has now, I believe, his fortune in
his hands. Mr. Phelps is an actor who does not fail in
high endeavour to give poetry its voice upon the stage.
Some individualities of manner are felt as defects. Art
absolutely perfect in any man does not appear once in three
centuries. But the playgoer has much to learn, let him be
sure of it, who does not feel the distinctive power of a true
actor in Mr. Phelps's delivery of Byron's poem. Costly
and beautiful as the spectacle of *Manfred* is, it really blends
with and illustrates Byron's verse. The best of the immortals is Miss Rose Leclercq, whose Astarte is all that it
ought to be. She has only to look like the mysterious
spirit of Manfred's lost sister and love, to speak Manfred's
name, say Farewell, with one or two variations of expression,
and to utter about four words besides. But small as the
part is, it is difficult, because it is one easy to make ridiculous.
Miss Rose Leclercq knows how to make it touching. The
piece deserves a long run, and its influence as an antidote
to some faults in the taste of the day will be all the stronger
for its want of effective dramatic action of the ordinary sort.
When the town has learnt to sit and hear poetry almost for
its own sake, and because it is well interpreted, it will have
made a safe step towards the right sense of what it ought to
look for in a play. There is plenty of vigorous dramatic
action in a wholesome English playbook ; but just now it is

very desirable to lay the emphasis on words and thoughts.
We get plays of action (from the French) worded only-with
feeble commonplace. The action and the actors are the
play; printed it usually is unreadable. I do not know
whether there was any deliberate design to lay stress on the
right point in reviving a dramatic poem that consists little
of action, and almost wholly of a poet's thought and fancy.

At the NEW ADELPHI Miss Bateman's *Leah* is an
American version of the German *Deborah*, in which
Madame Ristori acted one night in London, not very
long ago. Of Miss Bateman, let me say, first, that she
can hardly be said to act the part at all, but only recites
it, until she comes to the fourth act, in which she displays
some dramatic energy. But in the fifth act she gives the
greatest hope of what she may hereafter do. She is still
young, is unassuming, although it was her misfortune to be
on the boards as an infant phenomenon when one of two
"Bateman children" some ten years ago, she has no set
faults, and in the fifth act of *Leah* she plays with a genuine
tenderness. Her Leah is not of course to be named with
Madame Ristori's Deborah, but the difference is not altogether of her own making. The charm of the pastoral play
has been all trampled out by the hoof of the American
adapter. Deborah is to Leah as the cottage flower-garden,
neat and trim overnight, is to the same garden in the morning after a jackass has run loose in it. Leah is but a ghost
of Deborah, all the poetical elevation is trodden out of the
language of the rabbi's daughter, all the pastoral simplicity
has been rooted up out of the plot. Instead of a Jewish
maiden's spirit rising grandly in its brooding over the traditions of its race, beautiful in its abandonment to love of the
Christian who is made to spurn her—terrible in its kindling
of the Jewish spirit of revenge, and beautiful in its submission to rebuke, all set among the *Geschwätz*—we have no
word of our own so expressive of the twitter and tattle—of
the village; we have Deborah degraded into commonplace;

the villagers perverted into the stagiest of claptrap characters. The schoolmaster is transformed into a heavy
melodramatic villain, the doctor into the conventional low
comedian. A murder and a thunderbolt are added to the
story, and, after all is over, the heroine is fetched back to
draw daggers with the villain, talk melodrama, and die in
state among all the *dramatts personæ*. With all the play's
proportions overturned, every flower of the original writer's
fancy stamped into mud, very much credit is due to Miss
Bateman for succeeding even in a single act. All that I had
enjoyed was gone: Ristori's low undertone of the complaint
of the Jews captive in Babylon; the exquisite tenderness of
her farewell kiss on the brow of her lover; the simple expression of her great love and its great wrong, when one
after another they of her lover's household, and at last he
himself, spurn her, and go in and shut the door upon her,
and with one sharp cry she falls with her face against the
closed door; all crushed under the adapter's hoof, or overlooked by the actress. That last situation, for example, so
simple and pathetic in the original, is improved by the
American adapter into a long-drawn-out melodramatic scolding scene. Miss Bateman having grown to the part in this
version, a better one could not well be substituted; but by
anyone who knows what the play was before "adaptation",
this version of *Leah* may be studied as an ingenious collection of the vulgar claptraps that our labour now should be
to banish from the stage. Yet, in spite of all, Miss Bateman,
who goes through the first three acts as if she were slowly
dictating her part to a spelling school, earns credit in the
fourth, and in the fifth looks like an actress of true mark.

November 7.—It has been proved conclusively that scenery
alone will not draw full houses to DRURY LANE, yet *Manfred*
crams the pit and fills the theatre. There has seldom been
a piece mounted with more lavish and picturesque scenic
effect, or with a stronger host of supernumeraries, than Mr.
Falconer's *Bonnie Dundee*. Nevertheless, *Bonnie Dundee*

could be played only for a few nights to almost empty houses. It is quite true that beautiful and apt scenery, harmonising with the descriptions and the few incidents of the poem, is necessary to the successful stage-appointment of Lord Byron's *Manfred*. It is not less true that a play with so little dramatic action, even with all help of the scenery, and Mr. Phelps in the chief character, would not draw for a week, if there were not a high intellectual power in the thoughts and language. Therefore, after all credit has been given to the attractive art of the scene-painter, the complete and unquestionable success of a play rather of poetical thought and language than of action, in a theatre that it takes a very large audience to fill, may be received as evidence that I have not been arguing against the grain of the public, but expressing its right mind, in protest against plays of French incident and intrigue, that have no words in them worth a good actor's speaking, and no characters worth subtle study for their full artistic development.

But, we are told, the race of good actors is all but extinct: there are not half-a-dozen actors equal to those parts in which the language rises above commonplace, or where there is demand for anything not to be found in the usual assortment of conventional emotions. I don't believe it. Good plays and good parts, not in the conventional, but in the best and truest sense, would make many good actors. They would have to warm into the unaccustomed work of really expressing freshly observed niceties and varieties and harmonies of character, and they would not know immediately how to speak a language of which every word has to go forth with its soul in its sound.

I do not object to a play because it is romantic, and abounds in stirring incidents, of which a good deal is improbable and some impossible. It is the romance of the story, with good scenery to back it, that makes the success of a play like *The Duke's Motto* of last season, or the

inferior *Bel Demonio* produced last Saturday at the Lyceum.
But why give us plays without words ? There are not two
sentences worth hearing in *Bel Demonio ;* there is not
a flash of wit, not a thought, that does not belong, like the
incidents, to the most threadbare stock of intellectual
properties for the romantic drama. The piece itself reproduces, with variations, that which had been already
worked up, adapted and draughted into a play for London,
called *Sextus V,* by Mr. Boucicault and Mr. Bridgman.
There is an escape of a hunted couple in monk's garments
through the ranks of their pursuers, who bonnet to them
respectfully, as we have seen done, only it was to more than
a couple, in *The Crown Diamonds.* Mr. Fechter tumbles
wounded down a rock into a torrent, because, since the
successful header in *The Colleen Bawn,* melodrama has
bidden for favour by the introduction of gymnastics. Indeed,
in *Bel Demonio,* as Mr. Brougham takes a header after Mr.
Fechter, there is double fare for the gods of this particular
sort of dainty. The defect of a play like *Bel Demonio* is
not that it contains this kind of stuff, but that it consists of
it wholly. It is all sauce and no fish ; all action, bounce,
conventional stage-chivalry, agony of the boards, pop, enter-
at-the-nick-of-time, tableau, and flummery, without a morsel
of substantial thought or satisfying literature under it.

 1864, *January* 16.—With hearty satisfaction I record in the
first place the triumphant reception at the Princess's Theatre
of a poetical English version, by Mr. Westland Marston,
of the German version of Moreto's masterpiece, which has
long been reckoned one of the four classical pieces of the
elder Spanish drama, *El Desden con el Desden.* This was
the play which Louis Quatorze, when he wished to delight
a Spanish wife and mother, caused to be produced at his
Court with the utmost magnificence of appointment, and
with Molière for its translator. But Molière's version of
the play, under the name of *Princesse d'Elide,* was as complete a failure as his imitation of Spanish heroic comedy in

Don Garcie de Navarre; except that *Don Garcie,* produced
for the public, was immediately damned, while the *Princess
d'Elide,* produced for a Court fête, was received with polite
admiration, and supposed at Court to be a great success.
The piece is usually omitted, and very properly, from
editions of the works of Molière, for it was written in such
haste, to obey the King's wish and punctually to grace his
grand festival, that Molière had only time to put the first
act and the first scene of the second act of his version into
metre, and hurried the rest into prose ; wherefore the chan-
sonnier Marigny said this Comedy had been summoned in
such haste to Court that she had only time to put on one
of her buskins, and appeared half-naked, with one shoe off,
the other on.   More successful was the Italian version of this
famous drama, by the truest and wittiest poet among Italian
writers of comedy, Count Carlo Gozzi, familiar to Germany
through at least one work in Schiller's version of his
Turandot.   Gozzi Italianised Moreto's masterpiece under
the title of *The Philosophic Princess, or the Antidote—Prin-
cipessa Filosofa, o il Contraveleno.*   Germany, too, has its
popular version of *El Desden con el Desden* in the *Donna
Diana* of Joseph Schreyvogel, a journalist of refined taste
but little genius, who translated two of Calderon's plays as
well as the play of Moreto.   He was Kotzebue's successor
as secretary of the Viennese Court Theatre, and commonly
wrote under the name of West.   It is evidence of its
popularity at home that his *Donna Diana* has been one of
the plays chosen for acting in London by a German company, and that Mr. Westland Marston, except a serious
departure from his text in the last scene, has thought it
worth a close translation.   Direct from Moreto, Mr. Marston
evidently has not taken a line, but he translates him through
a conscientious German, and I only wish he had confined
himself at the end of the play, as elsewhere, to the few
changes that satisfied the man he followed.   Of that
presently.   Meanwhile there is, on the whole, reason to be

exceedingly well satisfied. Mr. Marston could find, perhaps, good critics to argue in support of the modification
of the *dénouement*, sacrificing poetry to stage-effect, which
is the one change he has made. He is a man credited
deservedly with good dramatic taste. Enough, and more
than enough, we have had of the contemporary rubbish of
the minor theatres of Paris. It is greatly to the credit of
Mr. Vining that he has taken from one of the few English
writers of our day of whom we know that they can raise
the dramatic taste of the public if we will let them, a
metrical English version of the Spanish masterpiece, which,
though but a translation of a translation, is indeed, in
itself, a careful and most creditable piece of English
dramatic literature.

Don Agustin Moreto of Cabana, son of Agustin Moreto
and Violante Cavana, by seventeen years a younger man
than Calderon, was born at Madrid in the year 1618, two
years after the death of Shakespeare. Lope de Vega was
born two years before the birth of Shakespeare, and in the
year of the death of Lope de Vega, at the age of seventy-
three, Calderon was a man aged thirty-four, and Moreto was
a youth aged seventeen, already displaying his turn for song
and drama. He had written at least two, probably more,
of his numerous comedies before the age of twenty-three,
and his career was smoothed for him by the affectionate
regard of Calderon, who appreciated heartily his genius, and
probably procured for him his introduction to the Palace.
When Moreto began writing, the Spanish drama, which had
just attained its topmost height of glory, was there wrestling
with the superstition by which it was to be toppled down
into the depths. Lope de Vega was but nine years dead
when the King's Council subjected the stage to a rigid
censorship, reduced the number of the actors, forbade the
production of original comedies that were not histories or
lives of saints, and condemned the works of Lope de Vega
as pernicious. Thus it is that we have from Calderon and

Moreto so many sacred plays.   But there was a true earnestness in those men, a spiritual expression of the religious
fervour that was hard intolerance in many, and this charac-
terised also their one fellow poet and dramatist, a man
younger than Calderon but older than Moreto, Solis y Riba-
deneira, at one time Secretary to Philip IV.   Solis died in
the unfulfilled resolve to take holy orders.   Calderon died a
member of the Congregation of the Apostle Peter at Madrid,
to which he had given all that he possessed.   Moreto, having
forsaken poetry and the world, became a priest, and died
Rector of a Refuge at Toledo, where it was his chief duty
to attend the afflicted poor.   In his latter days Moreto
regretted the lighter works of his wit, blameless as they all
were.   His graceful touch more than once gave new life to
a hasty work of Lope de Vega's that had passed into obscu-
rity, and even this play of *El Desden con el Desden*, which
has made his fame in his own country imperishable, is
founded on a poor play that preceded it called *The Avenger
of Women*, if not on Lope de Vega's forgotten *Miracles of
Contempt*.

The original play is, like Mr. Westland Marston's version
of the German version of it, in three acts, and, of course, in
the usual *rime asonante*.   Schreyvogel's version agrees with
Gozzi's in altering the name of the hero from Don Carlos
to Don Cæsar.   This change Mr. Marston adopts.   He
follows his German original also in omitting the character of
the Prince of Bearn from among the suitors, in altering the
name of the *gracioso* Polilla, confidential secretary to the
proud Princess Diana, into Perin, and in adding the short
character of a Fioretta, with whom Perin may have a little
comic business.

The *gracioso* was a popular addition made by Lope de
Vega to the stock characters of a Spanish play.   He was
a comic character, sometimes half a buffoon, like the
"fantastical person" of the contemporary English stage,
more frequently the lively representative of the shrewd

popular mother wit, and the person of his drama through whom the author might be with the first to laugh at any extravagance of plan or fervour of romance about his story. Not seldom, and especially in Moreto's comedies, he is at the very core of the play ; and it is so in *El Desden* or *Donna Diana.* Here it is he who suggests to the hero how he may touch in his cold Diana the warm heart of a woman ; how he may melt the snow on her proud heights till it shall come throbbing down upon the valley in an eager flood. True as his love is, let him leave the other suitors to provoke her scorn by their submission, but let him surprise her on her own ground, holding himself as grapes above her reach, though elsewhere all the vintage on earth may seemed to have been tilled only for her. He does so. When the warmth of his love rises to his lips there is the *gracioso*, the gay confidant on either side, to warn him back into a show of ice ; or, if the lady doubt her senses, there is the sly *gracioso*, a true friend though a deceiver, at her ear. He is her confidential private secretary, who affects to be of one mind with herself, and can she doubt him ? The part is well played by Mr. Vining with a true *gracioso's* breadth of comedy.

Mr. Herman Vezin, a quietly good actor, who can rightly speak blank verse and give true but unforced expression to a poet's thought, well represents the life and love under the mask of a suitor who coerces himself to surprise disdain with a disdain yet greater, though as a true Spanish gentleman punctilious of courtesy. Mrs. Charles Young, now Mrs. Herman Vezin, plays the Diana with much grace and feeling, and marks with variety of expression the gradations of her passage from a cold disdain to a piqued curiosity, a wound of pride, a growth of wonder, admiration, and the loosening of the whole woman's nature in the Princess. It is a wonderful part for a great actress, capable of displaying nearly the whole range of her power, and absolutely demanding, in the second act, that she shall put forth all

her arts of fascination.   Mrs. Herman Vezin is not a great
actress, but she is a charming one who has achieved her
best successes in the poetical drama, and the quality of her
Donna Diana has assured the success of this play on the
London boards.   The famous scene in the second act,
where the cold suitor, invited to speak commonplace of
love to the Princess, whose colour it has, by her contrivance,
fallen to his lot to wear, pours his whole soul out earnestly
at her feet, is triumphantly scorned, and, recovering his
guard, dexterously turns the tables on the lady and builds
new success on his humiliation, is remarkably well played.

But why could not Mr. Westland Marston have faith to
the end ?   I believe that he fell into the old snare of doubting the power of an English audience to enjoy the simple
play of wit and poetry.   In the original play, and in the
German version of it too, the disdainful Diana is in the last
scenes all a woman, with the passion of her love set free.
To provoke her indifferent suitor into a word of desire to
win her, she tells him she has relented from her proud
theory, and means to give herself to one of his rivals, but
she is caught in that poor little trap, and tied in a knot of
etiquette that seems to bind her to make good the word so
lightly spoken.   She is in the last scene as a caught bird
fluttering in the net, with none of the high concern about
yet saving her dignity that Mr. Westland Marston gives her.
She is all anxious dread when they seem to be binding her
to the man, and her disdainful suitor to the woman, she
and he have, in affected disdain of each other, professed to
choose for mates. Mr. Westland Marston makes her struggle
yet to brave it out ; makes Perin bid the Count fix his eye
on her while she repeats at the dictation of her father the
form of betrothal to the other man ; makes her catch his
eye, break down, cry out at the unsympathetic face of the
knight to whom she is plighting herself ; and, in short, gives
the British public something like the dose of claptrap it is
commonly considered to require.   The German adapter,

from whose text in this instance Mr. Marston has departed, with better taste follows Moreto, who in this last scene showed only a woman in a tender tumult of distressful love, until Don Carlos has been admonished by the *gracioso* that he must now give her opportunity herself to loose the knot by which she is restrained. To the expectation that he will now plight his faith to his mock love he replies, therefore, that, since he is the Princess's knight and wears her colours, he is not yet free to plight his troth elsewhere. He waits till she has formally released him from her service. Then the Princess herself, plucking eagerly at the knot where she is warned that she may loosen it, claims and obtains the word of both knights that they will abide by her decision. Her decision is, that she belongs to him who has conquered Disdain with Disdain. And who is he? asks Carlos. With two little tender whispered words—*Tu solo*—the softened woman timidly creeps forward and lays her heart of love down at his feet. Mrs. Herman Vezin would have known how to give grace to such a close, if Mr. Westland Marston had not resolved that the taste of the British public demands less delicate fare. And thus it seems that even our good dramatic poets, like our players, can fall into the mischievous error of adapting their work to an assumed standard of bad taste.

Here I stop for to-day, but will spare three lines and a half to say that Mr. Falconer's new play, *Night and Morn*, at DRURY LANE, is certainly the best he has yet written.

March 5.—The theatres have been deserving success lately and obtaining it. The only mistake made during the last month or two has been Mr. Sothern's appearance at the HAYMARKET, in a "piece of extravagance" called *Bunkum Muller*, which, although he is clever enough in it to maintain his popularity, is a step backwards instead of forwards. A caricature should at least be a caricature of something. Bunkum Muller is a caricature of nothing. There is an intention, of which Mr. Sothern makes the most, to provoke mirth by incessant tripping up of the false sublime with the ridiculous. Bunkum Muller seems to have been meant for a gushing dramatist with a scolding wife and nothing better than a penny pickwick to console him, except the bust of Shakespeare which he takes into his confidence, and which is the only other person who appears with him upon the stage. But the incidents that represent the story of the piece are not witty extravagance, they are flat nonsense ; and as the author has not been content with his antithesis between Bunkum's mind and the small things of life with which its aspirations are surrounded and infested, but makes Bunkum himself continually thrust asides of a conflicting sort into the midst of his burlesque of fervour, there is no character or caricature, but a piece of the most witless nonsense. The construction of the piece is in this respect as sensible as a child's notion of improving a bright red by painting over it with a bright green, the only possible result being a neutral smear. It is wonderful to see how much Mr. Sothern does with a bad piece ; and his make-up as a shabby Shakespeare is very funny.

I never liked Mr. Watts Phillips so much as in his *Paul's Return,* now acting at the PRINCESS'S, where Shakespeare's *Comedy of Errors* forms an afterpiece as merry as a shorter farce. At the ST. JAMES'S Mr. Leicester Buckingham's *Silver Lining* has a well-deserved success ; the piece, too, is acted thoroughly well. Mr. Falconer, again, I never liked so well as in his *Night and Morn,* which has had a good run at DRURY LANE.

May 14.—There is a particular enjoyment in the sort of criticism that the players call for, which should go far in aid of many better reasons for the well-being of the stage among a free people. In the real world any blockhead of a Hohenzollern may get homage when he plays in the worst manner his part of king, but in the playhouse let him who shall play the king look to it. For, as said Epictetus, "it is not to be considered among the actors who is prince or who

is beggar ; but who acts prince or beggar best." Bad as
may be any critical taste that thus touches the mimic world
as with a divine philosophy, it will be well for the spectators
of performances in the great world when they have caught,
rather more generally than they yet have caught it, something of this spirit of the theatre. For in the playhouse
even the dullest lout is something of a philosopher who
looks beyond the clothes of those who tread the scene.
Despotic governments abroad are never on good terms with
a free theatre ; and out of England there has been a long
stand made for the old theory that the kings and queens
and the people in fine clothes were upon the stage also to
be the leading characters. It was to be they only who
should do and suffer the great things and have the leading
actors engaged for their worthy personation. That was the
rule in and after Shakespeare's day, and kings and dukes
duly appear, as nominal chiefs, in Shakespeare's plays.
But alas for the theories of despotism in politics and
literature ! By Shakespeare's genius these golden lads
and lasses were all stirred down into the common mass of
humanity, and Bottom the Weaver makes a better morsel
in that broth than Theseus Duke of Athens ; the Jew
Shylock counts in English art for more than the Duke of
Venice ; or in the play now to be seen at DRURY LANE,
Falstaff and Hotspur for more than King Henry IV.
The literature of the English stage is rich in the true
freedom of the English character, and the critical habit
of looking through the King's robes at the man who
plays the King, to reckon him perhaps below a dozen
of his comrades, helps to keep up that attitude of philosophical republicanism which has sharpened enjoyment of
Shakespeare in the artistic mind of Victor Hugo.

The English theatre is, in fact, not something apart from
English life, but is so intimately connected with it that the
mind of our country has to this day found no better form
for the expression of its highest vigour. It is not to passing

fashion only, but to nature itself—man's nature—that our stage has held the mirror up. Bold and clear have been its best utterances of those deeper truths of life on which it is in the English character to dwell, not with a shadowy parade of word-philosophies, but as thought in action with a practical keen sense that they are real. An English audience with a thoroughly good English play before it should be one of the worthiest assemblies that the world can show.

Again and again, then, I say, let the players believe in their public. They are not the fast men who have given their success to pieces which have lately had remarkably long runs. There is a great playgoing public that includes all, except, perhaps, a still reluctant section of the educated classes, and, of course, the class, every year diminishing, of persons who retain in a religious dread of theatrical performances the tradition of a time when there was honest reason why the theatre should be in ill repute. London is now so populous, and the throng of strangers daily passing through it is so vast, while there is so much recovered goodwill to the playhouse, that it may take a year to pass through a theatre by the houseful all the people who will wish to see a play said to be good. This is, in fact, rather more success than actors should desire, for to the development of an appreciation of good acting, as much as to the development of good acting itself, it is necessary that each actor should in his time play many parts.

If it is to become usual for single plays, when attractive, to run for a year in unbroken succession of performances, it will be very difficult for the young actor to acquire or to display his utmost skill, and the public will also be ill trained to that sort of appreciation upon which the maintenance of the best interests of the stage must finally depend. Mr. Phelps wisely varied his Manfred with two or three performances of Sir Pertinax Macsycophant, and has now passed with his art cleverly from that gloomy state of metaphysical abstraction as a melancholy soul too ready to cast off its body, into the fat flesh of the gross and humorous knight who may owe God a death, but would be loth to pay him before his day. Such contrasts the good actor should take care to set before his audience if he would make them decent critics of his art; and it is only by having opportunity to show the whole range of his powers that an actor can ever hope to prove his right to a first rank among his brethren.

If Mr. Phelps played nothing else than Falstaff, it would be remarkable. Considered as one part in a singularly varied series it is unquestionably good. He lays stress not on Falstaff's sensuality, but on the lively intellect that stands for soul as well as mind in his gross body, displays his eagerness to parry and thrust, his determination to cap every other man's good saying with something better of his own, which makes him, according to the manner of the actor, thrust in with inarticulate sounds, as if to keep himself a place open for speech while he is fetching up his own flagon of wit from the farthest caverns of his stomach. And the fat knight who so familiarly cracks his jokes with the Prince or upon Bardolph is not vulgarised in Mr. Phelps' reading. When the Prince and Westmoreland meet Falstaff on the road near Coventry, and the Prince hails his old comrade with a joke, the change from the gay jesting answer to the courteous salutation of "My good lord of Westmoreland" is marked by the actor with a smooth delicate touch that stamps the knight distinctly as a man well born and bred.

Mr. Walter Lacy is good as the Prince, giving all ease and liveliness to his part of the scenes with Falstaff, but less at home in the blank verse, and least in the soliloquy, "I know you all", the only part of the play in which he seems to be quite out of his element. But on the whole his Prince Henry is a part remarkably well acted, and must rank next to the Falstaff.

With the Hotspur Mr. Montgomery takes much pains. The part is, in its different way yet for a similar reason, like that of Mercutio, a very difficult one; for there is an airy grace under the impetuosity of each of these characters which it can be in the power of few actors to express. In Hotspur it is especially difficult, for about the martial heat of his quick spirit, that must· be shown with a blunt vigour, there plays constantly the light of a gay untamed fancy, full of fresh life in mirth and sportive tenderness. This Mr. Montgomery paints rather well in his scene with Lady Percy, which is the best piece of his acting, but in the rest of the play his manner is too much that of an unpleasantly head-strong boy. The refinement of the character is absent. Hotspur's description of the lord with the pouncet-box, who came to him when the fight was done, is very carefully and cleverly given by Mr. Montgomery, but with a manner simply of rough, violent distaste. There is the same absence of expression to the lighter graces of Hotspur's character in his impatient jesting at Glendower; he is too heavily and offensively contemptuous, where he should speak lightly and with audacious gaiety on the quick impulse of young blood.

Falstaff is to be seen also at HER MAJESTY'S THEATRE, singing to the bâton of Signor Arditi in true Italian fashion, in an Italian version of Herr Otto Nicolai's *Lustigen Weiber von Windsor*. Except that a short name is convenient for an opera, we should call it a great mistake to have brought Falstaff thus to the front, for the *Donne Allegre* are the soul of the piece, especially when their parts are played and sung as they are played and sung by Mdlles. Titiens and Bettelheim ; by both equally well. It is saying much for Mdlle. Bettelheim, for Mdlle. Titiens sings and acts her best, but there is no inferiority in her performance. Falstaff is absolutely nothing in the hands of Signor Marcello Junca. The opera is light and pleasant, but it is no work of genius ; it is of about the calibre of Flotow's *Marta*, and is not received with any sort of enthusiasm, though it is impossible not to enjoy the pleasant musical impersonation of the two wives by Mdlles. Titiens and Bettelheim.

I believe that on the whole a theatre audience shows better taste than an opera audience ; probably because it has a more real understanding of what it has come out to enjoy. Real so far as it goes. But what are we to say to palliate the success of Mdlle. Stella Colas in *Romeo and Juliet* at the PRINCESS'S ? Let me be fair both to the lady and the public. The lady has returned to us not quite so bad as she was ; and the public applauds her not quite so much as it did. I saw her again on the first night of her reappearance, and compelled myself to sit out—as on her original first night I could not—all the five acts of Shakespeare murder. There was nothing like the frantic enthusiasm of the first reception. If the management had not dealt liberally in the morning with Covent Garden, and supplied the lady in the evening with the consequent apple-basket full of bouquets, her reception might have seemed to her a cool one. Yet her English was more intelligible, and she had got rid of some of the worst absurdities of action ; the upward gesture of snipping with scissors, for example, that accompanied Juliet's suggestion concerning Romeo, that Night, when he died, might " take him and cut him out in little stars", a line that, to a dressy second-rate French *ingénue*, inevitably suggested millinery, and Night as the editor of *La Belle Assemblée*. But although not so bad as it was, this Juliet is still abominable ; for not only it is not what it ought to be, but it is precisely all that it ought not to be. Juliet is an innocent Italian child, enjoying with an exquisitely simple honesty the first passion of love. Artless, guileless, pouring out all the beauty of a most pure girlhood in the newly-awakened poetry of an un-grudging, unsuspecting love, hers is the very last character to be represented to us by the stage-artifices and ghastly grimaces of a French *ingénue*, in her stage-innocence the most self-conscious of all forms into which the front of womanhood has ever been recast. Mdlle. Colas cannot even seem to forget herself. When Juliet, after her first entry, has only to stand at her mother's chair, hearing much, answering little, Mdlle. Colas perks her head, grins, twists, ambles from one side of the chair to the other, and looks obtrusively conscious of every part of herself from the tip of her nose to the tips of her toes. In the balcony scene her coquetry with Romeo is abominable ; and the way in which, for example, she speaks of their swift contract as

> " Too like the lightning, which doth cease to be
> Ere one can say—It lightens,"

jumping up to deliver the last two words dramatically with big eyes and a pretty surprised stare, is enough to make one gnash one's teeth till they break. Her great point with the audience is in the soliloquy before the taking of the sleeping-potion. It is done with a great deal of misdirected force, ending in a shriek and recoil of horror at "Stay, Tybalt, stay !" I am quite sure that no Juliet whom Shakespeare in his time had the advising of ever recoiled with such a shriek from the imagined ghost that sought the Romeo who, being thus suggested, was in the next instant yet more intensely present to her disordered vision. Mdlle. Colas spends so much force upon the shrieking at and cowering by the bed-side from Tybalt's ghost, that she can only add as an insignificant tag to that claptrap stage-effect the line in which a greater actress would have found the true climax, "Romeo, I come ! this do I drink to thee." Juliet drinks the potion with her mind full not of Tybalt, but of Romeo. Ghosts do not themselves stab, poison, or strangle, and overpowering sense of peril to Romeo certainly is not the thought indicated in these lines :

> " O look ! methinks I see my cousin's ghost
> Seeking out Romeo, that did spit his body
> Upon a rapier's point : Stay, Tybalt, stay !
> Romeo, I come ! this do I drink to thee."

Every word of that last line, which Mdlle. Colas shuffles through as an anticlimax after her great shrieking effect, is emphatic ; so emphatic, that it is the dramatic balance to the whole preceding part of the soliloquy. At sight of the potion that was to lay herself in imaged death, there coursed with a thrill through her girl's blood the gruesome images that it suggested, till to her disordered mind the image of Tybalt seeking Romeo turned her thought to the search for Romeo, on which she also was, by that dread way, bent.   Instead of screaming the "Stay, Tybalt, stay", Juliet more probably whispers it with abhorrent voice and hands, yet less indicative of supernatural dread than of returning thought of Romeo, whom not Tybalt, but Juliet, must be the first to find. Her eye meanwhile wanders distraught in search, until she sees the marriage-bed and Romeo there present alone to her mind's eye. Her cry of "Romeo" then pours out her heart's love towards him. Each word in the "I come" is emphatic—it is I, not Tybalt ; but the sense of this should be most lightly indicated, for always in this play the thought of Tybalt hardly lives at all when Juliet's mind fills with the thought of Romeo. Towards the imaged Romeo, towards the marriage-bed, she hurries, fluttering with love. Every one also of the next words, "This do I drink to thee", has its poetic force. The "this"—the phial in her hand, which, apart from Romeo, had suggested all those ghastly dreads in the lines beginning "What if this mixture"—now that the image of Romeo is present to her, brings joy, not dread, "This do I drink to thee". She drinks as from a festive bridal-cup, and as she is bending in endearment over the bridal-bed the form of death changes her face and fixes it. So she then falls, and lies upon the bed in her long swoon. A really good actress might, no doubt, find other and better methods of interpreting the lines ; my only purpose is to show that in every good interpretation the last line must inevitably be the great one, for it is, as it were, the clench-ing of all that had gone before.   When Mdlle. Colas makes a great scream at the ghost of Tybalt, and flies and crouches as if she would take refuge under the bed, then huddles anyhow over the last line, takes the poison, and gets into bed as best she can, she may bring great applause from an audience at the PRINCESS'S, but she is not acting Shakespeare. Neither do I think anything in the rest of the play really well done, except the Nurse of Mrs. Marston. Mr. Nelson is but a heavy Romeo. The part of Friar Lawrence is, with conventional stage-gestures, actually ranted! The gentleman who plays Capulet deliberately speaks the part as if it were a heavy-father in broad farce. Mr. Vining is out of his element, and gives but a low-comedy suggestion of that light-hearted gentleman, the airy, graceful, quick-witted, and quick-blooded Mercutio, of whom in our time Mr. Charles Kemble has been the only sufficient representative. There is nobody now on the stage able to play the part.

The nearest approach to the right tone and manner would probably be made by Mr. Neville of the OLYMPIC. Mr. Neville, who has been for more than a year playing the Lancashire lad in *The Ticket-of-Leave Man,* now adds to that performance a good contrast of character by playing Petruchio to the Katherine of Miss Hughes in the abridged stage-version of the *Taming of the Shrew,* treated as an afterpiece. This runs like a farce; indeed, the practical jests of the scene in Petruchio's house are heightened here and there unnecessarily into farcical extravagance; but the chief and the best of the fun is Shakespeare's, and the verse runs with delightful ease and smoothness from the tongues of Mr. Neville and Miss Hughes, rare as the gift has now become of speaking blank verse well.

June 18.—At the HAYMARKET Mr. Sothern has considered his dignity by discarding the mere nonsense of *Bunkum Muller,* and sustaining a character in a play which demands alternation of serious and comic acting. The play is a translation from the French drama of *Sulli-van,* and I wish, though probably Mr. Buckstone's Chancellor of the Exchequer has his reasons for differing from me, that the translator, Mr. T. W. Robertson, had not taken the liberty of considering *Sullivan* the French for *David Garrick*. The play-bill does, indeed, append to the name of the piece a note, saying, "This play is founded on an incident said to have occurred to Garrick, but which has no pretension to biographical accuracy"; euphemism for "This play is called *David Garrick*, but has nothing on earth to do with Garrick". But why should English actors deal so lightly with the memory of their great chief, that, for the sake of so poor and false an effect as the placarding of SOTHERN as GARRICK, they should falsify and confuse the memory of Garrick's life? Mr. Sothern, we think, should have resisted the temptation to have his name brought into such apposition ; for he is not a Garrick ; he is a very long way indeed from being a Garrick, excellent as he is in his own way of art. If he could act Abel Drugger, he could not act Macbeth ; and his serious passages in this French-English drama, though they are well felt, are delivered with a heaviness of intensity remarkable in one whose touch as a comedian is so light. He is cleverly supported. Miss Nelly Moore is the heroine, a young lady whom I remember having seen two or three years ago in some small farce at the ST. JAMES'S THEATRE, and having liked much as a genuine young English actress of the class which the French call *ingénue*, and which is on the French stage my particular aversion. She vanished almost immediately into the provinces, but has come back to London with a HAYMARKET engagement, and quite justifies the good hope of her I formed when she was first seen upon the stage. Let me not forget to record of *David Garrick* that it is so very moral as to proceed in the last act to the delivery of a long exhortation, unbroken by dialogue, which Mr. Sothern preaches with such quiet seriousness that we are almost invited to look under his chin for the band and bibs. In the main, however, it is comic, and it is now followed by a new and rapid act of Dundrearyism, written by Mr. H. J. Byron, entitled *Lord Dundreary Married and Done For*, in which Mr. Sothern's Lord Dundreary is amusing still, and the nonsense, though it *is* nonsense, is rather smarter than it was in the original piece, and so we laugh heartily and do not despise ourselves for laughing. We check the sense that will rise sometimes of flagging in the imitator's strain at a worn theme, while we appreciate the skill with which Mr. Byron has caught and repeated, and even mellowed with another humanising touch or two, all the characteristics of Dundreary as we knew him in his days of bachelorhood.

At the OLYMPIC Mr. Tom Taylor's truncated morality, *Sense and Sensation*, failed on the first night for want of connected and intelligible story, though, even then, several of its scenes had, I believe, been cut out. Since the first night, two or three more scenes have been omitted, including one in a milliner's work-room, which was well meant, but too stern and literal to be offered as occasion for amusement. One of the scenes was a burlesque by itself, an admirable jest upon the condition of the London stage, including caricatures of the "sensation" drama and the taste for a French Juliet. This, with the original head and tail, and a previous scene at a boarding-school, is nearly all that is now left of the piece.

The new plays produced at the PRINCESS'S have been of a better literary class than those acted recently at any other house ; and in the last of his new pieces, *Light and Shadow*, by Mr. Slous, the author of *The Templar*, there has appeared an actor, Mr. Dominick Murray, who is evidently an important acquisition to the London stage. Both the play and the actor are worth seeing.

June 25.—*Fidelio* is not only the best existing opera, but probably, except the same composer's *Mount of Olives*, the noblest musical work ever produced by the genius of man.

Mdlle. Titiens is already the best of recent Leonoras,

and she has not yet made the part all that she will make it.
There were quiet places on Thursday night which as Mdlle.
Titiens warms to the part will lighten up with new expression. Her determination evidently was to run no risk,
to attempt on the first night not a touch more than she
could make perfect. Her expression is throughout delicate
and true, but there are several passages in the first act which
she feels clearly, and which in a few nights she will make
the house feel more distinctly. More will be made, for
example, of Leonora's by-play at the opening of the
dungeons at the end of the first act. Her object was to
search for her husband among the prisoners, and Madame
Schroeder-Devrient, by her way of interpreting that, drew
tears. Mdlle. Titiens rightly avoids the merely conventional rushing about, and leaves the dramatic points yet to
be made ; content by no tone, look, or movement to break
the harmony of her entire performance. In the second act,
admirably supported by Dr. Gunz as the Florestan, her
acting of the part is singularly delicate and true in its
pathos, and she sings it, I believe, better than it has ever
been sung in England.

August 6.—At the PRINCESS'S, Mr. George Vining has
just set up a piece of transpontine interest derived by
Mr. Boucicault from the same mint that coined the original
of *The Ticket-of-Leave Man.* The PRINCESS'S version of
Les Pauvres de Paris, under the name of *The Streets of
London*, has its French origin uneffaced in ingenious
unreality of realism, in sentimental suicide by charcoal-
fumes, and so forth. But it is capitally acted by Mr. Vining,
who appears in it to much better advantage than he did,
however well-dressed to the part, as Philip II of Spain,
in *The Monastery of St. Just*, which was more unpleasantly
French, and had the disadvantage of producing Mdlle.
Stella Colas in two of its characters. To glance back for an
instant to that piece, I may observe that, although I went to
see it with the belief that one could not only endure but

like Mdlle. Colas in French melodrama, whatever we might
think of her in English poetry, I ended by giving her up
altogether. She is obtrusively self-conscious, showy, jerky,
artificial as a puppet. When she acted the convent-boy, in
a surplice like a night-gown, she was lively, but showily
feminine in all her amblings, skippings, and *minauderies*.
She is unquestionably an actress below the level of Miss
Terry, or Miss Nelly Moore, who played the heroine so
simply and gracefully in *David Garrick*, or of half-a-dozen
other young English actresses whose names never appear on
posters. To name Mdlle. Colas in the same line with
Mrs. Herman Vezin would be preposterous enough; but
she simply is not an actress at all in the sense in which
an English Helen Faucit or an Italian Ristori is an actress.
Enough of that. I am glad she is gone; and coming back
to the PRINCESS's new drama of *The Streets of London*, I
may commend the acting in that piece not only of Mr.
Vining, but also of Mrs. Marston, Mr. David Fisher, and
Mr. Dominick Murray, and record that it has two scenes, a
set scene of Charing Cross and Trafalgar Square as seen
from the corner of Hemming's Row, and a scene of a house
on fire, which take the place of literature to secure a long
run for the drama. The house on fire, which occupies the
whole breadth of the stage, is a wonderful scenic illusion.

October 1.—Of the *Second Part of King Henry IV*,
at DRURY LANE, it will suffice to record that Justice Shallow
is in Mr. Phelps's hands, as in Shakespeare's, anything but
a merely comic character. Comic upon the surface, it is at
the core terribly earnest, and was meant, with a profound
seriousness under the jest, as a picture of grey hairs without
honour, age looking back to a false heaven of youthful lusts
that in its imbecile youth it had ill realised, instead of
forward to the well-earned rest, and downward to the open
grave before its feet. There is nothing more sternly earnest
in Shakespeare, and more tragic in its undertone, than the
dialogue between Shallow and Silence at the beginning of

the second scene of the third act, and so Mr. Phelps feels it, as his acting shows. We have in this play the un-honoured age of two old men, Shallow and Falstaff ; with these men on one side of him and the venerable Chief Justice on the other, Henry the Fifth speaks his closing speech, that begins,

> " I know thee not, old man ; fall to thy prayers ;
> How ill white hairs become a fool and jester !"

There is a particular contrast between the unhonoured poverty of wit and soul in the old Shallow and the premature decay of the King weighted with mighty care for earthly dignities, that makes the representation of the two characters by one competent actor fully possessed with their significance a source of true artistic pleasure. It is well, also, that the untaught in dramatic art should see how far the skill of a true actor is removed from dull monotony, and through how many differing conceptions it is able faithfully to follow with its impersonation the true poet's mind.

October 8.—DRURY LANE reopened last Saturday, not only with the most creditable programme it was in the manager's power to produce, but with evidence of added strength in the performance. The *First Part of King Henry IV*, as it has been performed this week, gains largely by the substitution of Mr. H. Marston for Mr. Ryder in the part of the King. Mr. Ryder declaims very well, but he only declaims : Mr. Marston puts some of their life into the lines.

Mr. Creswick has profited well by experience ; and while he has plenty of energy on occasion, now and then rather too much, he knows how to be quiet, and can tone his per-formance into pleasant harmony with other business of the stage. Mr. Montgomery's Hotspur, with all its faults, was more interesting than I find Mr. Creswick's to be, with all its merits. There was an independent strain and energy about that actor, a desire to do worthily, and a rare power

of correcting faults, that won goodwill. When looking in
again upon the play towards the close of the last season, I
was surprised and pleased at the frequent skilful modifications by which Mr. Montgomery had brought his performance nearer to the poet's standard. His Hotspur as I last
saw it was a performance of a higher quality than Mr. Creswick's.

November 5.—At DRURY LANE the reappearance of Miss
Helen Faucit brought us *Cymbeline;* for Imogen, the most
beautiful of Shakespeare's female characters, is that in which
this lady seems most to delight and to excel, and with this
she desired, in returning to the London stage of which she
was some years since a chief ornament, to make her first
impression. The play had been formerly acted at DRURY
LANE with very good scenery of its own, so that on its recent
revival it was found to be in all respects well mounted, and
the acting did not greatly impede the sense in following the
exquisite freedom of the poet's fancy through the swiftly
changing scene of British court and Roman camp and
royalty of man in savage mountain-life. No mortal actors,
perhaps, can fitly speak the lament of Guiderius and Arvira-
gus over the body of Fidele. There was inevitably much
that jarred in the representation. But Miss Faucit was on
the whole well supported, and she had Mr. Phelps for
Posthumus and Mr. Creswick for Iachimo, parts that no
living actors could have better filled. In its tenderness and
grace of womanhood, in the simple piety that looks to the
gods when Imogen commits herself to rest or is about to
read a letter from her husband, in the wife's absolute love
and perfect innocence, void of false shame, slow to believe
ill, strong to resist it, Miss Faucit's Imogen is eloquent to
our eyes, even when she fails, now and then, to satisfy our
ears. She is an actress trained in the school of the Kembles,
careful to make every gesture an embodiment of thought,
too careful sometimes, as when, after the cry, "What ho,
Pisanio!" she remains with upraised arm throughout half

the speech of Iachimo that begins "O happy Leonatus!" There is a graver fault of excess in the first part of the representation of womanly fear when, as Fidele, she calls at the mouth of the unoccupied cavern, and runs from the sound herself had made. The warning of her error might be found in the fact that her pantomime here excites rather general laughter, where surely Shakespeare never meant that even the dullest boor should grin. But that short sin of excess is followed by the entry into the cavern, which is made most charmingly.

Miss Faucit's voice is more often at fault; it fails her whenever she has a violent emotion to express, and passion sounds often like petulance. The voice may not obey the prompting of the will, or there may be defect of that higher dramatic genius which can make words sound as "thoughts that breathe". Whatever be the cause, she fails to express by voice such phases of the character of Imogen as we have in the scene with Pisanio near Milford Haven. Yet where the mere emotion to be expressed is more tender than violent she attains often—though even then, perhaps, with a too visible art—to the utmost delicacy of expression. An example of this is in her picture to Pisanio of how she would have strained her eye to look on her departing lord,

> "till he had melted from
> The smallness of a gnat *to air; and then*
> Have turned mine eye and wept."

The sense of the final vanishing, and of the tears that follow it, is here exquisitely rendered by the actress.

Another incident of the week has been the opening of the OLYMPIC, on Wednesday evening, under the management of Mr. Horace Wigan, with two farces and a drama, all adapted from the French. The staple entertainment is *The Hidden Hand*, a French melodrama of poisoning, called *L'Aïeule*, adapted into four acts, with the scene laid in a Welsh castle in the reign of James the Second. It is a play of a bad class, remarkably well adapted for acting throughout the second and third of its four acts, and cleverly acted by Miss Terry, who, emancipated now from the LYCEUM panorama, gives evidence of a dramatic energy that may secure, even for *The Hidden Hand*, a long lease of the public favour.

December 3.—It is to be wished that, by way of special favour to a portion of the public for which it already shows a wise respect, the management of DRURY LANE would announce that their *Macbeth* would be acted, for a few nights at least, *without* Locke's music, and the corps of witches jigging to Davenant's misfitted rhymes. The very substantial Hecate, who looks like a cross between a beef-eater from the Tower and a ghost from the Styx, talks of anointing herself, and sings of the pleasure it is "to sing, to toy, to dance, and kiss", belongs to the stage of a very different sort of Restoration than that which the DRURY LANE management has now in hand. To those shadowy weird sisters who lie at the heart of the tragedy, this singing and jigging corps de ballet is—so far as their poetry is concerned—a ruinous accompaniment. By untuning the key-note they spoil the harmonies of the whole play.

Mr. Phelps's Macbeth is a half-barbarous warrior chief, around whom the powers of evil weave their fatal spell. The strife of the elements that rolls over the acting of his crime suggests the co-operation of the fiendish spirits who have him in thrall. By nature he is a rude, impulsive soldier, "valour's minion", "Bellona's bridegroom", turbulent of mind, restless, imaginative, quick of ambition, but with a religion strong in leaf, although fruitless and weak of root. As his wife says, in words to which Miss Faucit rightly gives clear, unmistakable emphasis,

> "not without ambition, but without
> The illness should attend it. What thou wouldst highly
> That wouldst thou holily : wouldst not play false
> And yet wouldst wrongly win."

The last words of the witches before Macbeth's entry are
of a "pilot's thumb, wrecked as homeward he did come";
at the words, Macbeth, who has been piloting through storm
the vessel of the State, is heard approaching, and on his
homeward way they wait to wreck him. An evil influence
that fastens on his soul comes with the foreboding of royalty.
His heart has been stirred by a breath from hell, that has
warmed into life damnable thoughts of the swift way to the
promised height of sovereignty. In the subsequent scene
with Duncan, Macbeth, still preoccupied, starts from his
reverie at the naming of Malcolm as Prince of Cumberland.
But though under the fatal spell of the weird sisters, unless
a power of earth, in the urging force of his wife's will, join
itself to the powers of hell, Duncan yet will sleep unharmed
in Macbeth's castle.

And here, in the acted play, appears the chief defect of
Miss Faucit's Lady Macbeth, which is weakest in the scenes
before the murder of Duncan. Miss Faucit is too essentially
feminine, too exclusively gifted with the art of expressing all
that is most graceful and beautiful in womanhood, to succeed in inspiring anything like awe or terror. The lines
beginning,

> " Come all you spirits
> That tend on mortal thoughts, unsex me here,"

are simply spouted : at the closing passage—

> " Nor Heaven peep through the blanket of the dark
> To cry ' Hold, hold !' "—

Miss Faucit shouts "Hold ! hold !" in a most unheavenly
manner, and throughout the early stage of the character it
may be said that her Lady Macbeth is too demonstrative
and noisy.

Of Macbeth's "letting I dare not wait upon I would",
her censure is vixenish in manner. The famous passage in
delivering which Mrs. Siddons is said to have transformed
herself into a terrible she-fiend, " I have given suck," etc.,

is poured out by Miss Faucit in a way that, by tones and
gestures, vividly recalls a common spectacle of passion in
our London streets—the scold at the door of a gin-shop.
The comparison is by no means so degrading as it sounds,
for the gin-shop scold pours out a true passion ; and in
passion, whatever the cause of it, high and low display alike
the common nature. But such tones belong to an out-
pouring of emotion inconsistent with the self-possessed
determination that makes Lady Macbeth terrible in this
part of the play. In the latter part of the scene Miss
Faucit is still too noisy ; and when she suggests how upon
Duncan's death they will make their "griefs and clamour
roar", she ends her part in the scene with voice pitched to
its highest key and outspread fingers all abroad. There is
the same excess of displayed emotion when she chides
Macbeth as " Infirm of purpose", and tells him " 'tis the
eye of childhood that fears a painted devil", spitting out at
him the word "painted".

This defect in the representation disappears, of course,
when the second phase of the character, that which is far
more congenial to the actress, has to be represented. Miss
Faucit's voice fails physically to express high tragic passion,
and it possibly is part of a softer, though, we think,
erroneous view taken by her of Lady Macbeth's character,
to make her at the outset of the play passionately womanish,
and herself impulsive.

The reaction of disappointment and hidden suffering
after the crime is delicately shown by Miss Faucit. From
the words opening that new phase of the character—

> " Nought 's had, all 's spent,
> When our desire is got without content :
> 'Tis safer to be that which we destroy,
> Than, by destruction, dwell in doubtful joy"—

Miss Faucit's Lady Macbeth becomes a performance that
no other English actress can approach. When Macbeth
hints to her of a new deed, a new crime, admirable in

various expression is his wife's tone of weariness of wonder and of dread in the question "What's to be done?" And when Macbeth replies—

> " Be innocent of the knowledge, dearest chuck,
> Till thou applaud the deed"—

she stands averted as he crosses, and mechanically follows as he leads. In the murder of Banquo, Lady Macbeth is no accomplice. We have seen Miss Faucit praised for representation of smooth treachery in the tender playing of her fingers about the head of the child Fleance while Macbeth is sending father and child into the toils set for them. Miss Faucit knows her Shakespeare better than that. The fingers of the woman who has been a mother, and has murder on her soul, wander sadly and tenderly over the type of her lost innocence. In the banquet scene, where it should be remembered that she, ignorant of Banquo's fate, believes it to be the murdered Duncan of whom Macbeth speaks (save only a weakly scolding note or two in the private warning to Macbeth, "O, these flaws, and starts", etc.), Miss Faucit is admirably good. Her by-play during Macbeth's speech, "What man dare I dare", is perfect, and her collapse into weariness of life-long torture after the departure of the guests, with all that follows to the close of that scene, shows our best actress at her best. The sleep-walking scene is very carefully delivered, but has too much the air of a well-studied dramatic recitation. It is Miss Faucit's Lady Macbeth, not Lady Macbeth, whose nature sinks under the weight of her fatal secret, even in the sleep that has brought no rest to her guilty soul.

December 17.—A visit this week to Drury Lane showed us that Miss Helen Faucit has, like a true actress, profited by information given from before the curtain, and now, in expressing the first phase of Lady Macbeth's character, avoids all the louder tones in which her voice failed physically to express the thought in her mind, skilfully substituting for them methods of expression perfectly within her range and. far more impressive.   The result is a most harmonious interpretation of the part according to that reading which finds all its womanhood in Lady Macbeth's character.   Some of the passages in her opening scenes, which used to be weak, from a physical cause really beside any question of the genius of the actress, are now to be felt as even among the gems of the performance.   I observed also a point in Miss Faucit's acting which had, I believe, always been part of her reading, but which I had previously overlooked.   It had been seen that during the tumult after the discovery of Duncan's murder Lady Macbeth's assumed surprise and terror passed into a real and sudden fainting, but in the general bustle of the scene had not been observed why.   I see now that .she faints at recurrence to the image which recalled her father when he slept.   It is at Macbeth's words—

> " Here lay Duncan,
> His silver skin laced with his golden blood"—

that the swoon comes over her.   It is the right place for an overpowering emotion.

On Monday and Tuesday Miss Faucit repeats her impersonation of the most pure and womanly of Shakespeare's heroines.   There are parts of her performance of this character that once seen few can forget—not the least beautiful, Imogen's simple presence at Cymbeline's court in the first scene, modestly clinging to her husband, shrinking from the rough life outside their love, and stretching out towards him, as he departs, the hands that return to her empty.   Last year there were passages in both her Imogen and her Lady Macbeth that were like false touches of a painter whose hand by disuse has lost its unerring correspondence with the movements of the mind.   Wherever the physical strain passed a certain limit, the expression would sometimes fall short of the conception.   But Miss Faucit soon succeeded in adjusting her performance to her powers and to the house in which she was acting. It was like the adjustment of an opera-glass to the sight, and in some parts of each character the difference of effect between in range and out of range is quite as striking. It has been notice-able this week in one or two of the scenes of her Imogen, chiefly the scene with Iachimo, and that with Pisanio near Milford Haven. It is no light honour to an actress, that the part in which she excels most should be that which represents the purest and most womanly of Shakespeare's women; in the whole range of poetry the most delicate embodiment of all the qualities that blend to form a womanly perfection—simple piety, wifely devotion, in-stinctive, unobtrusive modesty, gentle courtesy, moral heroism with all physical cowardice,—no thin ideal, but a very woman, who includes among her virtues aptitude for cookery.

In the important scene with Iachimo, Miss Helen Faucit is unfortunate in the change which gives her Mr. Anderson instead of Mr. Creswick for a tempter. Iachimo is no doubt a brutal sort of villain, yet he is outwardly a well-bred Roman, shamelessly but luxuriously dissolute. As practised conqueror of women, he must have known better than tempt virtue, even in the wildest British princess, with the roughness of a cattle-drover, or by standing por-tentously behind her with his nose in her back hair. There is a spiritual way of rendering even such a part as that of Iachimo. Mr. Creswick left much to desire; Mr. Anderson leaves everything to desire, yet he is skilled in the stage-business that pleases an uneducated public. His bedroom scene, spoken throughout in an oppressively ostentatious stage-whisper, is an intolerable blunder. Does he suppose that Shakespeare's soliloquies are pieces of mere realism, representing the defects of people who can't keep their tongues still even when they are alone? In all the solilo-quies—and Iachimo's part in Imogen's bedroom is especially and most necessarily of this sort—we are supposed only to be following a train of secret thought. We can thus, by slight exercise of imagination, pass into the innermost recesses of the mind depicted for us, watch its secret workings, and look for the mainspring of its action. It would be the densest stupidity to suppose that Iachimo uttered a sound he could suppress while he was at his base work around the sleeping Imogen. Let his part here be unostentatiously spoken, and we understand well enough that, in the usual way, we are enabled to penetrate to the thoughts that direct his silent action. But let it all be ostentatiously whispered, and we have the foolish spectacle of Iachimo, with a tongue too loosely hung, making noise enough to wake fifty Imogens, and huskily struggling to keep his importunate hissing and breathing as much as he can below the standard of an engine blowing off its steam. The laboured stage-effect hopelessly ruins the illusion of the scene. The Posthumus of Mr. Walter Montgomery is played in better taste, with energy that never passes into rant, and with manifest appreciation of good poetry.

On Wednesday, Miss Faucit played Rosalind in *As You Like It.* In *Love's Labour's Lost* Shakespeare jested at euphuism; in *As You Like It* he played euphuist himself in pleasant mood, and out of quips and fancies built a wise and tender day-dream of the world. Starting from one of the fashionable Italianised novelets of his day, Shakespeare wrote with a subtle waywardness this exquisite masque of life. His forest of Arden is an Arcadia, and there shall be lions in it if he will. With the Arcadia the court contrasts, the court with its wicked and usurping duke, and its good-hearted popinjay Le Beau; with its pitiless wrestler who breaks the ribs of youth and hope, and at its gate the grasp of the world of cruel brothers and hard masters. They who escape from the contest into that Arcadian shelter find how sweet are the uses of adversity. And Rosalind, the girl-woman, with her girlish devotion to her cousin Celia,

her soul of pity, her innocent mirth and bold playfulness;
first bashfully conscious of her mannish dress when she
hears that young Orlando, too, is in Arcadia, then recklessly plunging into enjoyment of his love; what bold profit
she takes out of his mystification, and how merrily she forces
from him oaths of love that are, as to her, to her and not to
her ! . Girlish abandonment to exquisite delight, womanly
depths of feeling shown from time to time when any rough
wind sweeps across the rainbow mist, these lie together in
her as the depths of its wisdom lie near to the playfulness
of the whole exquisite dramatic show, and through breaks
in its golden cloud-world we seem to see all kingdoms of
the world of thought spread out before us. In all the
scenes with Orlando, Miss Faucit's acting is delightful. If
she has not the art to conceal art, the art she does not
conceal is true, is founded on quick and refined perception
of the poetry she is interpreting. She can realise line by
line, with tone and gesture, more of the spiritual grace and
beauty of true poetry than any lady who now acts upon the
English stage. Mr. Walter Montgomery plays Orlando
without rant and with much excellent expression. Mr.
Anderson is a heavy stage-Jaques, who takes pains with
the business, and especially with the delivery of the lines,
" All the world's a stage". I protest, whoever plays the
part, against the transfer of the description of the melancholy Jaques

> " as he lay along
> Under an oak, whose antique root peeps out
> Upon the brook that brawls along this wood,"

from the mouth of one who had been observing him, to the
mouth of Jaques himself. It may seem very legitimate to
steal " lengths" of good poetry from a " first lord" who
might be a stick and not a gold one, and the transfer may
be usage of the stage; but if Shakespeare were stage-
manager he never would permit it. It is a special fficulty
in this play, and more or less a difficulty in all plays of

Shakespeare, that the small parts are worth great interpreters. Shakespeare himself played the part of old Adam, which is honoured by that pleasant tradition ; and the part, it is right to say, was played on Wednesday by Mr. J. Neville better than, so far as I know, he has acted anything before. Mr. Walter Lacy is a good Touchstone, and has a most pleasant Audrey in Miss Hudspeth. Mr. Belmore came on as Audrey's rustic lover William, and, as the part is a very small one, thereby did himself double credit. From such a company as DRURY LANE is gradually collecting we shall look for many who are free from the false dignity in which bad actors take shelter. In a first-rate play no part is unimportant ; and if a company enters worthily into its work —necessities of rest allowed for—every part, whatever its technical importance, should be filled by simply the most competent actor or actress of it who is not otherwise employed.

1865, *February* 25.—Mr. Phelps has been representing two great Cardinals, Wolsey and Richelieu, and is now acting Richelieu in Sir Bulwer Lytton's play to honestly full houses, which enjoy throughout not only the acting but the fine dramatic writing also that it worthily illustrates. The skilfully woven plot, the character of Richelieu expressed by touches very various yet all well harmonised, the thoroughly dramatic dialogue that elicits character and is instinct with thought, the language that has in its measured cadence a true music and an unaffected dignity, all this—the genius, in short, of the author—is felt as it should be, through the actor.

In Richelieu, how careful is the dramatic painting of a character worth dramatising well. It has ambition, honesty, dominant love for France. There is delight in the sense of a power that survives and surpasses the old vigour of arm. To the craft of the fox are added touches of love for the orphan girl whom the old statesman guards as a trust from his dead friend of old. There is a clear worldly insight, with the flattered and waylaid minister's bitterly low estimate of men ; dry humour, genial enjoyment of the gallantry of manhood; a touch of Richelieu's literary vanity in regard for the young critic who knew where to applaud his play. All this we have in the person of an old man, strong only of wit, now dallying playfully with power over those who come near to his heart, now bitter in pursuit of his own foes and those of France; now defying and now counterfeiting death; a feeble old man whose life ebbs with his power to serve France, clasping a feebler girl to his heart, and against the lusts of a king rising in her defence armed with the thunders of the Church ; a subtle minister, in the hour of his fall turning defiant upon his triumphant enemies ; a dying man into whom strong life flows back as there return into his care the fortunes of his country. In these and all other phases of the character, Mr. Phelps by numberless touches of an art kindred to the poet's genius gives to Sir Bulwer Lytton's Richelieu life again, and a strong life, upon the English stage.

Miss Atkinson is of the company who took honours when graduating at SADLER'S WELLS, and she has lately played Queen Katherine here in *King Henry VIII.* The grace and dignity with which from her place by the King's side she pleaded the cause of oppressed subjects, the quiet womanliness with which she warned Wolsey and Buckingham's accusing steward to deliver all with charity and to charge not in spleen, were admirable. In the scene before the court in Blackfriars, her womanly scorn and utter repudiation of Wolsey as her judge was delivered with a poetical intensity artfully heightened by the coming forward of Campeius at Katherine's words, " Lord Cardinal ", to be saluted by her with the humblest courtesy before she points to Wolsey with averted figure and imperious scorn, as she adds, " To you I speak ".

Mr. Phelps's Wolsey is remarkable for the impression of busy power subtly given through a marked quietness of demeanour. He moves easily as a Cardinal familiar with courts, and meekly, except in the first proud glance at defiant Buckingham, and in the short scene wherein Wolsey, left alone with Cardinal Campeius, lays aside his mask and shows the proud face underneath it. Everywhere, until the scene that shows his fall, Wolsey is the Cardinal in presence of the world. He sits still under the imputations cast on him by Katherine when she tells the King of the exactions suffered by his subjects. He is as humbly quiet at Blackfriars, and it would be a shrewd critic who could define exactly how by gesture, turn of head, nice management of voice, the proud ambitious spirit makes itself felt in that unobtrusive figure. In the last scenes showing Wolsey's fall there is a quiet restlessness of scheming that precedes collapse, and in the fall itself a pathos in the quietness with which the old man stands at bay amid the mocking courtiers; a dignity of pathos in his pointing of the moral of his life at court. Colley Cibber, if I rightly understand the records, was a Wolsey without ease of movement or of action, and with much display of a proud speech and bearing; the Wolsey of Mr. Phelps is the reverse of this. His movements are perfect in ease and in the quiet self-possession of a man who always surely steals towards the end he seeks. With help only of a flash or two of haughty spirit, as in the gesture that, when they are alone, denies his fellow-cardinal, Campeius, precedence of exit, it is usually by a visible attempt to veil the inner pride that its intensity is the more strongly shown. Shakespeare has painted it all in his verse—in Wolsey's relentless crushing of defiant Buckingham, in the meek Cardinal who is hard in council, who is pitilessly watchful of all those who come between him and the King, a luxurious host, a scheming servant of the Pope, but with high aims that give him dignity in the last hour of his disgrace. Shakespeare's Wolsey speaks to us most intelligibly when he comes free from distortion by a violent interpreter.

March 18.—Having now seen Miss Bateman in two characters, one may estimate the measure of her ability. Her acting as Julia in *The Hunchback* too exactly repeats the impression made by her Leah. In Leah it was only for a strain of pathos in the last act, and for a few touching notes of the voice then, that she was to be credited with a power of pathetic expression that came of her own genius, and not of mere stage-drilling.

But in other respects I find Miss Bateman is just as monotonous in the part of Julia as she was in the part of Leah, showing no original ability of any sort, save when she has to give pathetic expression to her voice, and there, and there only, again succeeding. She says marvellously well the words of distress, " Clifford, why don't you speak to me ?" but acts lifelessly in the first scenes of country simplicity, and almost lumpishly, certainly without a trace of real vivacity, in the succeeding scenes of town gaiety, standing almost unexpressive while Clifford is cruelly wounding her pride, and putting only the monotone of her pathos into the few words she utters. She is heavy even when rattling out words in stage-declamation, with the speed of a patter-song, but with no more soul in the sound they make than in the shaking of a bottle of shot. So I feel when she forbids Clifford, in his character of Earl's secretary, to put his arm about her waist, or when she pours on the Hunchback, in the last scene, a swift volley of monotonous sound instead of a full utterance diversified, as the whole acting of the character should be, with a quick play of thought and feeling full of the liveliest contrasts of expression. It was in this part of Julia that so spiritual an actress as Miss Helen Faucit chose, when a girl of sixteen, to make her first appeal to a London public. The part should be a favourite one with every actress of quick sensibility, and with a wide range of expression in voice, feature, and manner. Miss Bateman has almost no range. Her American intonation adds to the natural monotony of her delivery;

although its nasal tendency may lend itself to the effect of those pathetic tones which are her one strong recommendation to the public favour. When she is loud or swift, or anything but pathetic, she is never thoroughly expressive. When Helen is scoffing at Clifford's fall into poverty, her interpolations of "Helen!" convey no more feeling than the half-idle warning of a nurse to a child who is spilling the salt; and when she follows them up with a loud "I hate you, Helen!" the words have no more soul or propriety of tone than there would be in the same nurse's sudden outbreak of temper against the small offender. She walks over to stand before Modus and lecture him on Clifford as an American lady lecturer might walk up to her place at the lecture-table, and recites her admonitions with less animation. Whatever her mood—as simple, heart-whole country girl, as girl with her heart turned by town pleasures, as woman with her love spurned and her pride stung, as wrathfully contemplating vengeance, as tenderly conscious of her wounded love—Miss Bateman's notion always is to settle herself into some quiet, well-looking attitude, and save herself all awkwardness by keeping in it as long as possible. Even when Clifford is telling her, in her country-girl days, of the joy of country life, she stands still, turns up her eyes, and keeps them unwinking for a wonderful length of time; as if she were standing for a *carte de visite* before an exceedingly unsusceptible plate, and wouldn't have a hair stir till the cap is clapped over the lens. Miss Bateman's Julia is, in fact, so monotonous—although a part which most fairly good actresses would find it singularly difficult to make monotonous—that the variety of expression in Miss Simms's pleasant acting of Helen, and that young lady's flexibility of voice, seem by comparison almost miraculous.

March 25.—*Arrah-na-Pogue*, at the PRINCESS'S, is in the first two acts cleverly constructed and well written, but the interest does not pass into the third act, which is weak and strained, though it is supported by the greatest scenic efforts, and what is meant to be the great "sensational" effect of a climb up an ivy-covered tower wall. The play is, nevertheless, thoroughly and deservedly successful. If the third act were as good as the first and second, it would be the best piece Mr. Boucicault has written. *Faces in the Fire*, at the St. James's, is a play without a backbone. It is a French drama with its corrupt plot drawn, and nothing left in the way of adequate motive for the overwrought passion of the acting, which nevertheless brings down applause.

Mr. Watts Phillips's *Woman in Mauve*, at the Haymarket, is the work of a well-intentioned man who invents his own stories, and always desires to read some wholesome lesson to the audiences attracted by his plays. He has written a solid melodrama, *The Dead Heart*, which still keeps its ground as a stock-piece at the Adelphi. He has written also a comedy of *Paper Wings*, to which Mr. Tom Taylor's *Settling Day* bears obvious resemblance, and which is on the whole decidedly a more satisfactory play than *Settling Day*. He has written other pieces also, and I acquired from them a great esteem for the good intentions of the author. Latterly Mr. Phillips's dialogue seemed to have brightened and grown more compact. And so I went to see his burlesque upon sensation-writing with a decided inclination to be pleased, although there was, founded upon half-effaced reminiscences of the respectable heaviness of his earlier dramas, just a doubt whether the author had a wit nimble enough to provide three acts of extravagance, without flagging into a mere strain to produce nonsense.

What I did see was a combination of popular actors and remarkably good scenery employed in making the best of probably the clumsiest and poorest piece that has been acted in a London theatre for many years past. The author's good intentions, and an occasional cleverness in the dialogue, will save his own credit; but for the credit of the Haymarket, the shorter the run of *The Woman in Mauve* the better. And even the intention of the piece is

ill-defined. The author seems no more to know what to
attack than how to attack it. Using the now popular
Americanism introduced by Mr. Boucicault, his play is
meant as wholesome ridicule of what are called "sensation" novels and "sensation" plays. But the attack is
made, or rather seems to be intended—for the piece is so
weak that no attack is really made—upon stories of absorbing interest in which there is crime or mystery. Now that
really is not the object of any attack made on behalf of
literature. A good story cannot be the worse for taking a
very strong hold on attention. They are the crimes and
mysteries of life that stir the depths of human character
and bring into play all the passions. If plays and stories
turning with strong interest upon incidents of crime are to
be put down as "sensational", let us bury our Shakespeares
fathoms five, cry "Out upon Marlowe, Ford, Massinger, and
all the rest of them", and burn half the best novels in our
language. Only mischief is done and confusion produced
by following the unthinking multitude when it feels the
shortcoming of a certain class of novels and plays nowa-
days called "sensational", and ignorantly mistakes the nature
of the fault. Nobody can feel less mercifully than I do
towards some of the claptrap dramas of Mr. Boucicault,
and the corresponding school of fiction. Always, however,
the complaint should be not of their strength of incident,
but of their poverty of wit. The sort of "sensation" novel
or play against which protest cannot be too constant and
too strong, is that which depends wholly upon the heaping
of crime, mystery, and surprise, and relies on tricks of plot
or stage-effect, without making any use of the story as
means for the subtle development of character, and without
any charm of wit or wisdom in the language through which
all is told. Dialogues full of the bitterness of commonplace, a threadbare narrative style that is not even gram-
matical, and that never once flashes into a phrase of
independent thought—these are the evils to be fought

against. The same tale of bigamy and murder that excites
a merely vulgar curiosity when told in the Braddonian way
might be exalted into an immortal work of genius by the
mere difference of mind through which it comes to us.
For example, after reading Shelley's *Cenci*, fancy what Miss
Braddon would have made of such a story.

April 22.—DRURY LANE takes new honours by producing Milton's *Comus* as a brilliant Easter piece. The
stage-version used places too little reliance on the whole
and unadulterated text. But *Comus*, pure and simple,
never has been acted yet at any theatre, and the present
DRURY LANE management has done so much well that we
must not ask it to be over-bold. The masque of *Comus*,
as most people know, was written by Milton at the age of
five-and-twenty, as an entertainment to be presented at
Ludlow Castle on the arrival and installation there of the
Earl of Bridgewater as Lord President of Wales, Ludlow
Castle being the Lord President's official seat. The masque
was to be acted by members of the family ; and the
fourteen or fifteen year old daughter Alice was to represent
the principal character. In Milton's masque she was herself simply, but by the incidents of the scene became an
embodiment of temperance and purity. Her two actual
brothers took the brothers' parts in the masque, one a boy
of twelve or thirteen, the other a boy of eleven or twelve.
The attendant spirit was acted by Milton's friend, Harry
Lawes, who had been commissioned to write the music,
and doubtless, as in the case of *The Arcades*, recommended
as writer of the words the young poet whose genius and
worth he knew.

Given the occasion, there was to be produced a poem
fitted both to it and to Milton's early devotion of his life's
service to God, as one who, according to that sonnet which
was the sacred prelude to a life throughout attuned to it,
resolved that he would, as he said,

" Do all as in my great taskmaster's eye."

There was not only the young company of actors to be fitted to parts suited to their age, and words suited to their innocence, and the Shropshire guests to be gratified— as they were, by the use of the chaste nymph of their own Severn to cut the last knot of the story—but there was God to be served by the poet in a place noted for licentious revelries. Richard Baxter, who had, for a year and a half immediately before the writing of this work, been living in Ludlow Castle as a lad in attendance on the chaplain to the Council of Wales, tells in his autobiography how the chaplain only sneered at Puritans; how there was much tippling and other profanity in the castle and town, crowded with officials and their servants; how a good friend of his own, who had been zealously pious, was there transformed into a drunkard and a scoffer, and he believed that, had he remained in Ludlow, the bad influence of the place would have erased from his own mind the good impressions of his father's teaching. There can be no doubt that a knowledge of this character of the court and capital of the Welsh Presidency was among the materials upon which Milton founded the most exquisite plea for temperance and chastity that ever poet penned.

A marked feature in Milton's character was his entire purity of mind. He who in his youth spoke from the lips of a young maid those counsels of perfect purity, and to his chaste ideal gave victory over the sensual rout, was he who in his mature life and in the days of Charles the Second, when the common stews were less ignoble than the English Court, produced, even among a rout as sensual as the Court of Comus himself, a naked Eve as the embodiment of purity.

Κῶμος originally meant a licentious dancing revel. In Hesiod's shield of Hercules it means the promiscuous band of revellers who followed with their wilder dance and song after the trained chorus of a procession. In later times Comus appeared as a god of festive mirth and joy. Philostratus describes him as painted drunk and languid after a repast, his head sunk on his breast, asleep standing, with his legs crossed. And so he passed into a type for use of moralists; appeared, fourteen years before Milton's poem, in Ben Jonson's masque of *Pleasure reconciled to Virtue*, and had appeared, eleven years before that, in a Latin poem entitled *Comus,* by Henri du Puy, of Louvain, which Milton had read and liked, for at least one passage in it has been distinctly imitated. In Peele's *Old Wives' Tale* there are two brothers rescuing a lost sister from the spells of an enchanter. So much for what Milton had in his mind when he accepted the mission to write, for the Ludlow masque, poetry to the music of his friend Henry Lawes. Of the poetry, as spoken on the stage, much of the true spirit is retained by the care of Mrs. Charles Young, who represents the Lady. Let it be said by the way that it is a mistake to admit colour in her dress, which should be all white, or enriched only with emblematic ermine. But there is need of the force of every line in the poetry to maintain in the acted masque the triumph of the spiritual over the sensual. When the Court of Comus forms the whole attraction in the way of spectacle, and the piece appeals to the eye most strongly by brilliant pictures of licentious revel with a grand display of ballet-dancers' legs, it is essential that by every word the soul of Milton should be a clear-voiced interpreter of what is shown. The right emphasis of the poem is weakened by every stage-alteration; and how must the point of the work be broken to the sense when a singer, Mr. Henri Drayton, takes the place of the actor who should speak the part of Comus, and dissipates into unmeaning musical shakes those words of the reveller, after the pure song of the Lady has awakened even in his heart some echoes. Those words are in the highest degree emphatic, and contain, more than any other single passage in the poem, the key to its spiritual import. Comus says that he had often heard the charmed song of his mother Circe and the Sirens—

> " Yet they in pleasing slumber lulled the sense,
> And in sweet madness robbed it of itself.
> But such a sacred and home-felt delight,
> Such sober certainty of waking bliss,
> I never heard till now."

April 22.—The late Mr. Robson's son and namesake has appeared this Easter for the first time in London, at the ST. JAMES'S THEATRE, as Ulysses, in, as burlesques go, a merry burlesque of that name by Mr. Burnand. Mr. Robson the younger looks young, has family likeness to his father, especially in some forms of expression, and acts in his father's manner very agreeably and without obtrusive imitation, giving pleasure now, with promise of vigour when his acting shall have ripened with the ripening of his own physical powers into perfect manhood.

June 3.—There are two kinds of good acting : one is that in which a true artist can pass into the nature of the person represented ; and the other is that in which a performer with a pleasant personality can identify the character represented with himself or herself. To neither class does the new singer, Mdlle. Ilma de Murska, belong. She has not the genius that would enable her to be for the time what she would appear ; but she is cumbered with enough of conventional stage-action to prevent her from identifying her part with her own natural personality. Mdlle. Adelina Patti belongs to the second class, and is a delightful example of it ; for her natural perceptions are so quick, her ways so pleasant, as to secure, for every part that has any harmony at all with her own nature, a representation more delightful than can be accomplished except by the very highest efforts of true genius in another way. Mdlle. Patti uses her delicious voice with lively natural expression, never jerks her arms while she is singing, after the manner of a marionette, but is always a charming little lady giving pleasure and creating sympathies. In a thoroughly congenial part, it is hard to distinguish acting of this kind from the best efforts of genius. Indeed, it is only by observing the range of the performer's art that one can rightly appreciate its character.

June 10.—The HAYMARKET is well set up with a whimsical character in *Brother Sam*, whom Mr. Oxenford has connected with a play derived from a good German writer of dramatic whimsicalities, Herr Görner, director of the COURT THEATRE, Mecklenburg-Strelitz. As the smaller adapters all live by the copying of other folks' ideas, we may think, by the way, it would be a blessing to the public if one or two of our burlesque-writers would add a smattering of German to their smattering of French, and look up Herr Görner's *Possenspiele* and Children's Plays, which are popular holiday entertainments at extravaganza time on many a German stage, are meant to please the young, and do amuse children infinitely more than a splutter of bad puns, enlivened with airs from the street-music and idiotic dancing. And they contrive, too, plenty of bright work for the scene-painter and cunning effects for the machinist, besides having in their incidents and dialogue an essential whimsicality that would be a new thing in burlesque to the old London playgoer. In *Brother Sam* Mr. Oxenford has dealt as he pleased with a play of Görner's and made it his own. Dramatically that is not saying much, perhaps, for he has exaggerated its whimsical suggestions into incoherence.

But good nonsense is a legitimate source of fun, and Mr. Oxenford presents, in a play of capital nonsense, happy burlesques of character in merry dialogue. If the plot were less absurd it would be bad. As in good hyperbole the exaggeration must surpass truth, lest, being mistaken for it, the effect be simple falsehood ; so, in a burlesque upon life (which this play on *Brother Sam* is, rather than farce or comedy), where the end to be obtained is pure and simple fun, apart from any other purpose, there must be a disjointing of cause and effect, a whimsical exhibition of irrational for rational motives, to prevent the comical extravagance of action from being in any way whatever connected with the serious business of life.

July 1.—At the OLYMPIC we now have *Twelfth Night* and Miss Terry. The delicate poetical charm in the character of Viola has been acutely felt by her. All that she does feel she seems, as a true actress should, to feel in every nerve. Her sensitive nature speaks not only by refined expression in a face over which the changing emotions pass visibly and swiftly, but by every gesture of the body it adds eloquence to a speech in which not seldom the soul of the speaker is felt passing in quick sympathy along the poet's line. Thus we have from Miss Terry, with youth and all natural grace and aptitude, a near approach to the embodiment of Shakespeare's Viola. Viola's love for the Duke, to whom she plays the boy page, is defined vividly, but with the utmost delicacy, from her first quick turn at the sound of his voice in the question "Where's Cæsario?" to her lightening up with pleasure in his reference to her as "this boy whom somewhat I love", and her last act of fond readiness to suffer at his hands. The spiritual charm given by Miss Terry to the whole part becomes especially manifest in the skilful rendering of particular lines, to which an ordinary actor might not suppose that any particular care was to be given; as that line to Olivia, "I see what you are—you are too proud", and the "She loves me sure", following a most charming rendering of the scene of Malvolio's delivering of the ring, "I left no ring with her". Miss Terry heightens the poetical illusion of the play by representing both the brother and the sister whose resemblance breeds perplexity. Her Sebastian is skilfully distinguished from her Viola, by the more firm walk and tone of voice, the use of a few simple male gestures, as the folding of the arms, and by a spirited display of firmness and skill in fence that contrasts with Viola's womanly fear in the charming scene of the mock duel. The playfulness as well as the poetry of the drama has been delicately appreciated by Miss Kate Terry; nor should one omit to note the touch of true pathos which she put into Sebastian's reference to the sister whom he supposes to be drowned.

Mr. G. Vincent's Malvolio is not only an admirable stage-figure, ih its Elizabethan costume, with the hard Quixotic face over the stiff Elizabeth ruff, but it is a thoroughly successful impersonation that adds much to the already high credit attained by this young actor.

Miss Lydia Foote, known to be apt for serious and earnest parts, who has sometimes mind in her voice and speech in her face, obtains also one of her best successes in this play as the light-hearted Maria. Mr. Sutar, again, as Sir Toby, showed that the public has not yet seen to the end of his capabilities, and so with some others of the company. Given, in fact, certain necessary general conditions of fitness, and no actor at the Olympic is asked or, it would seem, allowed to hold by the mechanical iteration of a simple dramatic formula, to creep along one narrowly-defined line to which parts written for them must be servilely adapted.

August 19.—Mr. Tom Taylor's new drama of *The Serf* is constructed on this principle with great success. It is a thoroughly interesting play, having that essential unity which all good English dramatists observe, little as they care for the artificial unities of the French classical school; that is to say, it has one central idea, that is its soul; an idea, in this case, with the strongest hold upon the feelings of an English audience—resentment against tyranny. In Count Karateff Mr. G. Vincent finds opportunity for another strongly-marked dramatic sketch, and skilfully represents the cruel Tartar under a thin varnish of civilisation. Mr. Neville and Miss Terry, as hero and heroine, make every point felt. To be critical, I may say that, although the last dialogue between them may be held to be a sufficient justification of the second title of the play, *Love Levels All*, the final explanation, that the Serf is no serf, but the noble heir whom a

wronged serf had got hold of in his infancy and bred thus
an instrument of revenge, is a begging of the question, a
flinching from the uttermost development of the idea upon
which the whole drama turns.

However that may be, Mr. Tom Taylor's play is a most
interesting one. The plot is unhackneyed, the dialogue
throughout written with literary taste and skill, the emotion
healthy and strong, the spirit of the piece English, its whole
tendency wholesome.

September 23.—Mr. Jefferson's Rip Van Winkle is preceded by the Nan of Mrs. Mellon (Miss Woolgar) in *Good*
for Nothing; and that picture of the true-hearted, neglected
girl, who plays hopscotch with the street-boys, and, when the
woman's heart in her is touched with jealousy, breaks awk-
wardly out of her tattered slovenliness, familiar to London
eyes as are the actress and the part, is set before us in
a piece of acting certainly as good as the new actor's Rip
Van Winkle.

Mr. Jefferson's Rip Van Winkle is Washington Irving's,
set in a play that seeks dramatic effect by tasteless variations
from the tale as Irving told it. As the village schoolmaster
in *Deborah* was transformed for the American *Leah* into a
conventional stage-villain, so here the harmless schoolmaster,
Derrick Van Bummel, is selected for the villain's part. The
first act is brought to a melodramatic close by Rip's wife
driving her husband from her hearth into a thunderstorm.
He goes out snivelling. She of course cries in vain to him
to return, and, as the curtain descends, plumps on the
ground in the orthodox melodramatic swoon. This may be
great improvement in the eyes of an American audience ;
but an English audience, with a really good actor before
them, would have entered, perhaps, quite as readily into the
original notion of Rip's wandering off for a lazy autumn
scramble, escaped from the labour of the farm and his wife's
clamour.

In the second act we have the adventure on the moun-

tains with the ghost of the old discoverer of Hudson
River and his solemn crew of nine-pin players. Here the
story is closely followed, except in the poor melodramatic
change that substitutes for Rip's attendance on the company
and his sly pulls at their flagon, a formal attendance of the
company upon him as the drinker, and the conventional
"Ha! ha! ha! ha!" when he drinks. The original story
made them absolutely mute, allowing no sound but the
thunder produced by the rolling of their bowls. The
adapter, however, having ghosts on hand, could not dis-
pense with the conventional effect of the "Ha! ha! ha! ha!
ha!"

In the third act all the delicacies of the rest of the story
are smothered in the garlic and onions of the melodramatist. Yet all this latter part of it is precisely the
dramatic part of the original. The happy notion of making
the American Revolution fall within the twenty years of
Rip's sleep, and bringing the dazed man, who had left his
village as a subject of King George, back into the bustle
of a republican electioneering crowd for which the story
supplies figures already sketched, would suit the humour
alike of a good dramatist and a fine actor. Surely there can
be no actor of high mark who would not rather have his
Rip left on a bench, astonishing the gossips by the door of
Doolittle's hotel, than presented with the claptrap effects
of a wife who has been borrowed and improved during his
absence, and a magnificent collection of town lots to make
him happy ever after. As an actor, Mr. Jefferson marks
Rip's weakness of character by giving very skilfully an air
of picturesque and easy indolence to all his postures and
movements, while his good-humoured Dutch-English is
spoken with a quiet laziness. When, as he sits out of doors
by the innkeeper's table, the innkeeper's little son Hendrick
tells him how he means to go to sea in a whaling-ship, and
has promised to come home and marry Rip's little daughter
Meenie, and the two children kneeling at Rip's knees tell of

their true love, the twinkle of humour in Rip's way of listening to them, as one who finds a quiet luxury in his admission to communion with children's happy thoughts, and his nod to them over a wine-cup with his customary toast, " Well, here's your health and your family's. May they live long and be happy," is acted with much quiet delicacy. In the scene with his wife in the cottage—the wife's part being so acted by Mrs. Billington as to be one of her marked successes—it is impossible to cover the defect of bad invention by the dramatist. A long story about shooting at a rabbit and not hitting it is very tedious fun, and it is but a coarse stage-effect to make Rip drink out of a spirit-flask over his wife's back while she is embracing him because he has again " swored off" his evil habit. Rip was good-hearted, and his faults came of his laziness. Such a situation, though it may be a broad stage-effect, degrades him far too low. It was necessary, it may be said, to degrade Rip in this and other ways to account for his wife's turning him out of doors into a thunderstorm. But it is. a pity that the dramatist could not deny himself that incident, and be content to carry through from first to last the lazy humour of the story.

In the second act, Mr. Jefferson, as Rip Van Winkle among the ghosts, acts as well as the dramatists will let him. But the words put in his mouth are poor, and the variations from the original story are, in a dramatic sense, for the worse. Rip falls to his twenty years' sleep, and the ghosts leave him.

The opening of the third act shows him at his awakening with rotten clothes and long white hair and. beard—an exaggeration not required. The story had said that his beard was grey, and grey would be, in the dramatic rendering, more truly effective. The drama in this act is at its poorest, but Mr. Jefferson is at his best. Retaining his old Dutch-English with a somewhat shriller pipe of age in its tone he quietly makes the most of every opportunity of

representing the old man's bewilderment. His timid approaches to an understanding of the change he finds, his
faint touch of the sorrow of old love in believing his wife
dead, and reaction into humorous sense of relief, his
trembling desire and dread of news about his daughter,
and, in a later scene, the pathos of his appeal to her for
recognition, are all delicately true. It is doubtful whether,
in such a drama, more could be done by the best effort of
genius to represent the Rip Van Winkle of whom Washington
Irving tells. It is certain that in a play more closely in
accordance with the spirit of the story, Mr. Jefferson's
success, real as it is, would have been yet more conspicuous.

At the PRINCESS'S THEATRE, Mr. Charles Reade's play of
Never too Late to Mend is a weak three-act piece with a
fourth interpolated act, during which the plot stops while
the audience is edified by a transformation of the stage into
a treadmill, and of the supernumeraries into convict gangs,
under the rule of a demoniacal governor, who is touched at
last by the Ithuriel spear of an angelic chaplain, but not
until a boy who has only stolen a few potatoes from a rich
man's cart, to keep himself from starving, dies of his prison-
tortures when upon the point of hanging himself in presence
of the audience. Upon this repulsive excrescence, which
does not advance the story by a syllable, the manager spent
his chief energies in the way of scenic effect; for it has
yielded the most costly scene in the play, a perspective of
radiating prison-corridors seen from the centre of a model
prison, with practicable tiers of galleries, and iron stair-
cases, and cells, and gaslights. For the rest there is
enough scenic effect. Real water comes out of a stage-
pump, and there is a fine stage-picture of an Australian
ravine. The play is a commonplace transpontine drama in
plot and in language, with only a chance gleam here and
there of the genius that produced, in conjunction with Mr.
Tom Taylor, one of the best dramas of our time—*Masks*

and Faces—and to which we owe so admirable a novel as *The Cloister and the Hearth.*

1866, *February* 10.—*The School for Scandal* is now eighty-eight years old, but it holds the stage yet with the liveliness and grace of youth. Sheridan wrote it at the age of five-and-twenty, and it will stand as long as there are theatres in London. For permanence of interest it is indebted not to the good wit alone. For we should note that the good wit is spent, not merely on a story suited to the taste of its own day, or in ephemeral satire of a passing folly, but in attack on a vice of society that must always arise out of the imperfect lives of men. No literature lasts that does not found its argument upon the inner truths of life. The lightest wit, if it be true wit, is durable as granite when it deals with the essentials of human nature, and not with the mere accidents of passing fashion. Though several of the actors have yet much to learn, the play runs well enough to support the one important feature in it, the good acting of Miss Herbert, who has too seldom given fair-play to her genius by spending it upon stuff worth the study of an artist. Her Lady Teazle, like Mrs. Abington's and all that have followed, "plays her part in all the extravagant fopperies of fashion and the town with as ready a grace as if she never had seen a bush or a grass-plot out of Grosvenor Square"; and in raiment of white satin she looks as handsome as my lady should. But while Miss Herbert plays the lady to perfection, she colours her part with a natural joyousness that separates her altogether from the town-bred members of the scandalous college, and that well accords with the position of the country squire's daughter who has changed her figured linen gown and her work upon fruits in worsted for sudden enjoyment of unlimited adornment to her beauty, and a thousand new amusements for her wit. The fine lady is copied to the life; but the copyist is a quick-witted, joyous, home-bred woman, who delights in the new pleasure of spending, and enjoys the social triumphs of the home-bred wit that had found, before her marriage, no livelier exercises than in a game of "Pope Joan" with the curate. It is here, in the essentials of character, that Lady Teazle's country breeding is apparent, not in the trivial accidents of an external awkwardness; for those the squire's fair daughter was too naturally graceful and too quick-witted to find any difficulty in effacing speedily, while, with models enough before her, she could learn in a week to mimic all the ways of fine-ladyism to her heart's content and the distraction of Sir Peter. It is in the true natural gaiety, based on the in-nocence of her old way of life, and in essentials of character allied to it, that a good actress should make Lady Teazle's home-bred character appear. Miss Herbert thoroughly succeeds in doing this. There is not a trace in her Lady Teazle of the hardness of character shown by the scandalous colleagues, to whom society has been a nurse, a mother, and a god since they were born. When Sir Peter's tenderness and generosity towards her have stirred the wife's heart in her as Joseph's treachery had stirred the woman's, the natural shame, the outspoken sim-plicity of truth in all that, after this, is said or done by Lady Teazle, the actress has brought into complete harmony with the preceding phases of her character. Miss Herbert's is a womanly Lady Teazle, acted with much care and finish, every word and gesture thoroughly well weighed, yet with less than we are used to see of defect in the art to conceal art that sometimes impairs the effect of her graceful and very skilful acting.

April 7.—Miss Herbert has since appeared as Miss Hard-castle in *She Stoops to Conquer*, and passed from that to Shakespeare's Beatrice.

Mr. Westland Marston's comedy, *The Favourite of For-tune*, is another strong move in the right direction. The author has given himself pains to write a dialogue worth hearing, and he has invented a plot of his own which now

and then yields charming dramatic passages, marked by unusual delicacy of contrivance.   It is a curious fact that,
although this play was written for Mr. Sothern, Mr. Sothern's
own part is so far from having been "written up", or
seasoned with marked eccentricities, that it is even a weak
one ; while a part calling for a wide range of power in the
actress has to be intrusted to Miss Snowdon, now Mrs.
Chippendale, who does more with it than might have been
expected from her, but is unequal to the full expression of
strong serious emotion.   Mr. Buckstone gives a very genial
version of a part designed with so little direct reference to
his own manner of acting, that it would suit Mr. Neville, of
the OLYMPIC, quite as well or better.   Miss Kate Saville
does herself credit as the heroine, but the best acting in the
piece is that of Miss Nelly Moore.   When she represents a
girl with lively generosity of character assuming the mask of
a she-Gradgrind with business notions upon marriage, to
avert an offer, which she is half bound not to refuse, from a
visitor who is himself hoisting false colours, her playful
humour of strongmindedness is touched with a right sense
of the purest comedy.

   Mr. Fechter is also, I trust, now to be claimed as a recruit
in the real service of our drama.   His recent version of *The
Bride of Lammermoor* skilfully and effectively followed Scott,
even in dialogue, and gave a sense of overruling fate, as in
the old Greek drama.   Some changes were necessary at the
close, but those made were not good.   And yet one ought
to admire the accommodating quicksand that allowed Edgar
to stand on it with Lucy in his arms till he had quite finished
his theatrical business, and then let him go suddenly down,
together with the curtain.

INDEX.

LONDON : WHITING AND CO., 30 AND 32, SARDINIA STREET, W.C.